BEAUTIFUL INTENTIONS

HEALING ONE SOUL AT A TIME

MICHELE SCHRADER

Beautiful Intentions
Copyright © 2023 by Michele Schrader

All rights reserved. No part of this publication may be reproduced, distributed, or transmitted in any form or by any means, including photocopying, recording, or other electronic or mechanical methods, without the prior written permission of the author, except in the case of brief quotations embodied in critical reviews and certain other non-commercial uses permitted by copyright law.

Tellwell Talent
www.tellwell.ca

ISBN
978-0-2288-8390-6 (Hardcover)
978-0-2288-8391-3 (Paperback)
978-0-2288-8389-0 (eBook)

DEDICATION

I dedicate all my Beautiful Intentions to my father and loved one's who supported me on this journey

TABLE OF CONTENTS

Dedication iii
Introduction: Inspirational Message vii

1: Our Spirituality Revealed 1
2: Changing Our Perspective 6
3: Rediscovering Our Purpose 10
4: Our Soul's Intention 12
5: We Are Energy.. 15
6: World Energy Shift 20
7: Taking Our Power Back... 23
8: Recognizing Ego 27
9: Emotion As A Catalyst For Healing.............................. 31
10: Our Soul's Intention Through Divine Healing 35
11: Understanding Divine Healing..................................... 37
12: The Divine Healing Process.. 45
13: Self-Reflection Through Divine Healing 55
14: Divine Healing In Practice 57
15: Our Soul's Journey Into The Afterlife.......................... 65
16: Triggers And Free Will 93
17: Synchronicity And Serendipity..................................... 99
18: Intuition 102
19: Intention 104
20: Exit Points 105
21: Karma And Dharma 108

22:	Discovering Our Soul's Purpose Through Life Challenges	112
23:	Grief	116
24:	Miscarriage and Loss of a Child	126
25:	Abortion	134
26:	Suicide	136
27:	Cancer and Critical Illness	141
28:	Challenges of Being a Caregiver	151
29:	Relationships	157
30:	Dysfunctional Relationships	165
31:	Addictions	170
32:	Sexual Identity and Orientation	173
33:	Depression and Mental Health Awareness	177
34:	Rape and Sexual Assault	188
35:	Evil Acts	195
36:	Covid	201
37:	Marginalized Souls	208
38:	The Cycle Of Growth Through Our Life Challenges	211
39:	Healing Through Our Life Challenges	220
40:	Communication With Souls In The Afterlife	236
41:	Past-Life Experiences And Reincarnation	274
42:	Our Life Purpose Revealed	290

Citations	299
Acknowledgements	301

INTRODUCTION: INSPIRATIONAL MESSAGE

The journey to realizing who we are and what our purpose is will be challenging yet incredibly rewarding. It requires being aware of all aspects of ourselves: mind, body and soul. My mission is to unlock the knowledge that is within all of us.

The Universe has created an ideal environment for awareness of who we are on a spiritual level. There is a palpable shift in our world energy that will unearth our pursuit for answers.

There has never been a moment in our Earth's existence where the veil that separates us from the Higher Energy Realms has been thinner. This allows us to access information on the big picture of our life plan and why it is such a challenging journey. When we are aware of this truth, we open ourselves to discover our purpose in this lifetime.

My personal journey began as a child when I realized I could communicate with loved ones in the Heavenly Realm. Throughout my life, I denied and questioned my abilities due to fear of judgment from my family and society. When my father crossed over to the Afterlife, he opened a portal for me to receive incredible inspirational messages. I could no longer deny the strength of my abilities and embraced my divine gift of communication and healing.

Initially, the writing of this book began as a love letter to my family and friends. The messages contained within were a legacy to my children and grandchildren. As I wrote, the scope of my original intent exploded into an inspirational journey that astounded me.

Throughout my life, I began to understand that personal repetitive experiences held underlying critical lessons. As an R.N. in a palliative care setting, I was witness to remarkable spiritual events. The accumulation of all these revelations created the ideal foundation for the messages I was about to receive. My soul was being called to share my gift of spiritual awakening with those on a quest for clarity.

We begin this journey together with a concrete plan on how to heal our emotional pain and deepest fears. When our hearts are open to embracing love and forgiveness, we unlock the mystery of our purpose in this lifetime. Through this process we are elevating our personal energy, which contributes to raising positive energy throughout the Universe. This energy shift encourages authentic experiences and people to enter into our lives. What we project into the world is reflected back to us in equal measure. Like reflects like. I will guide you on your journey to achieve this state of being, which will give you a renewed sense of joy and self-love. Not only is this healing critical to our personal journey, but we are also contributing to a universal shift towards an elevated compassionate world energy. When we work together on a common goal, we have the potential to change the trajectory of the collective experience.

I will explore an enlightened perspective on specific life challenges and how we can heal through each experience. All our decisions come from a place of either fear or love. Our most important job on Earth is to clear the stagnating and low-energy emotions that hold us captive in a state of fear. Through this process, we begin to understand that there is a reason for every life challenge and how everything works out exactly as it was intended.

To fully embrace our life experiences, it is imperative to be aware of how our soul journey continues into the Afterlife. This will help alleviate some of the fear around our body's demise on Earth.

We will discover how our soul transitions to the Heavenly Realms and my experiences witnessing these miraculous events. Here we will also learn about synchronicity, triggers, free will, intentions, exit points, Akashic Records and many other fascinating aspects of the Afterlife.

The Afterlife is not some elusive place thousands of miles away. The love from Source and our crossed-over-loved-one's energy surround us in an embrace of soul-blending love at all times. This is the intense love that never ceases to exist with our loved ones in the Afterlife. Soul love encapsulates a sense of being and transcends even the greatest love we experience here on Earth. Our newfound awareness gives us the opportunity to communicate with family and friends in the Afterlife. We will explore many avenues on how to tap into this energy through the language of love.

I will then reveal many aspects of reincarnation and share incredible adventures of myself and others that are difficult to dispute. It is fascinating to explore how past-life experiences complete the circle of life and help us understand some of our critical life lessons.

When we approach all these concepts with an open heart and alternative perspective, we witness how beautifully and seamlessly our journey flows. My sincere hope is that you embrace the lessons revealed for you to discover your life purpose. I am divinely guided to share all my Beautiful Intentions with you on this journey of the soul.

OUR SPIRITUALITY REVEALED

"Who am I?" and "What is my purpose?" are questions we have asked ourselves since the dawn of human existence. There is a palpable shift in our world energy that is creating the ideal environment for us to unearth the answers we seek. The knowledge we are searching for is within each one of us. My soul has been called to share my gift of spiritual awakening with those who are on a quest for clarity. I have been blessed with the ability to receive messages from a Higher Power and to communicate this knowledge through my writing. The journey we will embark on together will empower each one of us to discover who we are on a deep soul level. As the truth is revealed, we will witness how beautifully and seamlessly our journey flows.

We are all spiritual beings having a spiritual experience in a human body. When we are aware of this truth, we open ourselves to discover our purpose in this lifetime. We are never alone on this journey and are always surrounded by Divine Love. We are blessed to have been the chosen souls who came to Earth at this critical time. There has never been a moment in our Earth's existence where the veil that separates us from the Heavenly Realm has been thinner. This allows us to access awareness of ourselves as the spiritual beings we are.

Our greatest purpose on Earth is to heal our deepest fears and emotional pain so that we may become aware of who we are at a soul level. When our hearts are open to embracing love and forgiveness, we unlock the portal to our true Higher Soul Self. Our Higher Soul Self is our most intimate selves at the core of our being. My intention is to help guide you in rediscovering your Higher Soul Self and life purpose.

We are the privileged generation who have been blessed with the gift of enlightenment. If we choose not to acknowledge this revelation, we are forfeiting one of the greatest opportunities to heal ourselves and in turn contribute to the healing of the Universe.

We are the brave souls who have chosen to be present during this renaissance of renewed spiritual awakening. We have been empowered with this divine knowledge from Source so that we can become aware of our purpose. Source is an energy that radiates love and forgiveness at the highest state of consciousness in all the Universe. As we realize who we are at a soul level, we are blessed with the understanding of a Higher Power. Source, or the Highest Power, is that greatest love that resonates within us and around us at all times.

The path to realizing who we are and what our purpose is will be challenging yet incredibly rewarding. To fulfill our destiny, we must confront and release the traumatic and painful emotions that hold us captive in this life. This requires becoming aware of and healing all aspects of ourselves: mind, body, and soul. I will provide you with a foundation of knowledge, tools and empowerment to guide you along this path.

My main motivation for writing this book is to share an important message of love and hope. I have been reassured by Higher Powers that this information will benefit many on their spiritual journey. I pray that you embrace the healing messages so that you are alerted to your higher purpose. I am offering a new perspective on how to deal with the challenges of life and unlock some of the mysteries of our journey into the Afterlife.

Even if you are a skeptic, which is a good place to start from, my hope is to present an alternative perspective on healing and our life purpose. I only ask that you approach the material with an open heart and mind. Take what resonates within you and allow the rest to marinate in your soul.

In the past we have forfeited our spiritual awareness to the distractions of the human experience. We are blessed to now have the opportunity to become the enlightened souls who can change the trajectory of universal consciousness. We create positive change simply by alerting the Universe to our intention to grow and learn at a deep spiritual level, one soul at a time. When we initiate this process, there is a perceptible shift in our consciousness that triggers our soul to begin remembering our purpose in this lifetime. A critical step is to process our fear, pain and hurt so we can heal our soul and contribute to healing the souls of humanity. When we release our fear and pain, we open a space for forgiveness and love to enter. The purpose of this love is to alert us to what requires deeper healing so that we may come back to our Highest Spiritual Self. When we rediscover our Higher Soul Self, we are gifted with the ability to fully comprehend our soul's journey and life purpose. Through this process, we are elevating our personal energy, which contributes to raising favorable energy throughout the Universe. This positive energy shift gives us the opportunity to experience life with a renewed sense of joy and self-love. I will empower you with the knowledge and tools to assist you on your personal healing journey.

The information I am sharing with you is an expression of my truth. It originates from the most intimate aspects of my heart and soul. My spirit has been called to share my personal experiences with you and to communicate messages sent to me from a Higher Power. This venture has been both terrifying and exhilarating. It exposes aspects of myself that I have never shared with anyone. It has been and continues to be an authentic and inspirational labor of love.

From my earliest memories, I have always had the ability to communicate with family members and friends who had crossed over into the Afterlife. I refer to these souls as Spirit or spiritual beings. As a young child, I felt a powerful and reassuring energy outside of myself and yet a part of me. It was an elusive knowing that my purpose extended beyond my immediate reality. I sensed energies around me that I could not explain. When I began writing, I was able to channel thoughts and feelings from loved ones who had crossed over to the Heavenly Realm. Initially, I did this through poems and creative writing.

Instinctually as a child, I sensed that my abilities would not be accepted by my family or friends. When I innocently spoke of crossed-over loved ones, my messages were received with skepticism and silence. I quickly learned to keep my experiences to myself. In my youth, I did not share my abilities and revelations with many people, as I did not fully understand them at that time. At some level I knew these abilities were a beautiful part of who I was, yet fear held me back for many years.

After my father crossed over to the Heavenly Realm in 2016, my abilities could no longer be muted. The veil to the Higher Realm thinned and a portal to the Afterlife began to open. I was soon receiving messages from my father and Higher Powers at an accelerated rate. I could no longer deny the strength of my abilities. What my father could not grant me in this earthly life, he more than rectified from the Afterlife. My purpose took off in a radically prophetic direction. I began to embrace my revelations with a renewed passion and slowly started sharing my truth with those I trusted. Meditation and prayer were instrumental in initiating my discovery of my Higher Spiritual Self. A common theme of love and being of service to others wove its way into my consciousness. I was directed by Spirit and my personal insights to share what I have learned and experienced through my gift of writing and channeling.

If anyone had told me that my life would take this spiritual path eight years ago, I would have been extremely skeptical. My awareness and faith has grown with every challenge I have experienced in my journey. I have dedicated an enormous amount of time and energy into discovering who I am at a soul level and strengthening my spiritual knowledge. My intention is to assist you in navigating your journey through a more purposeful and joyful life passageway.

As with many of us, my journey was not a smooth one. I have had to battle insecurities and vulnerabilities in writing my story and embracing my abilities. Since every challenge has led me to this pivotal moment in my life, I now sit in gratitude for all my critical life experiences. I am dedicated to assist you in finding your truth through a renewed perspective. My intention is not for you to deny your experiences, but to grant you the tools to navigate your journey in a purposeful and enlightened way.

It is my calling to be of service to others, so I welcome the opportunity to share my truth with you. I am confident that my message and the wisdom of my spiritual supports must be presented to those outside my inner circle. I understand that my message will not resonate with everyone, but I strongly feel in my heart that the messages contained in my writing are key for the healing of many people. I have also been shown by Higher Powers that by healing ourselves, we empower the Universe to mend collectively.

CHANGING OUR PERSPECTIVE

Discovering the answers to our questions of immortality, life purpose, who-am-I-and why-is-life-so-challenging are all within our grasp. The concept is simple but requires shedding some aspects of what we have been taught throughout life. This may include releasing some societal ideologies and organized religious dogma. My goal is not to negate the positive aspects of your belief system, but to enhance your knowledge through an enlightened spiritual view on faith and forgiveness. There is power in knowledge, and my message comes from a place of love from a Higher Power.

The first step is opening our hearts and minds to a new perspective on how to achieve this awareness. We are on this Earth to learn through life experiences and to grow in spiritual awakening. As a human race, our most impactful life lessons are learned through experiencing opposites. To fully appreciate happiness, we must first encounter sadness. To understand acceptance, we must first be rejected. To truly know love, we would have been exposed to hate. To appreciate peace, we must endure times of conflict. We are given this knowledge to understand that every challenging experience is actually an opportunity for optimum growth. We will explore this concept in great detail, as it is difficult to comprehend why our souls would choose suffering and pain for us to learn our most profound lessons. There is no growth in neutrality. It is imperative to understand this perspective for us to embrace the lessons required for growth and learning.

Earth is the classroom and life is the learning center for our soul. We are currently living the story of our spiritual existence on this planet. Use any tool presented to create a narrative you are proud of. The challenges of each individual involve learning the lessons needed to progress on Earth and into the Afterlife. Take advantage of all the knowledge available so you may advance in this lifetime to a level beyond all your aspirations.

My life's purpose is to share what I have discovered in my soul as truth. You will hopefully gain knowledge to grow and experience life in a more positive light. Allow that glimmer of hope to help expand your belief in yourself and in the potential greatness of humanity. Be patient and kind with yourself. Allow your soul to view life with a new perspective. The concepts introduced are straightforward but will take commitment and effort on your part. During the process you will begin your journey towards self-love and inner joy. When you internalize your truth, you are empowered to release love and peace into the Universe. This gives you the opportunity to heal and live a higher awakened life. When we open our hearts and allow love into our lives, we are creating an opening for a fulfilling existence. The lesson for us to discover collectively is to know love through forgiveness and gratitude.

For us to open ourselves to discovering our purpose and truth, we must step out of the myopic view we currently experience life through. Changing our perspective can help us visualize life with a much broader lens. We are given the answers every day; we have just lost the faith to trust.

Accepting a Higher Power in our life is a key factor in our spiritual journey. This Highest Power goes by many names and concepts. I will be referring to this Highest Power as Source, Creator, or God. Labeling this divine essence is not what we should focus on. God is not a concept granted to us from some elusive entity. The Divine Love of Source is a state of consciousness or a state of being that resonates within us and encapsulates all life within the Universe. When we accept the unconditional love of Source, we are on the path to rediscover our Higher Soul Self. When we embrace ourselves as the loving souls we are, we become aware of our life purpose and soul journey.

When we open ourselves to reframe our spirituality to the true meaning of love instead of what we have been taught, we open ourselves to the pure essence of spiritual love. When we are alerted to the unifying aspects of spiritual love, we empower ourselves to eliminate fear from our lives. Every decision originates from a place of either love or fear, and we have the power to always choose love. I will help you become aware of the tools required for you to embrace love and eliminate fear from your life. When we release our fear and pain to a Higher Power, we are granting ourselves the opportunity for awareness and understanding towards the meaning of our existence on this Earth.

As a society, we do not openly discuss or understand what role spirituality has in our lives. My calling is to present the information I have been shown in a clear and concise manner. Spiritual growth is a lifelong journey that builds on each learning venture. Do not feel rushed in getting to the next level before fully experiencing this level. Be patient. We are spiritual beings having a human experience. Embrace the pleasures and pain of our humanness. All of life's challenges are necessary for growth and are part of a divine plan. When we can reframe challenges as blessings, we are another step closer to embracing our life purpose. It is within our power to work through all our challenges and transform our mistakes into learning experiences. In the spiritual sense, these perceived mistakes are imperative for growth and every misstep is viewed as an opportunity. There is truly no downside to embracing this inspired view on spirituality and discovering our life purpose. Our spirit is strong and needs to learn the lessons at its own pace. Above all, be kind, loving, patient and forgiving of yourself and towards others.

Life is the school for our soul. We learn lessons in the Afterlife, but our greatest progress occurs in this classroom called Earth. Life as we know it here on Earth is the catalyst we require to accelerate our awareness and growth. As enlightened souls, we have chosen the most challenging learning center in all the Universe. Our true home exists within the Heavenly Realm. Our life here on Earth is a practice ground to accelerate our knowledge of who we truly are on a deep soul level.

REDISCOVERING OUR PURPOSE

There are millions of people all over the world searching for awareness of their life purpose. As a society, we have become distracted from understanding the meaning of our existence. We have relinquished our spiritual selves to the ego-driven temptations of the Earthly Realm. Once we are able to return to our Higher Spiritual Selves, our purpose becomes clear and we are awakened to the true meaning of our soul's path.

I have been directed by my spiritual guides to assist in returning us to a state of understanding and knowledge that we all possess on a deep soul level. As we rediscover these answers, we will become aware that this has always been our truth.

By simply committing to the process, we are activating a shift in our consciousness and alerting the Universe to our intention for soul growth and learning. The Universe reciprocates by elevating our vibrational energy, which results in placing positive experiences and people in our life.

Our purpose on Earth is to embrace and learn the lessons we came here to fulfill. These goals may include working through jealousy, low self-worth, shame, guilt, greed, anger, selfishness and many other human frailties. This entails confronting these painful emotions, working through each feeling as it emerges, and releasing our sentiments that do not serve a higher purpose into the Universe. Our next critical step is to forgive those that have harmed us so we may create space for love to enter our hearts.

This level of forgiveness is for personal self-growth and is very different from society's definition of forgiveness. Embracing this fundamental sentiment will inspire your journey towards spiritual enlightenment. We will explore this concept of forgiveness in great detail, as it is the most challenging aspect of this process to comprehend. Through this awakening, we begin to rediscover our Higher Soul Self. When our hearts are open to this truth, we embrace Divine Love, which is the highest state of consciousness that is within us and surrounds us at all times. As we become aware of our Higher Soul Self, we are empowered to process the lessons we came to Earth to learn. Our purpose in living this challenging life on Earth is to work through critical lessons our soul agreed to embrace in our pre-life plan. All efforts towards this goal are rewarded and any setback is viewed as a necessary aspect for growth. With every lesson learned we achieve spiritual advancement on our soul journey. Earth presents the greatest and most challenging opportunity to achieve these goals. Shedding our feelings of fear, anger, guilt, judgment, shame and all other debilitating emotions are crucial for our journey to progress on a forward trajectory. This is the foundation for embracing every lesson we commit to encounter on Earth. With every goal accomplished we achieve a higher vibrational frequency, which affords us increased opportunities for favorable life experiences. Through this process we are also projecting elevated positive energy into the world and are contributing to the enlightened shift in the universal experience for the collective.

OUR SOUL'S INTENTION

For us to fully embrace our life challenges, it is imperative to be aware of our soul journey in the Afterlife. As we explore this concept throughout the book, attempt to open your heart to the flow and beauty of our spiritual path. When our soul is planning for our life on Earth, we do so in conjunction with our soul family in the Heavenly Realm. This collaboration creates a pre-birth soul plan that we all agree to incorporate into our earthly existence. We have spent many lives with this soul group and our intention is always from a love-centered approach. Our Higher Soul Self is highly motivated to experience the hardships of life because it is able to view the entire process of our spiritual journey from an elevated perspective. In Heaven, our soul is free from all the restrictive emotions we experience on Earth. This allows us to optimistically plan for a life that may be very challenging. Our soul understands that with every accomplishment we achieve on Earth we are rewarded with an elevated station in Heaven. As we embrace our lessons on Earth and in the Afterlife, we graduate in the spiritual energy levels towards our greatest heavenly rewards.

We are given many opportunities to accomplish the goals we set out to learn in our pre-birth plan. We are also gifted many lives to work through these challenges. We are continually working towards the ultimate reward in the Heavenly Realm. It is important to note that whatever stage we are working on during our soul's journey, we are all welcomed into Source's Kingdom with forgiveness and unconditional love. This includes every single person regardless of race, religion or any societal ideology of the time.

Source resonates in the highest energy frequency level in the entire Universe. Our greatest achievement is to become enlightened spiritual beings or Ascended Masters who reside in Source's inner circle of light and love. At this stage, we have achieved our soul goals of learning all the lessons we agreed to fulfill on Earth and in other realms or galaxies. Our primary mission then involves being of service at the highest level to assist other souls on their spiritual journey. This process may take many lifetimes to achieve, so it is imperative we are alerted to all the aspects of this grand adventure.

As humans, it is extremely difficult to understand the challenges in life without being aware of the purpose for all our hardships. Through an incredible spiritual experience as well as messages I have received from crossed-over loved ones and guides, I have become enlightened to of one of the greatest rewards we are blessed with from Source. Immediately upon crossing over to the Heavenly Realm, our soul witnesses the most immense abundance of Source's love that far exceeds any emotion felt on Earth. Our earthly selves could not endure this extremely intense emotion for more than an instant, as it is the most powerfully exquisite state of being within the entire Universe. On a deep soul level, we are always striving for that perfect state of being, or Highest Love, that resides in the Heavenly Realm.

My personal experience occurred shortly after my father crossed over from this Earthly Realm. He gifted me with a miraculous glimpse into that most powerful and profound feeling of Heavenly Love. I will share that experience with you in greater detail in the following chapters, as this event created exciting revelations for me. I was only present in this love for a brief moment, yet I was astonished when I felt my soul absorb this incredible infusion of Divine Love that resides in me to this day.

When we become aware of the eternal life of our soul being, our fear of death of this body drastically decreases. We can then embrace the truth that our core essence, who we truly are on a deep soul level, continues on forever. Our fear of death may diminish so we are able to experience this lifetime for the amazing journey it is meant to be. I have also been shown that our life in the Heavenly Realm is exciting and reflective of the joyful aspects of our life on Earth. Our options are greater and beyond our imagination for all the adventures awaiting us in the Afterlife.

Our ultimate reward for all these intense life lessons is beyond our capacity to fully comprehend from the perspective of this Earthly Realm. When we achieve our earthly goals, we are blessed with a more joyous and meaningful life. With each accomplishment, our soul is rewarded with achieving a higher elevation level in the next realm. The exquisite consciousness that exists in the Heavenly Realm is even more powerful than what anyone can grasp on Earth. This awareness of Source's encapsulating Higher Love for each one of us becomes a primary motivation to achieve our earthly goals and challenges. When we have faith that this is a universal truth, we open ourselves to experience our life in a more optimistic and enlightened state of being. We are also given insight into what our life purpose is and the incentive we require to accomplish our soul mission.

WE ARE ENERGY

Understanding energy is a key element towards embracing our soul journey. All matter consists of energy. Once energy is created it cannot be destroyed. This is not only a spiritual truth, but also a scientific fact.

Our soul energy is created from the highest energy source in the Universe. When our soul enters our earthly bodies, we must conform to a low energy state or realm. Just as we are energy, so is the atmosphere surrounding us. Our bodies keep us grounded in a lower vibration. All our emotions are part of this dense energy state that only exists on this Earthly Realm. One of our greatest challenges is to clear this heavy lower energy to attain a lighter and positive state of being through forgiveness and love. All around us are progressively elevated realms or layers of increasing energy states. Once we shed our earthly body, the tether to our confining low energy shell is severed, and we are transported into a heightened energy state. Some refer to this state as Heaven or the Afterlife. Heaven is not some elusive place thousands of miles away, but is an energy surrounding us in a beautiful warm embrace at all times. This foundation of knowledge helps us understand how we begin to gain awareness of our spiritual journey and how to access the Higher Realms while residing in our earthly bodies.

The veil between our Earthly Realm and the Afterlife is thinning. The portal, or opening, to the Spiritual Realm is becoming available for us to access so that we may enlighten ourselves to our true purpose. We are witness to this evidence every day. Thousands of people all over the world are speaking of their Near-Death Experiences (NDEs) and are sharing the message of a divine Higher Love beyond anything we can imagine. Children and adults are talking about their past-lives and spiritual encounters with crossed-over loved ones in significantly greater numbers. Psychic and mediumship abilities are stronger and more prevalent than ever before. I will be presenting a variety of methods for you to recognize messages from your crossed-over loved ones, and how communication exists between these realms. Simply by elevating our spiritual energy and awareness, we are creating an opportunity for connection to the Heavenly Realm.

For us to learn and grow, we must be aware of how energy contributes to our daily lives and greatly influences our experiences. The energy we put out into the Universe is reflected back at the same vibrational level. Like reflects like. When we reside in the past, we sit in a depressed and regretful state of being. Our energy vibration is lowered, and we attract other people and experiences that share similar adverse energies. When we are consumed with the future, we live in an anxious and fearful state of impending doom. When we project fear into the Universe, we increase the likelihood of unfavorable experiences reflecting back on us. Living in the moment creates a state of awareness for us to achieve optimum opportunities for learning and growth. It is imperative we ground ourselves in the present, so that we create a balance in our energy center. We become grounded when we immerse ourselves in the here and now. Allow all distractions to flow through you and sit in the moment with peace and love in your heart. We are all capable of grounding ourselves during our daily lives to reconnect and balance our energy center. This practice may take only seconds during our busy day, or we can choose to dedicate more time later in the evening or early morning. We will explore many methods of grounding ourselves to elevate our soul energy throughout the book.

This knowledge on energy is a tool for us to begin our healing journey. Everyone and everything on this Earth has their own vibrational pattern. Our soul and emotions carry their unique frequency into all aspects of life. When we are filled with love, our vibrational frequency is very high. When we stray from love, we vibrate at a lower frequency. We attract people and experiences with similar frequencies as our own. Happiness and peace attract those that are joyous and reflect an optimistic vibration. Pain and sadness attract people and experiences that reinforce a lower vibration. Grief and fear reflect the lowest frequencies for humans. Our Highest Power (Source) vibrates at the highest frequency of all. That is why prayer, meditation, intentional thought, gratitude and love naturally raise our vibration.

It may help to understand energy from a basic earthly concept. I will use water as a metaphor for soul energy. Water changes form depending on the amount of energy surrounding it. When water boils, it is activated to ascend into the upper atmosphere. When water freezes, it stagnates into a low dense energy state that is immobilized. Water in its natural state can ebb and flow depending on the environment it is in. This is similar to how energy affects our soul's state. As our energy vibration increases, we are in an elevated state of being and are freely able to access a higher vibration and enlightened experiences. When our energy is low, we stagnate in an inert state that is incapacitated to move or change. If we can maintain our energy in a free-flowing state, we are then able to control our experiences by elevating our energy level when we choose. This analogy allows us to visualize how our soul energy performs.

Our ability to raise our vibration has given us the gift of being able to communicate with our crossed-over loved ones. Our connection occurs through the language of love. When we quiet our brains through intentional thought, meditation, prayer and dreams, we are greatly raising our vibration to become aware of our connection with the Higher Realm. There is no great distance between Earth and the realm on the other side of the veil. I will refer to this place as the Afterlife, the Higher Realm or Heaven. We are connected to every soul on Earth and in the Afterlife through symbolic cords. We have a symbiotic link that is the life pulse to every soul, and every soul is connected to Source. The cord that links us all is never severed and is our lifeline to Source and our loved ones' souls who have crossed over to the Afterlife. The Heavenly Realm is surrounding us at all times. Their energy encapsulates us in a beautiful dance of soul-blending love that never ceases to exist, even after the death of the human body. When we engage in forgiveness, gratitude and love, we are increasing our energetic frequency to merge with that of our crossed-over loved ones. They must simultaneously pull down their energy to meet ours. It takes dedication and perseverance to accomplish this form of communication on both sides. I will be presenting many methods of increasing our ability to connect with our crossed-over loved ones' souls. I will help you understand even the most subtle ways our loved ones send us messages. I will empower you with the knowledge and tools required for you to progress on this aspect of your journey.

Every person is exactly where they need to be on their soul journey. When you open your heart to the concept and tools I am presenting, you may greatly elevate your soul growth in this lifetime. We are all unique individuals and will experience this journey at different levels. Advanced souls who have embraced their lessons through multiple previous lifetimes may be living their truth already. Younger inspired souls will have to diligently work through the steps and information presented to progress on their soul journey. There are no coincidences in life. If you are reading this book, then know that your soul guided you to this exact moment in time.

Even those that struggle with the idea of God and the Afterlife can acknowledge the concept of vibrational energy frequency. Choosing to live in a higher energy will lead you to a state of living your best life. One of my greatest priorities is to empower you with the knowledge on how to accomplish this. By raising your vibration, you are raising the vibration for all humanity. When we sit in a higher vibration, we attract people and experiences which pull positive situations into our lives. By shifting our consciousness and perspective, we will elevate our soul growth and that of the Universe. We are evolving souls growing towards the highest energy levels, one soul at a time.

WORLD ENERGY SHIFT

There is a palpable energy shift occurring in the world today. People who are aware of their Higher Soul Self are recognizing this increasing energy frequency within their core essence. As a society, we are witness to this shift through pandemics, radical atmospheric changes like droughts, fires or flooding and unprecedented wars and behavior changes not previously experienced at this level. These powerful energy changes were pre-planned by the Universe and orchestrated through our Creator. We are moving from a dense three-dimensional state into higher energy dimensions. Although this shift may feel uncomfortable for some people, it is important to understand that our world energy must evolve for the survival of Earth and the human race. As a collective, we are recognizing the unsettling result of unequal energies competing against each other. This manifests for some as feeling unsteady, off-balance, physical aches and pains, anxiety or a knowing sense of instability in the world.

Recently, I have received a strong message regarding our current world energy shift. Since 2019, there has been an incredible energy surge that has never previously occured on this Earth. As challenging and extreme as this shift is felt, it is important to be aware of the reason why we are going through this transition. This is a wake-up call for humanity to embrace a more love-centered approach to heal ourselves and the collective. We have approximately two more years of this heightened energy state to go before the world shifts to a calmer and more peaceful time. It is imperative we gain awareness of why our life is currently so challenging and that we are prepared for all the changes to come.

When we become conscious of this shift into higher dimensions, we are alerted to another universal truth. When we sit in our dense three-dimensional state, we view the world through a low vibration. This stagnating energy holds us in a condition of fear and pain. This creates a harmful perceived reality where we feel seperate from everyone and everything else in the Universe. When we raise our vibration, by becoming aware of how we can change and heal ourselves, we move into a higher state of being. Once we are able to release judgment of ourselves and embrace forgiveness and love for all humanity, we are able to come into a state of wholeness of self.

Embrace the understanding that you are not alone. When you are conscious of this elevated frequency, you are receptive to a Higher Power. You now have the clarity to understand that everything happens for a reason and that you have pre-planned for all your learning opportunities on Earth. You are now empowered to recognize your purpose when you feel joy in life's challenges. You are coming to the realization that you are pure Divine Love. When you internalize this love, you are motivated to be of service to others. What we do for ourselves, we do for all. We are all energetically connected. Through this enlightened state of being, you are also elevating universal energy into a higher dimension. While entering into this higher vibration, you are still able to experience human emotions. Allow yourself to feel from your human perspective, but understand that you are not the pain and fear. Embrace this higher energy level so you can view this experience from an elevated perspective while remaining in your power. This is our purpose on Earth. When you live your purpose, you are elevating universal energy into a higher vibration. Being aware of this transformative time in history is helpful in moving towards the higher dimensions. Be observant to the signs of increased consciousness that surround us every day.

As discussed, our lower energy has the potential to hold us in a state of fear and anxiety. Sitting in judgment towards others also greatly decreases our energy frequency. When we serve others, our vibration rises exponentially. As we elevate our frequency, we increase the probability that joy and love will enter into our lives. Simply by embracing the knowledge of this transition into a higher energy shift, you are not only increasing your personal frequency, but are contributing to elevating universal energy. We will be exploring this concept throughout the book, so you may alerted to how energy affects our daily lives in critical ways.

Every individual on Earth has a choice to remain in the lower world vibration or elevate their energy into a higher dimensional state. We have free will to remain in the lower frequency and there is no judgment in doing so. My role is to provide you with the tools and information available, so you are able to make the best decision for your personal journey. Approach the information with an open heart and embrace what resonates in your soul for the journey you are about to embark on.

TAKING OUR POWER BACK

It is of vital importance to be aware of the role our emotions play in our spiritual journey. The evolution of human feelings will help us understand why we have stagnated in our spirituality and how imperative it is to process these emotions to take our power back. One of the most important factors is to stay strong in your personal power. You have always had the sovereignty and strength, and now you will gain the knowledge to manifest the experiences you have designed for yourself. Be the warrior of your destiny; you control the narrative.

All our lives we have been exposed to the concept of victim mentality. Every time we ask ourselves "Why me?" or "What did I do to deserve this?" we are placing ourselves in the victim role. When we are able to release the debilitating entrapments of viewing ourselves as victims, we will begin to allow our spiritual journey to flourish. Our life's path will become clear and the obstacles that block our way will fade. Divine Healing is the cornerstone for embracing our soul's pre-life plan. This concept will be discussed in detail throughout the following chapters. It provides the foundation for many challenging interactions: past, present and future. This process takes inner strength, self-love and patience. It requires extracting much of what we have been taught and shifting our perspective to an alternative way of processing pain and forgiveness. It is a crucial step in creating understanding towards our intended life plan and releasing the confining aspects of victim mentality. This creates an opening for us to become empowered to take our power back.

Awareness of past and present cyclic occurrences in history are beneficial in discovering our current life path. This has become even more apparent in our post Covid existence. There are signs all around us supporting this great renaissance we are experiencing. The Universe is crying out to be healed. Nature will benefit greatly from the world being forced to slow down at this time. As a result, there will be positive atmospheric adjustments and a renewal period for nature to heal. We are also seeing signs of personal awakening. Through the consciousness of the "#MeToo" "Black Lives Matter" and Indigenous reconciliation movements, we are witness to society engaged in taking their power back. These developments are reflective of this critical time and highlight unresolved ancestral suffering. People are bravely speaking their truth and are uncovering the pain of repressed emotions that have gone unhealed over multiple generations.

For our society to heal, we must first resolve the adverse emotions that arise on an individual basis. This is a strong example of how we must heal ourselves in order to alleviate universal suffering. It is not a coincidence that these issues are coming into our awareness all at once. By changing our perspective, we can recognize this as being an essential series of events that must occur to heal the Universe.

As we work through the process of Divine Healing, we empower ourselves to heal generational pain that we have carried within us. As we resolve our personal core issues, we are freeing our souls from ancestral fear and anger that we have internalized for possibly many lifetimes. This also enables future generations the gift to not burden their souls with past and present pain. By freeing our souls and thereby the souls of future generations, we are creating an unobstructed and clear path towards greater healing and soul growth for universal enlightenment. This is the greatest gift we can give to our children and generations to follow.

We are taking our power back from centuries of oppression, abuse, ridicule and a myriad of atrocities committed against humanity. Part of the process is having our voices heard through the courts, rallies, marches, parades and other peaceful demonstrations. Violence begets violence and only exacerbates pain and anger. Violence is not an effective means to healing. It is imperative to acknowledge the detrimental emotions that arise within each of us, heal the pain and release those feelings into the Universe. If we do not change our perspective at this time, from fear and anger to healing, we will have missed one of the greatest opportunities in humankind.

As a society and as individuals, we already realize that what we are doing now is not working. The brave souls who have chosen to come to Earth at this time understand that the world is preparing for radical change and growth. Society today is in a state of great fear and turmoil. This causes division, judgment and victim mentality to emerge to the forefront of humanity. We are bombarded with messages of anger, hate and pain. It has become difficult to filter out truth from fiction and conflicting sentiments so prevalent in the human experience today.

Conversely, we are also in a time of enlightened spiritual awareness. As discussed earlier, we learn our greatest lessons through opposites. The Universe is presenting us with a perfect opportunity for optimum growth. As a collective, it is imperative to change our perception of the current world situation so we may embrace the opportunities presented to us. This is a perfect moment to radically alter and heal the consciousness of humanity. We need to relinquish the victim mentality by changing our perspective on life's challenges. This is the ideal environment to take our power back. It is important to acknowledge that all these adverse events occurring in the world today are present to alert us to what requires healing. Awareness is key to begin our mending journey. A lifetime of conditioning will require a lifetime of acceptance of a new reality. This new reality will help give our lives purpose and meaning. When we begin to forgive and love ourselves, we begin to heal all.

RECOGNIZING EGO

The original sin concept helps us understand the foundation of separateness, anger, pain and the emergence of ego. For growth to occur, we must become aware of the purpose ego has in our life. It is true that our souls must learn through experiencing extremes of emotions. Unfortunately, many of us get stuck in these debilitating feelings and struggle daily to find a way out. As a young child, the first Bible story I heard was about Adam and Eve. When the story ended, I felt confused and upset about everyone being so angry at each other. This was my initial indoctrination into organized religion. I now have a very different interpretation of this parable.

In the Bible, Eve "tempted" Adam to eat forbidden fruit and he succumbed to the temptation. This set the stage for blame and guilt that follow us today. This is a prime example of how generational pain is carried throughout centuries of time. As a result of the misinterpretation of this biblical story, men have been angry at women for leading them into temptation. Women have felt guilt and the burden of responsibility for original sin. This guilt was repressed by both men and women and expressed as fear within ourselves. What we internalize we project onto others. Behind anger is fear. This created separation and judgment towards our fellow human beings and God. Anger and guilt became permanently internalized and set us up for lifetimes of generational pain. This misconception was never Source's intention. This "original sin" was perpetrated and misinterpreted by humans, not God.

Being aware of the role regarding ego and its contribution in our life experiences is important in understanding our soul's journey. Ego developed from the misunderstanding that original sin separated us from Source. Ego reinforces this pretense of separateness which creates anger and pain. We then internalize this false belief of abandonment and are consumed with fear. This then creates the foundation for misperceptions of our life experiences. We misinterpret our distressing experiences and emotions as being punishment from God. We mistakenly perceive these actions as happening to us. In actuality, these human experiences are there for our learning and growth. We are the authority figures who orchestrated all these events in our pre-life plan. When we internalize these false messages from ego, the external world will reflect back increased adverse events to reinforce what we are sending out into the Universe. This is our egocentric existence working to pull us away from our intended purpose and Higher Soul Self.

As a society we have become trapped in the temporary and false rewards of power, wealth and control. Our ego reinforces the instant gratification that our world so readily provides. We have internalized the inaccurate messages from ego to dictate who we perceive ourselves to be. The ego is fear-based and attempts to control us at all times. Our ego contributes to our feelings of separation, fear, pain, dependency, self-doubt, depression, anxiety, unworthiness and judgment.

This is a simplistic explanation for a very complex concept of our history with guilt, anger and ego. Whatever the root of humankind's experience with adverse emotion, we must deal with the present. To heal present pain, it is not necessary to know the exact origin of that emotion. Our energy needs to be focused on all the emotions that emerge in our life today and relase the feelings that do not serve us. Healing present pain will help to resolve and heal past pain.

The agenda of the soul is to undo the misinterpretations of ego. In this respect, ego is a trigger to create an awareness of returning back towards love and compassion. It is beneficial to change our perspective on the role ego has in our life. Ego creates awareness of our spiritual path and triggers our soul to remember the lessons we came to Earth to learn.

Our soul in its purest form does not embody ego. Ego is developed throughout our life on Earth as a manifestation of who we think we should be. Ego clouds our ability to embrace who we truly are on a deep spiritual level. When we work on releasing the false messages of ego, we open a space to allow our intuitive heart center to embrace the loving and beautiful souls we are at the core of our being. Acknowledge ego as a stepping stone to spiritual growth and not as an end game to rewards that do not serve our Higher Soul Self. These are triggers for our soul to return to our authentic self and become aware of our life purpose. Love conquers ego and resolves fear.

We can escape our egocentric life by first processing the debilitating emotions that arise from embracing our soul's journey. We must process and move through these emotions to feel love, acceptance and joy. Through this discovery, we become aware of our true purpose on Earth. We recognize this in how we relate to and treat others and how others respond to us. Our shift is felt when we move from a life of material gratification to a life of being of service to others. This looks different for every individual, and there is no judgment in how we choose to serve. The act of service may be as simple as acknowledging our fellow human beings and authentically sending a beautiful intention or smile their way. It is the every day acts of kindness that have the potential to positively transform the world into a loving and joyful experience for all humanity. When we set out to heal the world on a grand scale, we may become immobilized with the complexity of accomplishing these grandiose plans. Be the pebble thrown into the water to initiate a movement of positive change and enlightenment for all. This could potentially empower others to embrace their healing journey and create a universal wave of love energy. Achieving wealth is not a negative accomplishment unless it is done through ruthless or nefarious means. When the intent of accumulating wealth incorporates being of service to others, this becomes an act of love and not ego. Simply by being aware of the role ego has in your life is a powerful tool in your journey. Knowledge is the foundation for positive change and growth.

EMOTION AS A CATALYST FOR HEALING

I will closely examine the role emotions play in our daily lives. Every emotion has a specific function to alert us to what requires healing within ourselves. The resolution of our adverse emotions is a key factor in helping to recognize our life purpose. In the spiritual sense, there are no negative emotions. Every emotion has a purpose and is therefore necessary for our personal growth. I am only using this terminology to clearly understand from our human viewpoint. Our next step is to recognize why these deep emotions reside so persistently within us. We do not have to pinpoint the exact incident to begin to heal, but it is important to be aware of the process for our healing journey to begin.

When we experience extreme emotions from critical incidents in our life, we often suppress those feelings. We block the painful emotions as a protective mechanism and bury them deep in our being. When we repress a memory, we unconsciously block the emotions attached to that memory. When we suppress guilt, we are reacting to something we feel we have done wrong. When we suppress shame, we give it the power to become a part of who we are. When we block shame and guilt, they become embedded into who we perceive ourselves to be. We will eventually have to deal with the consequences of not releasing all this detrimental energy. Just as we are created from energy, our feelings are generated from varying degrees of vibrational energy. When we absorb this distressing energy, it eventually invades every aspect of our being. Our lowered energy vibration may then attract unfavorable experiences to repeatedly enter our lives. If we do not process our feelings, they may come out in destructive and unhealthy avenues. These internalized adverse emotions carry a high probability of leading us into a myriad of physical and mental health issues.

Our history with guilt is extremely complex and convoluted. In prehistoric society, guilt and shame were used as an enforcement measure to control behavior. When a member of society chose to experience life outside of the norms of the clan, they were threatened with abandonment. Our survival was totally dependent on our family unit within the greater community. Guilt and abandonment became intertwined as a deeply ingrained motivator for our survival as a human race.

Our ancestors also developed the concept of organized religion as a means of control through guilt and fear-based indoctrination. At the time, our ancestors believed this was necessary to keep society in a strict and conforming structure. Once again, this does not diminish the importance of religion in our lives today. There are many genuine aspects of religion that contribute to a positive world energy. The information I am providing is to assist us in processing our emotions that stagnate our spiritual growth. It is important to be aware of how our emotions have been deeply entrenched into our psyche through a rigid social structure and the onset of organized religion.

Historically, judgment was used by the powerful of society as a means of control to keep humankind in a compliant and fearful state. The concept of guilt-based customs was contrived by humans to manipulate and control human behavior. Judgment became a means for ego to justify condemning others for acts, thoughts and actions that were deemed unacceptable at that time.

In actuality, when we judge others, we are projecting judgment from within ourselves. We direct our own insecurities and infallibility onto those we falsely feel superior to. It is imperative to recognize this detrimental attitude within ourselves to continue on our healing journey. We can create change by viewing this strong feeling as the trigger required to address an emotion we have subconsciously not dealt with. When we feel an absence of hostility and judgment towards others, our heart is open to forgiveness and love.

Fear has a greater influence more than any other emotion we experience. We are fearful of many things in our life, and this resulting anxiety may create a stagnation in our progression of life's journey. When we live in fear, we are not open to the joy that life offers us or to the lessons we need to learn in this lifetime. We can alter our perspective and understand that many things we are afraid of generate some of our greatest opportunities for healing. Fear can often be a trigger to alert us to the need for change in our life. When we are given the tools to work through this anxious state, we allow ourselves the opportunity for awareness and the path to happiness. Guilt and anger are reflections of fear. Guilt is anger directed inwards and has no genuine purpose in our soul development. I will be exploring many positive ways to process fear and use it as a catalyst for healing.

If we are to embrace the spiritual truth of life, we are encouraged to re-examine this archaic attitude of control through guilt and fear. I am offering an alternative perspective on how to view a concept that does not serve our best interests anymore. Empower yourselves with the knowledge of a greater spiritually-based existence. Again, take what resonates as truth for you and keep an open mind to all concepts presented.

Source granted us the gift of free will and humans have since attempted to control that freedom through the manipulation of guilt, shame and fear. We need to reframe our relationship with these emotions to be aware of how they were used against us throughout history. Recognize guilt, fear and judgment as a trigger to release our victim mentality and to embrace our purpose in our soul journey. It is imperative for us to understand the history of feelings so prevalent in our life today. Now that we are empowered with this knowledge, it is critical to move forward with resolving the emotions that hold us back from discovering our purpose.

When we are deep in the emotions of guilt, shame and other debilitating feelings, it can be difficult to break free from the emotional prison we feel we are in. It is human nature to get comfortable with what we are familiar with. As destructive as these feelings are, it is sometimes terrifying to see who we are without them. It takes courage to release these emotions and discover our authentic self underneath the heavy burden we have adapted to and carry within us.

It is natural to fall back on coping strategies we have embraced our entire lives. Be aware that when guilt and shame come up, we may be defaulting to these emotions to prevent going deeper to the feelings that genuinely require healing. Release guilt and shame so we can become conscious of and expose the underlying emotions that are critical in our healing journey. The first step is to acknowledge that these feelings exist within ourselves. Next, work on processing and releasing these emotions in any healthy manner we choose. Understand that guilt, shame, fear and ego do not serve any positive purpose in our lives other than to trigger what requires healing at our core essence. Processing our pain is the primary reason why we came to Earth and took on these challenges.

We are not the debilitating emotions; they are only temporary visitors in our life until we work on their departure. If our body is a temple, then these are the squatters who have invaded our being. These emotional parasites become very stubborn as they may have resided there for some time. You are accumulating the tools and knowledge to empower yourself to guide them out into the world. The Universe's job is to then convert that adverse energy where it can best be neutralized and dispersed appropriately. Nature is a strong ally on our emotional and spiritual wellness journey. This is the path to increased joy and spiritual freedom in our daily lives.

OUR SOUL'S INTENTION THROUGH DIVINE HEALING

Now that we are aware of the role our deeply ingrained emotions contribute to our daily lives, we will explore a method of releasing these feelings into the Universe. I have discovered that an effective means of working through unresolved emotional trauma is through a process I call Divine Healing. This tool will be instrumental in allowing the release of emotions that stagnate our spiritual journey. Self-doubt, shame, pain, guilt, anxiety, depression, unworthiness and fear are some of the emotions we may potentially release through this process.

The concept of Divine Healing that I am introducing may be completely new to some. To others, this is the reality they live every day. My sincere hope is that you learn, grow and accept love into your life so you may share that love on a deep soul level. I will present what I have been shown and what I sincerely believe is the path to personal healing, and how we can collectively contribute to a positive universal shift. Attempt to objectively and openly approach the material presented, and you will observe how smoothly and beautifully our soul's journey flows. It is a miraculously simple concept that holds immense truth. Again, take what resonates within you and use that to formulate a spiritually-guided life plan. It is in your power to choose the tools that best suit your journey, so you may focus on discovering the best version of your soul's path.

We often ask what one individual can accomplish. I am offering each person a chance to discover themselves, and by doing so, you are contributing to the positive shift in the Universe. You can be the pebble thrown into the ocean that sends ripples out into the water. If we all do this, we have the potential to create a tsunami of favorable change and enlightenment for humanity.

When you begin the journey of Divine Healing, you may feel resistance and doubt within yourself. This is your ego trying to paralyze you with fear. Trust the process. Repeating the same past behavior pattern only creates the same result. This is an opportunity to jump off the negative and stagnating loop of fear you have been living. It is in your power to take the initial step that may alter the trajectory of your life. There will most likely be hesitation before taking that initial plunge, but the result may create a life of renewed passion and purpose.

UNDERSTANDING DIVINE HEALING

I understand that change is challenging. My plan is to introduce you to a manageable strategy of approaching challenges and conquering fear. Forgiveness of self and others, at a soul level, is a critical aspect of living your best life. Forgiveness is an act of love at its purest form.

One of the most important tools to begin our journey of self-discovery incorporates the concept of Divine Healing. Attempt to approach this new perspective on healing with an open heart and mind. The focus of Divine Healing is to free our souls from the heaviness and burdens that prevent us from living our most authentic lives.

Divine Healing incorporates an alternative perspective on forgiveness. It is unlike traditional forgiveness in many ways. The process does not involve directly confronting any individual who has caused you pain. Divine Healing works by releasing our inner suffering and frees our soul to alleviate the heavy burden of fear, anguish, judgment and anger. The priority of Divine Healing is to deal with the emotions elicited from unresolved buried feelings. To be able to deeply experience the authentic emotions, we must feel, expose and process the detrimental feelings. This is a crucial aspect of spiritual growth. It is difficult and challenging but necessary in discovering our true selves. We were gifted this life on Earth to learn and grow. We can make great strides in this lifetime to uncover the knowledge required to unearth our life purpose and personal identity. When ingrained adverse energies are transformed into love and forgiveness, your purpose will begin to reveal itself. The Universe will present the ideal circumstances directly in our path for healing to occur. Our ego falsely informs us that this person or situation transpires only to bring suffering and despair in our lives. In actuality, it is we who have brought this person in so we can learn to heal by releasing our unresolved debilitating feelings. These negatively perceived people and situations are reflecting what requires healing within ourselves. This was a crucial aspect of our pre-birth soul plan and karmic obligations.

I will be discussing pre-birth soul plans and karma in a spiritual sense in the following chapters. This will dispel many preconceived false perceptions of what we have been taught regarding karma as a punishment. When we embrace karma as another tool to enhance our awareness, we empower ourselves to become closer to discovering our life purpose. When we balance our karmic energies, we heal at a soul level. We not only carry that healing into our lives today, but also into every incarnation we experience. While healing karmic energies at a soul level, we are helping to balance collective karma out in the Universe. In this sense, one person can change the world. As we resolve our emotional challenges, we raise our energy and begin to achieve karmic release. While increasing our vibrational energy, we contribute to raising the vibration of the Universe. What a beautiful gift to yourself and for humanity.

Even if you are struggling with aspects of reincarnation, karma or a Higher Power, at the very least you can potentially improve the quality of your current life through Divine Healing. My intent is to introduce many tools and knowledge on how to improve and deal with your daily challenges. My goal is to promote intelligent dialogue for the expansion of your life experience and guide you towards a more optimistic outlook in your personal journey.

If we do not resolve these emotions now, another scenario will present itself that produces those same sentiments. Through Divine Healing, we will recognize a situation and the underlying emotions that may be healed at a soul level. We are then empowered to lessen the probability of these distressing experiences from recurring in our lives. We can continue to lay blame on everyone else, but until we accept responsibility and create change, the pattern will continue.

When you go through life walking in pain, you transmit a cloud of low energy sorrow into the Universe. Without consciously recognizing this, you project your hurt and anger onto others. It is imperative that you acknowledge this aspect of yourself for true healing to occur. This is often an intuitive reaction to protect yourself from being victimized. For a brief moment, you may feel empowered in causing someone else pain. It requires hurting others and ultimately yourself. Sentiments of being right and others wrong is also a slippery slope of empowering yourself in an unfavorable and potentially destructive way. The debilitating energy we are sending out will be returned by lowering our vibration and inadvertently pull negative energy and experiences back into our lives. This is our ego falsely allowing pride to dictate our emotions. Pride interferes with forgiving and is a manifestation of ego. Healing and awareness potentially alleviate all these ego-driven emotions.

It is important to understand that these emotions have been an integral part of who you perceive yourself to be. When you release these deeply embedded emotions, you may experience a sense of loss that feels overwhelming. You will have to rediscover who you are by filling that void in a renewed positive light. Your healing journey entails being aware of all these aspects of yourself. All your work must come from a place of honesty. For some, this brutal honesty often feels uncomfortable. Again, embrace the emotions that come up and work on healing and releasing them into the Universe.

When you can fully forgive yourself, you are able to forgive others. The realization that you have hurt others to protect yourself is an important aspect for healing to occur. By forgiving yourself, an opening for clarity emerges. Do not sit in shame and guilt. Objectively observe that this was always part of the plan to alert you to what requires healing within yourself. We can now honestly observe that we see aspects of ourselves in those who have hurt us. This awareness comes full circle for us. We are reminded that we chose these people in our pre-life planning. They are reflecting what requires mending within ourselves. When we can accept and acknowledge this, we increase the ability to heal and release the suffering that accompanies this experience. To break the vicious cycle of judgment and pain, we must embody love and compassion for ourselves and ultimately for others. Relinquish the pull from adverse emotions and actions attributed to ego such as pride, control and judgment. Forgive yourself for your role in this experience and the anguish it has caused you and others.

For Divine Healing to be effective, it is not necessary to confront any individual who caused you harm. Divine Healing is on a deep soul level and incorporates forgiveness as a method to heal inner personal trauma. It is a tool to open your heart to self-love and love for others. The first time you put this into practice may feel unnatural and uncomfortable, but the healing you experience may be transformative in your personal soul journey.

Traditional forgiveness is ego motivated. It is black or white, good or bad. It is polarizing and often leads to judgment. We are forced into an us against them scenario, victim vs. perpetrator. We perceive this action as being done to us. The event is viewed as a random act that we have no control over, and we internalize a victim mentality. We have been conditioned to accept these experiences without exploring why they are so persistent in our life. We are transported into a downward spiral that may become difficult to crawl out of. The result of these assumptions creates grief, anger, guilt and shame, causing a low vibrational frequency.

For Divine Healing to occur, we must completely change our perspective on forgiveness. Reframe your understanding of forgiveness to incorporate the concept that divine forgiveness is a state of being and not a concrete feeling. It is the avenue towards emotional freedom that we pre-planned in the Heavenly Realm. Accept that we chose this experience out of love, so that healing will set us free from the destructive emotions attached to our soul. In actuality, the Universe creates situations our soul requires for spiritual growth and awareness. We draw in people and events to fulfill our planned pre-birth life lessons. These individuals and situations reflect what requires healing within ourselves. Even the most traumatic circumstances may be the key factor to heal our souls from a deep wound that has kept us in a state of despair. We cannot control others; we can only control how we respond to other people's actions. We are not a victim, and we have sovereignty over how we respond to every situation that occurs in our life. The lessons we need to learn are contained within the situation. The only way for inner peace and growth to occur is by working through our emotions.

The first step of Divine Healing is to feel the impact of your experience and emotions attached to that event. Simply by alerting the Universe to your intent to heal, you are creating an opening for a shift in awareness. The Universe opens a space for change and growth to occur. Document your emotions to help organize your thoughts. Recalling the experience is not necessary for this process to work. The main goal is to focus on the emotions that emerge once you begin your healing journey. Any healthy method of processing your emotions is effective; you are in charge. Next, examine how you interpreted that experience or emotion. This is often where the victim mentality spirals us into a state of despair, and we relinquish our power to the perpetrator and the situation. It is imperative to now reframe your experience and approach it with an entirely new perspective. View the situation as a life lesson necessary for your growth and spiritual enlightenment.

Empower yourself and redirect your energy into healing. Reframe your thought process to allow an enlightened perspective on any life event you previously viewed as debilitating. Every critical experience occurred to alert you to what required mending within yourself. You have always had the control and power.

These concepts may seem foreign and difficult to process initially. Acknowledge that incidents and people keep recurring in your life that elicit these similar emotions that require healing within you. This may be a very difficult aspect of your life challenge to accept. We will explore an overwhelming amount of anecdotal evidence that supports this alternate perspective. This is a reasonable and enlightened explanation for why our life presents itself in this format. When we can accept this concept, we may begin to drastically alter our life to a purposeful and spiritually-motivated existence.

Do not put effort into analyzing the situation; focus predominantly on redirecting your energy into healing the emotions that arise. You do not have to revisit every incident that caused you pain in the past. Divine Healing is at a soul level and does not require human interaction. It requires strength, commitment and soul-searching on your part. My hope is that the end result will alter your life experience to alert you to the power of forgiveness and allow love and joy to dominate the space that previously held pain.

In life there are no random events or coincidences. The Universe is reflecting a deep wound which needs to be healed. This is an opportunity, not a punishment. You can continue giving your power away or you can take your power back. When you are resolving present suffering, you are alleviating and releasing past trauma. You are also empowering yourself to deal with future situations that may create similar strong emotional responses.

It is human nature to misinterpret many experiences that occurred in our childhood. We lay blame within ourselves from events that were totally out of our control. Throughout our lives, we may be subconsciously drawn to people and circumstances that reinforce these untruths. Now is the time to alleviate the burdens of a lifetime. Heal the inner child with the perspective of your spiritually enlightened self. When you return to that memory where the inner child was abused and shamed, recreate the event by infusing your love and enlightened intentions into the experience. Speak to your inner child with compassion and kindness. Attempt to refraim your experience with a higher awakened perspective. You can continually lay blame on those that wounded you. This action places you in a revolving door of re-experiencing the pain and suffering from your childhood and entrenches you in a victim mentality. Give yourself permission to step out of this trauma and take control of the narrative. By re-discovering and loving your inner child, you have opened the door to identify your most genuine path to healing. You have the power to live this experience with a forgiving and compassionate perspective. Understand that those who have hurt you are likely coming from a place of pain and anguish within themselves. They may never have truly loved themselves, so they were unable to fully love you. Attempt to internalize the favorable aspects of your chidhood and focus predominantly on those emotions that fill you with love. It is important to work through the feelings that hold you back from living your most authentic and joyful life. Always remember to be kind and forgiving towards yourself during your healing journey.

 It is normal to experience an increase in fear and emotional pain during the initial stages of this process. This is an expected and necessary response to working through buried emotions. Use these triggers as a tool to alert you to what requires healing for growth to occur. Experiencing life through contrast is the key to every meaningful lesson. We must feel the impact of retrieving painful emotions to experience the freedom of releasing these debilitating sentiments into the Universe. This may be the catalyst you require to create purpose and meaning in your life. When we re-discover who we truly are by healing the most critical aspects of ourselves, our life purpose may reveal itself. This is the reason we bravely chose to experience these challenges on Earth. Seek out any healthy avenue that will support you in dealing with the strong emotions that come to the surface. There are professional, spiritual and many other resources that can be helpful at this stage in healing.

We will now explore a step-by-step process for Divine Healing. It will require repeating the exercises multiple times for healing to occur. This may be the most challenging aspect of your life journey. Approach it with patience and an open heart. Divine Healing may conceivably be the catalyst for a more peace-filled and loving existence. Documenting your thoughts could be beneficial for future reference. You may want to share this experience with a trusted loved one or use it as a tool to continue on your healing venture. This is your journey, and you are in control. Trust the process and your ability to take your power back. We will now embark on a step-by-step plan to begin your healing journey.

THE DIVINE HEALING PROCESS

Alert The Universe

Send out your intention to the Universe that you are initiating your healing journey. This can be accomplished through prayer, meditation, documentation, speaking out loud or creating a dialogue within yourself. This will trigger your consciousness to alert your emotions that require attention. This shift in awareness sends out an elevated energy into the Universe to create an opening for healing to occur. Intention for positive change is an extremely powerful tool to initiate the healing process.

Honor Emotions

Allow your emotions to freely surface and release all judgment surrounding the experience or feelings that emerge. These emotions may be shame, guilt, fear, grief, abandonment, rejection, hatred, panic, depression, anxiety, self-loathing or any combination of emotions that come up for you.

For this process to work, it is not essential to recall the exact memory or incident associated with every emotion. There are often many events that contribute to our most profound sentiments. Document every emotion as it surfaces and also the memory that emerges if there is one. A combination of emotions and memories may come up simultaneously. Start with the most prominent emotion and peel back the layers to discover deeper repressed feelings. I recommend repeating this process separately with each emotion or painful memory that emerges.

Release Victim Mentality

During this phase of the process, it is normal to view yourself as a victim. Honour your story from a victim mentality and allow your emotions to emerge freely. This critical step may become the trigger required to initiate viewing this experience with an alternative perspective. When we are immobilized within the depths of victim mentality, it is often challenging to release the confining emotions that accompany this perceived prison we feel we are in. It is imperative to now release the victim mentality and remain open to the process.

Change Perception

This step flips the switch and puts you in charge of every emotion and experience. Only you can choose to change your perspective regarding people and situations that cause you pain. Understand that they are resonating an emotion that requires healing within you. Objectively reflect on how these feelings continually re-emerge in your life. The lesson you need to learn is contained within the experience and emotion. You are awakened and your soul is gaining awareness of the job that needs to be done. The most important aspect of Divine Healing is that you release the emotion that has held you captive and thereby stop the cycle of repetitive incidents that incite this pain. While healing present emotions, you are subsequently resolving past pain. The stories we have told ourselves in the past are not accurate. They do not deserve the energy required to live with them. You are not the victim; they are not the perpetrator.

Our Soul's Perspective

When we approach this process with an open heart and mind, we are alerted to healing from our soul's perspective. This divine gift of knowledge creates an opportunity for us to embrace the answers to our life purpose and soul plan. To fully understand Divine Healing, it is important to be aware of how critical our pre-life soul plan is to this journey. It will be beneficial to incorporate our soul's perspective into the Divine Healing process. I will be discussing these concepts in great detail throughout the book, so for now I only ask you to remain open to the process.

Long before we were born, we pre-planned many critical experiences that alerted us to what required healing in this lifetime. This is called our soul contract. We created this contract with members of our soul family with whom we have experienced many lifetimes together. The primary motivation in the Heavenly Realm is to heal the wounds on our soul that may have plagued us throughout these lifetimes. We are the ones, through our Higher Soul Selves, who choose what is required for our soul to heal in this lifetime. Once these goals are achieved, we internalize that lesson on our soul for all eternity.

We are not privy to the emotions of our earthly bodies while in the Afterlife. Our Higher Soul Self may miscalculate the intensity of our life lessons and create burdens that may overwhelm us on Earth. The one factor we cannot plan for is the concept of free will. We must incorporate all these options into planning for our life on Earth. Every plan we create with other souls is out of love and enlightened intentions. We are able to orchestrate our life plan from a practical perspective that incorporates the needs of all members within our soul group. Once we enter our earthly body, we experience a state of amnesia, which clouds our ability to view the entirety of our life purpose. This is both a blessing and a challenge that we must work on throughout our lifetime. Once on Earth, our primary purpose becomes processing a scenario our soul pre-planned before we came into this lifetime. Our soul is aware of every possibility available to us on our healing journey and includes these tools in our life plan. Our Higher Soul Self incorporates triggers, synchronicity, premonition, intuition, dreams, signs, nature and many other factors into our experience. I will provide you with many options on how to become aware of these crucial tools. As you process each aspect of your spiritual plan, you come closer to realizing your life purpose and who you are on a deep soul level.

Re-examine Experience

We can now reassess our understanding of every adverse experience and the emotions that do not serve us in any authentic way. Approach these experiences as pre-planned events necessary for growth and learning and not as a punishment. In the past, we were projecting misperceptions of our own pain and fear, which often surface as anger. We then add shame and guilt to our story. Guilt is anger turned inwards and is one of the most destructive emotions to our spiritual, mental and physical health and well-being. Many of these feelings are a result of misinterpreting the original event. From this renewed perspective, we are empowered to process the underlying emotions and release the debilitating energy attached to that feeling. By re-examining the event and releasing the victim mentality, we are one step closer to reclaiming our purpose and discovering our Higher Soul Self.

Releasing Emotions

Sit with the emotion that arises. Honour that feeling as being a part of you. These emotions have potentially been embedded in your soul for a long time. In your mind's eye, envelop that emotion with love and tenderness. Visualize the pain getting smaller and softer until it dissolves. Bathe the emotions in forgiveness and compassion and release your debilitating sentiments into the Universe. This may be a challenging part of the process for you. The first time you put this step into practice may feel uncomfortable. You can choose to release your emotions in any healthy format that works for you. When you release your pain into the Universe, it will be absorbed and distributed appropriately by nature. There is an incredible energy field in nature that can redirect your pain into a learning opportunity for other souls. Some of that energy may be directed at those who have harmed you. This is not a punishment but an opportunity for them to experience and learn from their actions. As humans, this is done at such a subtle level that we are not consciously aware of what is occurring. Nature has an innate ability to disperse or absorb energy to create a perfect balance.

Allow forgiveness and love to replace the space where pain once resided. Understand that you had to experience these emotions and events so that you may recognize them as being a critical learning opportunity. Their job was to alert you to an important aspect of yourself that required healing. You have begun releasing the overburdening emotions, and they will cease to serve any purpose for you.

Awareness

Be aware that this is your soul calling out to heal the emotions that continually reoccur in your life. You have lived out this experience in many forms during your lifetime. You are becoming alerted to the triggers which are placed in your life for awareness of your soul's journey. You are retrieving energy from past emotions that have held you captive. You are now empowered to speak your truth. This enables you to release residual debilitating energy that is paralyzing your growth and happiness.

Be aware that when you allow your pain and adverse feelings to surface, you may experience intense emotional responses. This is a normal reaction and may require additional supportive measures to assist you in dealing with these emotions. Enlisting professionals and support on this part of your journey is a strength, not a weakness. Keep working through the process. The intensity of retrieving repressed feelings that have previously enslaved you in a state of despair will begin to dissipate. You are allowing forgiveness and love to dominate that space in your heart. You are now open to accept that you are solidly on the path to spiritual freedom through forgiveness.

Forgiveness

Forgiveness is understandably the most challenging aspect of this process. This step will take a lot of inner searching and self-reflection to achieve. Remember, you are accomplishing this at a soul level. You do not require any interaction with those who have caused you pain. This level of forgiveness is a state of being and not a traditional tangible action. When you send forgiveness into the Universe, you are freeing yourself.

Honour every emotion that surfaces as it emerges. Acknowledge the feeling, release the detrimental impact it has on your life and relinquish the victim mentality accompanying that emotion. View the emotion with an enlightened perspective. Accept that this feeling continually re-emerges in your life so that you are alerted to what requires healing. These experiences and resulting emotions are pre-planned events necessary for your growth and learning. Focus on healing the accompanying emotions while still honoring your strength in taking your power back from the experience. Visualize that emotion as being an unwanted guest you are now ready to set free. Feel empowered to encapsulate that emotion, and watch it get smaller and softer until you release it into the Universe. Fill that space with forgiveness and love.

If you are being challenged with the concept of forgiveness, attempt to approach this process from an alternative perspective. Journeying down this path to forgiveness is primarily centered around discovering your Higher Soul Self. In this sense, forgiveness is the path to release the paralyzing emotions that have held you in a state of pain and immobility. It is important to acknowledge that people and situations were placed in your life as a means to alert you to what is critical to heal within yourself. Divine Healing is accomplished through this process of awareness and may help you reawaken the powerful soul you are.

When you release these confining and restrictive emotions that paralyze your ability to accomplish your life purpose, you are empowering yourself to fulfill your soul contract. Forgiveness is the direct path to emotional freedom. Relinquish the traditional meaning of forgiveness to free your soul to continue on your life journey. Trust that your Higher Soul Self orchestrated every major life event with the intention of soul development through love and positive intention. Use forgiveness as the catalyst to emotional freedom that it was always intended to be.

Forgiveness creates peace in your heart, which in turn allows a space for harmony in your mind, body and soul. Your confidence and non-judgmental attitude are felt by others around you. When you are able to forgive others, even considering the worst of their actions, you are empowering yourself with the greatest healing potential. Forgiveness requires patience and commitment to work through the process. Living in a state of anger and pain requires an enormous amount of energy. Once you have worked through the layers of pain and hurt, your ability to forgive will become more comfortable. You are becoming aware of how ego has created a state of fear for you. Once this fear dissipates, you can begin to live your life with clarity and purpose. The initial times you go through these steps will be the most challenging. As you go on to experience life, the process of forgiveness becomes less complicated and requires less intense effort. Initially, forgiveness may feel disingenuous at this stage. By repeating the process, you will become more comfortable with your emotions. You are establishing a foundation for a future with hope and love. This frees your soul to live the life you were intended to live. Simply sending your intent to forgive will activate the Universe to reflect increased positive opportunities to heal yourself and the collective. When we send forgiveness to those individuals who we feel have hurt us, we open a path to emotional freedom for ourselves and create an opportunity for others to begin their healing adventure. Intention is a powerful tool to use on your journey. Your positive vibrational energy will resonate internally and will project out into the Universe. The end result will incorporate an increase in affirmative experiences and release debilitating emotions that do not serve your higher purpose.

Surrender

Surrender to the realization that life was never happening to you but is merely a reflection of you. What you project into the world is mirroring what you experience in return. When you internalize your pain, you allow that pain to become a cancer on your soul. When you surrender your pain, you allow a clear pathway to return to your Higher Soul Self. You are awakened to your purpose in this life and begin to focus on achieving your soul goals. Surrender to the realization that this was all orchestrated by you, in your pre-life plan, to free yourself from the confines of emotions that stagnate your spiritual progress. Surrender to the knowledge that you will achieve freedom through forgiveness. Surrender to the truth that love is the greatest healer of all, and that Divine Love surrounds and supports you at all times. Surrender to the belief that every experience leaves a permanent imprint on your soul.

Gratitude

Once you have worked through the stages of forgiveness and surrender, the next stage is gratitude. To fully experience the rewards that the Universe has for us, it is important to express gratitude. Gratitude comes from the core of your being. It frees you to become who you are truly meant to be. As part of your daily routine, express gratitude for at least one thing in your life. Gratitude reveals connection to the spiritual world. Gratitude is that final stage of acceptance that may be difficult to acknowledge. When we are pre-planning our future life ventures with other souls in the Heavenly Realm, we do so without all the emotions attached to our earthly bodies. In the Afterlife, we understand that even the most cruelly perceived experiences are motivated by love. In the Higher Realm, we view these events strictly as an avenue to heal deep emotions that have held us captive in this life and potentially many lifetimes.

You are well on your healing path when you accept the concept of challenges being blessings. You are becoming grateful for the incidents you once perceived as being debilitating. You are processing the realization that you pre-planned these life events with other souls in the Afterlife before you came into this lifetime. You have gratitude in knowing that you are not a victim and that you have control within every situation. You are becoming grateful for having the strength to allow this human experience to bring you to a place of spiritual growth. When you hold this experience in forgiveness, you understand that love has taken the place of pain. You are empowered to make decisions based on love and compassion and not fear or pain. Express gratitude for yourself in getting to the final stages of healing and peace.

Through gratitude, you may experience emotions that overwhelm you. Allow these genuine life-affirming feelings to absorb into every part of your being. You have opened a space for joy and pleasure, and this may initially feel unfamiliar. Sit with these emotions and allow them to develop into who you are becoming. This is the true essence of healing power. You may need to take baby steps to fully appreciate the enormity of this state of being. Build a solid foundation of love and gratitude.

As we all know, life is not a smooth ride. You will require this foundation when you encounter challenging events and emotions in the future. You now have the tools and well-earned strength to deal with whatever life has in store for you.

SELF-REFLECTION THROUGH DIVINE HEALING

Follow what your heart requires for healing now that you are open to the experience. Align your mind, body and spirit in perfect harmony. Continue meditating or sit in self-reflection, and work on living a healthy lifestyle. Always care for yourself first. Feed your body with nutritional food. Walk in nature. Sleep well and restoratively. Maintain an optimistic perspective on life and know that your intentions are powerful. Be grateful for each day and every experience. Surround yourself with like-minded people who support and strengthen your positive energy.

As you reflect on the process of Divine Healing, be aware that you always have the power in every facet of your journey. This is only one method to achieve soul growth. My intention is to stimulate your curiosity so you may research, discuss and explore any healthy avenue to further your spiritual journey. I am sharing with you what has been effective for myself and those I love. The greatest gift of healing is to awaken your soul to discover your passion and life purpose. We have entered into a higher dimensional vibration that allows us to find the answers we seek. My hope is that it leads you to a life of joy and happiness and ends the cycle of repetitive debilitating experiences from dominating your life. If I can influence even one person to live a more joyous life, then every moment of writing this book is worth it. My greatest motivation is creating an opportunity to help decrease pain and suffering through forgiveness and clearing a path to discover your Higher Soul Self. My love and prayers are with you all on that journey.

DIVINE HEALING IN PRACTICE

I have had to work through the steps of Divine Healing many times before healing occurred. I still revisit the process of Divine Healing when unresolved or residual depleting emotions re-emerge. The process is less intense and less energy-consuming every time I put it into practice.

Throughout my life, patterns emerged that reflected my internal feeling of unworthiness. I had low self-esteem and looked for validation in many unhealthy ways. I lived my life feeling that I had to do better and be better than anyone else to be loved and heard. I am now able to recognize the pain and shame I felt for so many years. I realize that all these incidents were brought into my life as an opportunity to heal. I did not have to go back to specific incidents that created these feelings within myself. I allowed those feelings to freely come to the surface, and that is what I centered my healing on. When the actual event surfaced for me, I focused on releasing the accompanying emotions while still honoring my strength in taking my power back from the experience.

Upon reflection, I recall many incidents where I projected my repressed pain onto others. I often viewed people and events as being a destructive force surrounding me. I was instantly transported into a victim mentality. I am now thankful to those who have been participants with me on my journey towards self-discovery. I required those experiences to learn and grow. I now understand that they were essential in fulfilling a great awakening within myself.

A critical aspect of my journey was to release my inner child's pain. As an adult, I did this by envisioning myself as the vulnerable child I was at that time. I was able to spiritually go back and convey reassuring words to that hurt child that I felt I had not received in my past. I could now revisit the painful experiences from my childhood and comfort my inner child self with compassion and love. I wrapped my arms around her and released all the pain into the Universe. I surrounded my inner child and adult self with a renewed sense of pure love, protection and forgiveness.

I now accept that I am a loveable, worthy and special person. I do not need to pretend to be someone I am not. I am me without apology. I send love into the Universe, including to those whom I previously felt wronged me. I realize this was all part of a divine plan to free my soul to be open to learning my truth. Part of that truth is knowing that this love and knowledge is imprinted on my soul for all eternity. I work daily on finding the joy and happiness I denied myself in the past.

Divine Healing works on a soul level, not always through specific memories or incidents. Often, it is many memories that elicit emotions of pain, anger, sorrow, guilt, shame, helplessness, rejection or any emotion that may surface. When these debilitating emotions come forward, you may require additional support for dealing with them. I have used counsellors, prayer, books, restorative yoga, meditation, breathing exercise, Body Talk counselling and guidance from spiritual supports and from Source. Family and friends have been an invaluable resource of healing for me. Use any healthy avenue you feel will help you on your journey.

Divine Healing is a gift I have shared with loved ones on their mending journey. The Universe creates opportunities for this process to take place when healing is required for spiritual growth. It is amazing to witness how this process is like a lifeline to those seeking answers. A dear friend of mine was tortured by a traumatic experience that occurred many years ago. He had never spoken about this incident but relived it daily in his mind for over forty years. The first step in his healing process was to verbalize the incident and allow his repressed emotions to emerge. He then worked on changing his perception of the incident. He was recycling past experiences and allowing ego (fear) to dictate his emotions. He was now ready to accept that his soul had pre-arranged this incident as an opportunity for immense spiritual development for himself and those involved in this experience. We discussed that there was likely a past-life connection to what he went through, and that it was time to release his pain into the Universe. It became imperative for his internal torture to end by moving through this experience. By processing his deeply ingrained emotions, he is not only becoming aware of an integral aspect of his life's purpose, but he is also gaining increased awareness to alert him to his soul journey.

In the past, this one incident in his life dictated many of his critical adult decisions. He is working diligently on releasing the detrimental hold these emotions have had on him. By viewing the incident with an entirely different perspective, he has embarked on a healing journey. Understanding that this was planned in a pre-life session with another soul gives him comfort. Releasing the pain and guilt from this experience has allowed room for forgiveness and love to enter his being.

During the process of Divine Forgiveness in my own personal journey, a recurring theme wove its way into many situations I was working through. I was shown that my low self-worth created a succession of events that were the foundation to many of my challenges in life. I felt judged, attacked and undervalued in my communication with those closest to me. This theme occurred with my close family members and partners throughout my life. I became a victim and played the role very convincingly.

From a small child into adulthood, I recall many times where my feelings were dismissed and I felt unworthy. As a child I was told, "You made your bed and now you must lie in it," or "Others have it much worse." As an adult, I felt my partners would use my emotions against me or try to fix me without hearing what I was feeling. This reinforced and further entrenched me in a victim mentality.

As I worked through Divine Healing, I began to fully comprehend the true purpose of all these interactions. I realized I needed to change my perspective and understand that my loved ones were reflecting an emotion I required healing within myself. As I accepted that this was all planned in my pre-life soul contract, I saw what my spirit required to grow in truth and love. I became aware of projecting my insecurities onto others and how that reflected back on me. I saw a distinct pattern of how this same theme recurred in my life with consistent regularity. I was able to forgive myself for the role I played in perpetuating my feelings of unworthiness. I forgave others for the pain I previously felt had been inflicted on me. I alleviated my suffering through the process of Divine Healing and releasing my debilitating emotions into the Universe. I accepted myself as the loving and worthy person I am. I felt my soul required me to be rejected and not validated for me to gain understanding of my life purpose. I am now grateful for every person and experience that alerted me towards my healing path and led me to discovering who I am at the core of my being.

The concept is straightforward, but the work required may often feel overwhelming and daunting. This is a lifelong process that will challenge you and also create opportunities that continually allow you to learn and grow. There is no growth in neutrality. I experienced many days where I felt I was taking one step forward and two steps back. To this day, there are moments that trigger my self-doubt and insecurities. I revisit the process of Divine Healing to work through the emotions that re-emerge. This now takes much less time and requires a less intense emotional process to return to that place of inner peace. Use every tool available on your healing journey that you feel comfortable with. The clarity that emerges will be transformative. Release the victim mentality, and embrace the powerful soul that you are.

There are many practical aspects to Divine Healing that have the potential to improve current and future relationships. Personally, I now attempt to view every life challenge through a clearer lens. Divine Healing has presented an opportunity for a transformative perspective on the big picture of life. As spiritual beings having a human experience, we will continually make mistakes. I now understand there are no mistakes in the spiritual sense, and every misstep is an opportunity for learning and growth.

When there is potential for conflict in a conversation, I attempt to consciously approach that interaction with an alternative perspective. I now understand that all parties are fulfilling a contract made with each other. I am alerted to the lesson much sooner and attempt to release the victim mentality before it is triggered. I still feel pain, frustration and anger, but I attempt to reframe my emotions from a less victimized approach. I realized I previously entered many discussions feeling judged and projected that judgment onto others who triggered that repressed emotion. Through this awareness I can now attempt to enter conversations with a new set of tools. This has resulted in more meaningful and honest relationships. I will still occasionally revert back to engrained detrimental messaging, but I am much quicker to flip the switch to my aware and rediscovered Spiritual Self. Along with the awareness comes the realization that this is an integral aspect of my purpose. As I absorb my lessons, I am given the gift of spiritual enlightenment to fully discover my soul's path.

We can also apply Divine Healing through incidents that occur regularly in life. It is a quick method to relieve stress when we encounter frustrating daily occurrences. For example, in a situation where a driver cuts you off, take a moment to process your anger instead of internalizing it. Slow down, take a deep breath and count backwards from five. Allow the anger to flow through you and release it slowly. Acknowledge that this person was put in your path to help you deal with the emotions that came up for you. Realize that this experience will recur in a variety of ways until the emotions you feel are processed. The incident may have brought up feelings of fear, anger, rage or any unresolved emotions. The anger you experience may be disproportionate to the actual event. Because of the instant intense emotions released, your normal protective mechanism for suppressing those feelings was set free. It is similar to opening a pressure valve of trapped steam, releasing it for a few seconds and slamming the lid back down.

The Universe is sending you a clear and direct message. Recognize this incident as a gift that has alerted you to what requires healing in your soul. Allow yourself to acknowledge the source of these emotions. You may need to process these feelings at a later date when you have time to delve deeper into their origins. Remember, only you can control your reaction to the incident. You cannot regulate the actions of others. Chances are the driver was not even aware they cut you off. You are well on your way to your healing journey when you can send forgiveness and gratitude out into the Universe for this experience and other incidents you previously perceived as negative.

You can also practice alleviating physical discomfort through the process of Divine Healing. When you release adverse emotions, you are empowered to lessen physical suffering. Focus your restorative energy around the affliction or area of disease. Mentally encapsulate that region, hold it with love and visualize the dissolving of your ailment. Intention and phrasing are powerful and may alter your perception of any life occurrence. Replace the word "pain" with "unwellness" or "hate" with "dislike." These are subtle changes that alert the Universe of your intention to a more optimistic result. Rephrasing of powerful unfavorable messages may also instantly flip the switch to alert your inner self to approach life with a more positive and hopeful outlook. Use these tools along with other healthy options of healing you choose. Be consistent and dedicated to this process. We are all a combination of mind, body and spirit. We must work on all aspects of ourselves to create harmony in our life. When we release emotional suffering, we begin to repair physical unwellness. When physical and emotional discomfort begin to alleviate, we make room for our bodies' natural restorative abilities. Spiritual strength is a powerful tool to incorporate into your healing journey. Embrace every modality of wellness available. There is Western Medicine, Eastern Medicine and Natural Medicine, which all offer their expertise in your recovery. You will discover that even by initiating the process of healing any aspect of yourself, you will begin to improve your overall quality of life.

Through Divine Healing, you are gaining knowledge and tools towards enlightenment of your life journey. When you reach the place of love and forgiveness, you will find that life will reflect genuine emotions and favorable experiences to enter into your world. This requires a lifelong commitment and a complete change in perspective. Ego, pain, pride and anger limit and cloud your ability to make optimistic choices in life. Sitting in these debilitating sentiments is energy consuming, paralyzing and unproductive. As fear and pain dissolve and love enters, you can open your heart to spiritual awakening. Love is energy-inducing. When love fills your being, you open space to receive divine messages. The information you receive will help you discover your true purpose and calling. It will open doors you never knew existed. When you choose love, it becomes easier to make healthy choices in life.

Once the negative emotions have dissipated and are released, you may find they re-emerge. Do not panic; this is normal. Repeat the process of Divine Healing from the beginning. Subsequent dealings with these adverse emotions will become less intense and smoother to resolve. Remember, this is a marathon and not a sprint. These feelings will ebb and flow through you. This is the main reason for our journey here on Earth. Our challenges will not instantly vanish, but now we have the tools and knowledge to deal with what life has planned for us. Or, more accurately, what we have planned for our life. Honour and process each emotion as it arises, and allow love to dominate. Sit in peace, not pain. Through Divine Healing, you are well on your way to spiritual freedom, one soul at a time.

OUR SOUL'S JOURNEY INTO THE AFTERLIFE

An important aspect to fully understand our life's mission and purpose is to become aware of our soul's journey in the Afterlife. For some, this may be a challenging concept to embrace. I only ask that you approach this section with an open heart and mind. There is a beautiful flow to our soul's journey that becomes difficult to dispute with the information presented. It is important to recognize the vital role our soul's journey in the Afterlife has on our daily life experience. By remaining open and judgment free, you will be closer to realizing your personal path and life purpose.

Altering our perspectives on our mortality can radically change how we live our lives today. I will help remove fear from this natural aspect of life. I am offering an alternative approach to how we perceive death and dying in our society. It is important to remember that our soul is energy, and energy cannot be destroyed. Our soul is on a continuum of life that never ceases to exist. We are miraculously propelled into a higher energy state when this current body stops functioning.

One of my most impactful experiences around witnessing the power of our soul energy occurred when I was a young newly-graduated nurse. I remained after my evening shift to stay with a patient, who was alone during her last moments on Earth. I held her hand and guided her to release her connection with this earthly body. As she took her last breath, I clearly saw a ball of light energy that shimmered and floated over her heart center. The room filled with such an overwhelming sense of love and peace. This ball of light energy slowly lifted towards the window, and gently exited in a slightly upward motion into the beautiful night sky. This miraculous event reinforced my belief in our soul essence and granted me the strength that I would require throughout my career. This experience was the foundation for many more spiritual occurrences in the future.

Through the demise of our bodies, our spirits are free to return to our true home and the unconditional love and compassion of Source. We are embraced by our soul family with an intense love beyond any earthly emotion. Our Soul Self is welcomed and celebrated for the challenging life we came from. Earth is the most desired destination due to its potential rewards, yet the highly demanding and difficult experiences it creates prevents many souls from ever exploring here. We are greatly admired for having the courage to choose to come to this Earthly Realm. We are praised and honored upon our entrance into the Afterlife. It is in your power to choose the tools and concepts that best suit your individual journey so you may focus on discovering the best version of your soul's intended path.

I will begin by explaining how our souls were first conceived. I will then fast-forward to the demise of our earthly bodies and proceed in a sequential format of our soul's journey into the Afterlife. I will refer to Heaven as our Eternal Home, Afterlife or Higher Realm. Again, the words we use are not important. What we need to focus on is the significance of this realm being only a thought within our grasp. I will disclose concepts of what to anticipate during our transition into Heaven and who will greet us on our way. Here we will meet with our spiritual supports and reunite with our soul family. This quest carries us through learning about activities in the Afterlife and who accompanies us in these exploits.

You will learn about spirit guides, soul plans, pre-birth planning, core personalities, triggers, exit points, Akashic Records, soul levels and many wondrous adventures in the Afterlife. I will introduce you to how life selection occurs and finally our rebirth into the next chosen reincarnation. I will present these concepts in a straightforward and organized format, as I have been shown.

A fascinating aspect of soul life is discovering where we originated from. At the very beginning of our existence, we were created from energy. This energy originates within Source and is gifted to us from God's pure love. We are always connected with our Creator and are interconnected with every other soul created. We are assigned our personal individual energy pattern that we maintain throughout our existence. We also have our own energy frequency we vibrate at. These vibrational energy patterns are imprinted on our soul for eternity. I like to use the analogy of our human fingerprints as our soul energy pattern and our personality as our individual vibrational frequency. Even if some people struggle with the concept of God creating us, we can acknowledge that everything on Earth carries their unique energy frequency. If you are still skeptical about Source being our Creator, approach this concept strictly from an energy perspective. View each soul as the result of a mini big bang of energy and love coming together. Imagine your soul being the creation of this miraculous blend of loving energy.

Our first home exists within a framework that resembles a honeycomb pattern. This realization came to me as I was observing my grandchildren playing in an enclosed structure in the park. We begin our existence as swirling energy encapsulated within each individual pod, which is contained in the larger honeycomb structure. Imagine the incredible workings of a beehive as the microcosm of this community of souls. We are loved and nurtured by the energy of Divine Mothers surrounding us in their tender embrace. Their chosen spiritual calling is to fulfill an extremely important role in our soul's infancy. I visualize these beings as similar to neonatal nurses on Earth caring for premature babies in the NICU. It is not a coincidence that many of these Divine Mothers were in nursing roles in their earthbound lives. How often do we refer to nurses as "angels on Earth"? The souls created in these neighboring pods are all members of our soul famiy. We are eternally connected in love and a similar vibration. Once our soul energy has fully formed, we are assigned a spirit guide that accompanies us for all eternity. These guides are very wise and experienced souls.

We will next jump ahead and address the event of our earthly bodies' demise and crossing over of our soul energies. People have commonly spoken of death with fear, avoidance and firm beliefs that this is where their journey ends. These common misconceptions could not be further from the truth. Our soul, the core of our being, continues on and returns to our Eternal Home. We shed our bodies with no remorse and little emotion. Visualize a beautiful butterfly emerging from a confining cocoon and now having the freedom to fly unencumbered to the Higher Realms. Our bodies served their purpose, and we are now ready to move on from their limited and restrictive earthly form. The tether that binds us to our bodies is severed, and our souls are free to continue on their journey. We are welcomed with overwhelming love and compassion within our Eternal Home. There is no judgment or blame for the lives we lived on Earth, only forgiveness on a divine level. All anger, fear, jealousy, pain and unworthiness are removed from our souls' beings. All these debilitating emotions are shed along with any physical aspect of our earthly existences. We are celebrated and accepted with a love that far exceeds anything experienced on Earth. Our core soul essence remain intact, and we only bring our knowledge and love with us during our transition.

We are never alone once we begin our soul journey into the Afterlife. When we were first created, we had at least one spirit guide which was assigned to us from Source. Our spirit guide has previously lived in the Earthly Realm in many lifetimes. They are chosen for us based on how they complement our needs. Depending on their level of experience, they may have a group of souls they oversee. We may also have been assigned more than one spirit guide. This all depends on the lessons we need to learn and the complexity of those earthly experiences. Our spirit guide is eternally attached to us. They are our constant companions on Earth and are instrumental in navigating our journey into the Afterlife. We may also encounter loved ones who have previously crossed over at this stage. Our loved ones will appear in a form that is familiar to us. They often present themselves at an age where they are in their prime. I often visualize spiritual beings coming to me around their mid-thirties. They always appear healthy with no residual disease or advanced age or illness marring their features. Spirit, or spiritual beings, are also recognizable through their personalities and soul energies. Our soul embodies all aspects of our individuality. We retain our talents, humor, passions, flaws and even less-endearing characteristics. We carry all aspects of our core beings into every reincarnation we choose to experience. Our soul family greets us so that we feel comforted and loved. Our soul family has been with us since the conception of our souls. We share many lifetimes and adventures with these valued members of our soul groups. They then step back to allow us to continue on our journey to the next stage with our spirit guide. Do not worry; we will encounter our soul families again very soon.

In this time of enlightenment, it is getting exceedingly difficult to deny that our souls continue on. We are increasingly becoming aware of our abilities to contact and communicate with loved ones who have crossed over. Communication with spiritual beings, through meditation or mediumship, helps to validate the continuation of life. Thousands of people who have had Near-Death Experiences (NDEs) consistently speak of the beauty and magnificent surroundings in the Afterlife. It is interesting to note that our past-life memories are forever stored within our soul, and we can retrieve them through a variety of methods in our current life. We all have the potential to access some of these memories, and I will explore this concept throughout the following chapters.

Every soul has their unique experience, but the general journey is remarkably similar. Immediately upon arrival into the Afterlife, we are surrounded and infused with the most glorious love. This love is the Highest Power's, or God's, love. It is a state of being resonating in the highest energy vibration. When our soul crosses over, we absorb this Divine Love that illuminates our entire entity. We do not have the words on Earth to comprehend the glory of Source or the Kingdom of the Afterlife.

After my father crossed over to the Afterlife, I prayed to him every day to help me understand what it is like in Heaven. My dad opened a space for me to briefly experience the love and light of the Afterlife. No other feeling on Earth can compare to that state of being. It felt as if my soul exploded out the top of my head and immediately entered a realm of pure joy and peace. Words are inadequate to describe the ecstatic love that permeated my entire essence. It was only a moment in time, as I do not feel my earthly self could endure that heightened state of emotional ecstasy for longer than I experienced. The beauty is indescribable and the love all-consuming. I sit in gratitude for my father and spiritual supports that presented this enormous gift to me.

I also learned that we have more of a significant role in planning for our transition into Heaven than we realize. I have been shown that our preconceived perception of the Afterlife influences our experience when we cross over. Through prayer or intentional thought, we have the ability to orchestrate whatever our heart desires for our passage into the Afterlife. We are in control even in the last moments of our earthly life. As a society, we have been conditioned to relinquish our authority in many facets of our existence. Take our power back and envision a beautiful transition back to our Eternal Home. This is a gift from Source to lessen the fear surrounding our earthly demise. I am offering a concept that may help you deal with the anxiety around your body's return to nature. There is no harm in presenting you with this one aspect of your life's transition. I strongly believe we can all conceive and plan for our journey into the Afterlife. I will empower you with the tools and knowledge needed to accomplish this miraculous transition into the Higher Energy Realms in later chapters.

In Heaven, nature is in perfect harmony at all times. There is no decay, just a life force resonating within all aspects of nature. The grass is always the greenest of greens, and the flowers are always in bloom. During meditation, I have been shown colors that are indescribable to our human eye. When we view a rainbow on Earth, we are aware of the seven basic shades existing in the spectrum of color. In the Heavenly Realm, there are a multitude of hues existing beyond every shade we visualize on Earth. The closest I have ever witnessed this intensity of color is within the Northern lights. During a very vulnerable time in my life, my husband and I were given a great gift that we will forever be grateful for. We experienced dancing and swirling lights in the northern sky in hues we had never viewed before or since. We were encapsulated in this miraculous energy of beauty and love. Every day we are given glimpses into what our life will be like in the Heavenly Realm. We just have to embrace the truth that is there for us to see.

Another aspect of the Heavenly Realm that we do not have to be concerned about is regarding communication. There are no language barriers in Heaven. We have the innate ability to receive messages through our soul directly into the core of our being. This is accomplished telepathically. We absorb the purest meaning of words and instinctually communicate in the most loving language. Many mediums are gifted with the ability to connect telepathically with souls in the Afterlife. This form of communication occurs instantly in the Heavenly Realm, but as mediums it takes time to fully comprehend the language of the soul. This process is similar to learning a foreign language on Earth. I will discuss how medium communication works in the following chapters and how everyone can tap into the language of our souls.

Time is a fascinating concept in the Afterlife and may be beyond our earthly ability to comprehend. Our perception of time is not present in Heaven as it is on Earth. Time on Earth is linear, but in Heaven it is multidimensional. In the Afterlife, there is no past, present or future. Time always is. We can transcend time in the Afterlife and be at more than one place at any given moment. We can relive times we envision to return to or move ahead at will. We can perceive many lifetimes simultaneously when we choose to do so. Years on this earthly plain may be perceived as moments in the Heavenly Realm.

Continuing on our transition, our spirit guide then brings us to the next phase of our journey. Throughout our adventure in the Afterlife, we are continually aware and comforted by the love energy of Source in every aspect of our journey in the Heavenly Realm. As we pass through the Divine Light, we are reminded of Source being the loving energy that envelops every soul and encapsulates the entire Universe.

Next, we appear in front of a Council of Elders. The Council is chosen specifically for each individual soul journey and is tailored for our personal needs. The Council of Elders is composed of souls who have lived many lives and are trusted to Source's inner circle. They are the Ascended Masters who have achieved this level of supreme knowledge through many lifetimes of conquering challenges and learning lessons in a variety of realms in the galaxy. They have earned their position and were chosen by the Highest Power to become a member of this esteemed Divine Council. We sit in awe and admiration of the importance and magnificence of the Council. One of the most intimidating aspects of this phase is when we are taken through our life review. The trepidation we experience comes mainly from within ourselves. Our life review consists of presenting us with every experience and interaction we participated in on Earth. Every action, thought, intention and motivation has been recorded. We are not judged but are held accountable for the life we came from. We not only discover how our actions affect others, but we also intensely feel the emotions we generated within others during that interaction. We become aware of the feelings and motivations of those whom we perceived harmed us on the Earthly Realm. We are gifted with a great knowing of every life event or emotion we ever experienced. The judgment comes only from ourselves to assist us in formulating a plan for our next reincarnation and to learn lessons for our soul to grow in empathy and love. With this knowledge, we are given insight into one of the greatest lessons we can learn on Earth. That lesson is to approach every interaction in life with love and forgiveness in our heart. Continually work on releasing adverse sentiments, such as pride and anger from your life, as they are strong characteristics of ego that block your spiritual journey. Our spirit guide remains with us at all times, including through our life review with the Council of Elders. This review is likely the most intense aspect of our journey back home. Our Elders know everything about our earthly lives, including our past lives and potential future reincarnations. These Ascended Masters have been specifically chosen for us to best suit our needs. They surround us with love and compassion while conducting their review with fairness and firmness.

The life you came from greatly influences where your soul goes from here. If you have lived a very challenging life or died a tragic death, your soul may require a prolonged recovery time. There are appropriate spaces for every life situation you came from. Some of these areas are specifically for healing, addiction recovery, or a private resting area. Our soul decides, in consultation with our guides, what the most beneficial course of action is at this time.

I personally do not believe in Hell or purgatory as seen through the teachings of many religions. I have been shown that the souls of people who have lived evil lives go to a special area where intense learning and reconditioning take place. Intent of the evil actions of these souls is heavily considered when processing where they will learn their intended lessons. There are many levels or realms where souls may choose to go or are assigned to reside in for healing to occur. The soul that has chosen to live an evil life with malicious intent may be assigned to a lower level in the continuum of realms in the Afterlife. If they perceive this place to be a hellish area, then that is where they will reside. No one is stuck in any area, and they are free to request to heal in a more enlightened section at any time. These evil souls will have to experience every emotion that they inflicted on others in the Earthly Realm exponentially more. Their journey is intense and challenging so they can become acutely aware of all the pain they created on Earth. This is not a punishment but is an awareness lesson for the betterment of their soul's progression. In extreme cases, only Source has the power and authority to manipulate and rearrange any soul's energy. These souls are still extended love and forgiveness but must undergo many steps of healing before they rejoin their soul family or are ready to reincarnate.

There are very few souls that choose to remain earthbound spirits. These souls may be referred to as ghosts and are generally young and immature in their soul development. There are no physical restraints that keep them earthbound, only emotional bonds that they have a difficult time releasing. The earthbound spirits may feel like they have unfinished business in this realm or have not come to terms with dying a tragic death. They maintain an obsessive level of attachment to a person or place on Earth. These souls retain only a small amount of energy while remaining in this realm. No soul is truly stuck as an earthbound spirit. The ghost entity is always welcomed back to Heaven when they are ready. In the Afterlife, every soul chooses a soul profession that they are called to perform. One important occupation is to become proficient at guiding wayward souls to return to their heavenly home. Their job is to assist these earthbound spirits on their re-entry journey into the Afterlife. Time is unlike our measure of time on Earth. Years in this limbo state may be perceived as only days in spiritual time. All souls retain the ability to return home at any time they choose. They only have to acknowledge our Higher Power and request to continue on their soul journey.

 These evil and ghost souls vibrate at a much lower energy level. I choose not to lower my energy level to theirs, so my interactions with these souls are limited. I have discovered that when I am in a depressed or lowered energy state, I can become vulnerable to their presence. I work diligently on maintaining an elevated energy state and protect my energy with love and light. If you ever feel a negative force near you, protect yourself by enveloping yourself and loved ones in white light. Firmly pray for their souls to enter into the light and reassure them they will be forgiven and loved. You are always in charge of your experience. Do not give your power away. Stay firm in your ability to take control of any situation that creates fear for you. You have always had the strength and power and now you are becoming aware of your God-given free will and abilities to take control of every life experience.

 These souls occasionally request to reincarnate before they have fully taken advantage of their healing opportunities. The Elders and spirit guides respectfully advise against this course of action, but we always retain our free will. These unprepared and unrepentant souls often end up repeating similar patterns from their previous life. Once again, we are given free will even if our guides are not in complete agreement with our wishes. I will later share what I have been shown regarding souls who choose evil lives in greater detail.

 Once the life review is complete, the Council of Elders releases our soul to resume on our journey. Our spirit guide continues to assist us with the process of reorientation. We now enter the phase of cleansing our souls from residual negative energy still attached to us from Earth. We go through the process of "showering our soul" from the lethargy and heaviness our earthly life has retained. We may choose to participate in a prolonged phase of rest and rejuvenation at this time. We may also be motivated to carry on our journey. Again, this is at the discretion of our spiritual supports and our Soul Self.

Once our guide returns us to our soul family, there is much celebration and an outpouring of love. Our spirit guide remains with us and continues to be available to us at all times. As previously stated, we can request what our family reunion looks like. If we want a huge party set in Roman times, we can ask for that. If we prefer a sedate return amongst nature, we can propose that scenario. I was so blessed when my father showed me his soul reunion in all its glory. He had a wonderful outdoor party with copious amounts of food and his favorite beverages. It appeared as a great banquet with a multitude of loved ones present. I recognized many crossed-over loved ones who were attending his celebration. I could even taste some of his favorite dishes that he presented to me and smell the green apple pipe tobacco he used to smoke on this Earthly Realm.

When our soul was first created, we were assigned to our primary soul group or soul family. This group consists of five to twenty souls that we experience many lives with. We have been with these souls since our incubation period. We are bound in love and a similar soul vibration that keeps us connected for eternity. After each earthly body dies, we are incarnated back to our original soul family in the Afterlife. Peace, comfort, trust and love are present within our family circle at all times. This is truly our safe place. We have lived many lives, choosing a variety of roles, to learn and grow with these souls. In one life we can be a mother, in the next life a best friend or brother, to the same soul. Each soul has a unique personality that is retained for eternity. There are serious, comical, determined and a myriad of personality types in every soul family. We role-play a variety of scenarios that most benefit each soul for their next reincarnation. We constantly learn from every soul in our soul group. In planning our next life, karmic balance and life purpose are all taken into consideration. We enter into a spiritual contract for our next life on Earth with our soul family. It is very likely that the souls we get most frustrated with in this lifetime are members of our soul family. Out of love, they are reminding us of the sometimes-painful lessons we require for our learning on this earthly plane. Often, these unresolved emotions have plagued us for many generations. When we embrace this concept, we are one step closer to realizing our purpose in this lifetime. Each lesson we learn on Earth is retained by our soul for eternity. The more advanced our soul gets, the less time we spend in this phase of the Afterlife and the less we choose to reincarnate. It may take hundreds of lifetimes to achieve this level of expertise.

We will now explore the education phase of our soul in the Afterlife. Our primary learning is with our study group. This group consists of members from our soul family and from other members of groups that are close to us. Every soul is unique and contributes diverse opportunities for growth. All our previous lives are imprinted on our soul, and we carry that into the Afterlife. Souls retain their humor and personalities in the classroom setting. We are there to do an important job, but we do not lose the joy of our inner core personality. All debilitating earthly emotions like pain and fear are left behind with the demise of our body. This opens our soul to learning on a unique level, without all the trappings of our earthly feelings.

There are a multitude of classroom settings. Each classroom focuses on specific lessons to be learned. Classrooms are as unique and varied as the souls studying in them. Spirits have the ability to place themselves in any setting they choose for optimum growth. Our souls can roam through the galaxy and participate in any experience we desire. There are a myriad of realms we may explore for advancement of learning. Souls discover how to manipulate energy for creating new life on other planets. Our souls can recreate any life experience that benefits learning and growth. The possibilities are infinite and beyond our comprehension.

The progression of learning is not unlike our earthly experience. We begin as young souls and advance to mature beings. The classrooms reflect the appropriate lessons depending on the maturity level of the souls. Each being is individual and learns at their own pace. We are always supported by our soul family, spirit guides, advanced teachers and Elders.

The beginner souls are very immature and must be gently nurtured. They are similar to preschool children in many aspects. These souls are in their infancy and must learn about empathy, teamwork and boundaries. They require much guidance and discipline. This is always balanced with love, compassion and patience. As the beginner souls mature, they are assigned to specialized soul groups who will best advance their learning and growth. Individual souls progress at their own pace but are always connected to their original soul family. The majority of soul members remain constant, but some souls require extra support and others accelerate quicker. At this stage, each group has a superior advanced instructor who oversees their education. Communication is through telepathy. There is no deception or ability to be untruthful in the Afterlife. Our Elders and guides always have the ability to access our communication center.

Our earthly life is a reflection of what we experience in the Heavenly Realm. Our life on Earth is extremely muted in comparison to the majestic atmosphere of the Afterlife. We could not endure the levels of extreme beauty, love and compassion that exist in Heaven while the cloak of our earthly life remains. While on Earth, amnesia creates an illusion similar to walking through a thick fog. We feel we are just on the fringe of seeing a clearing in the distance. As we soar towards our Higher Spiritual Self, the veil of amnesia begins to lift. As our truth is revealed, we become privy to our passion and purpose in this lifetime.

We not only learn in the classroom but also enjoy the pleasures of recreation, the arts, sports and celebrations. Every soul in the Afterlife decides how to balance work and play. Souls will often return to their core family group for recreational and role-playing activities. As souls, we have the ability to recreate any activity or experience that gave us pleasure on Earth. My sons will be happy to know that dodgeball is a game often played in Heaven. All activities incorporate learning as a key factor in their purpose. With dodgeball, souls learn about the exchange and power of manipulating energy. My husband will be ecstatic to be able to golf in the Afterlife. There are exquisite choirs, orchestras and bands. Souls may recreate their passions from Earth or explore new and fascinating interests they were unable to while here on this realm. All voices and instruments are in perfect harmony. Art, music and writing are all strong links between Earth and the Afterlife. When we access art in any form on Earth, we elevate our energy to become closer with our spiritual connections. I have witnessed many movies, documentaries, songs, and books on spirituality accurately reflect what the Afterlife is like. Art is a gift to help heal the soul of society. Many songwriters, musicians, artists, authors and screenwriters will reveal their inspiration was divinely motivated. I know my abilities of receiving healing messages through writing are directly linked to a Higher Power.

Souls can choose to partake in any event or experience available to them. This may include exploring other dimensions or multiple galaxies. The options are beyond our comprehension and imagination. Souls may use this time as a vacation or to further their learning horizons. Other dimensions may facilitate our souls' abilities to manipulate energy to enhance the viability of life on other realms or alternate galaxies. Souls may also use this opportunity to spend quiet reflective time on their own whenever they feel the desire to do so. We also have the option of planning elaborate parties and celebrations with incredible themes. We are in control of our souls' chosen paths. We have so much joy to anticipate in the next phase of our souls' journeys in the Afterlife.

As incredible as our souls' journeys in the Afterlife are, we feel a strong pull back to our Earthly Realm. Our souls have the ability to briefly return to Earth to recreate experiences we wish to duplicate. We take only a small percentage of our energy while temporarily returning to Earth, so we are unable to be seen by the average person. Mediums or highly intuitive people have the ability to sometimes tune into their subtle energy and recognize their presence.

A strong motivating factor for souls to reincarnate is the power of a sexual relationship in human form. The physical aspect of sex is unique to our earthly experience and is especially powerful for soulmates. In the Afterlife, soulmates may recreate aspects of their love through a deep soul connection. This interaction involves a beautiful melding of soul energy that creates a sensation that cannot be duplicated on this earthly plane.

Many people are curious about where the souls of our beloved pets and animals go. The souls of all animals cross over and reside in a very special area designed specifically for them. There is peace, love and harmony among all the animal souls that are free to roam together in this magical place. I have been shown that our domestic animals have a soul that is similar to our own. We are able to reunite with the souls of our domestic animals in the Afterlife at any time we choose.

I have had many pets, but I have a soul connection with my dog named Meeka. From the moment I saw her, I instinctively knew that we had shared previous experiences together. Meeka has shown me that once she crossed over, she was joined by our other dog Bandit in an incredibly beautiful area. Here, companionship and freedom prevail among all the animal spirits. Meeka sends me visions of herself and Bandit running free through spectacular meadows. Our entire family here on Earth experience both our dogs' spirits in a variety of formats. We often hear scratches at our back door or the sound of their nails on the hardwood floors. I smell "popcorn paws," which is a scent that Meeka carried on her paws her entire life, at random times. My youngest son will feel Meeka gradually nudge him into the corner of his bed at night, just as she did in her earthly life. My husband has momentarily viewed Bandit from across our street. It is wonderful to know that all our beloved pets enjoy a beautiful life in Heaven, and we will be reunited with them once again.

Our pets have the ability to manipulate situations here on Earth. They may maneuver circumstances to bring another pet into our lives at a time when we are open to the experience. They may often send a pet that reflects characteristics we need to address within ourselves. This is not a coincidence, but an active expression of love meant to assist us on our journey of self-discovery.

In the next phase of learning, the beginner souls gradually become advanced students. The process is similar to our school system on Earth. As the student soul advances in their education, they begin independent studies. When our souls are developing and maturing, they are exposed to a multitude of learning experiences and optional specialty areas of study. These specialties are specific areas of learning that we are drawn to. We will refer to this as our soul profession. Our soul profession is often reflected in the profession we choose on Earth. Many specialties in the Heavenly Realm are beyond our comprehension. Some recognizable ones are midwives, nursery caretakers, or teachers of preschool, youth and advanced learning. Specialties also break off into musicians, energy generators, librarians or socialization coordinators. By contemplating what your soul's true passion is, you may come one step closer to realizing your life purpose. Your soul profession in the Afterlife is often reflected through your life passion on Earth. I believe that when we are engaged in our purpose on Earth, we feel content and fulfilled. The further we drift from our soul profession, the more restless and dissatisfied we become. This knowledge presents us with one more tool to access our purpose in this lifetime.

I have experienced many lifetimes as a healer. I discovered this through meditation and past-life regression. My focus was mainly centered on midwifery and holistic healing. In this lifetime, I was compelled to become a nurse. From my earliest memories as a child, medicine was my calling. For over twenty-five years I worked in a high-risk obstetrical and gynecological oncology unit. The palliative care component of my career created many spiritual revelations that I will share throughout my book.

Continuing on with our education is a soul priority. Through many reincarnations and learning experiences, advanced students graduate to teachers and master status in their chosen soul profession. During this entire process, we have our guides and mentors supporting us. Eventually, we are assigned a core group of students whom we are responsible for teaching and mentoring. This may take hundreds of years and many lifetimes to achieve this advanced level of expertise. The final step is to become Ascended Masters. We are always one with Source, but upon reaching this status we sit within God's inner circle. This is the ultimate reward. When we achieve this divine station, there is no need to ever reincarnate again, if we so choose.

Spirit guides are a completely unique specialty. They are advanced superior spiritual entities. Spirit guides are powerful, and each has distinct and specialized characteristics. We are matched with a specific guide based on our individual requirements and needs. Once we have been assigned our spirit guide, they remain with us for all eternity. I have been shown that we may encounter many spirit guides during our lifetime. Our primary spirit guide orchestrates the necessity for additional guides at critical times in our soul journey. Just as people enter and exit from our lives at pivotal moments, so do our specialized spirit guides.

Even as a young child, I recognized a support system I could not see. As an adult, my spirit guide informed me that their name is Aridel. Aridel is both female and male in appearance but retains a more feminine aura. Aridel orchestrates many of my spiritual interactions. Aridel and my father are my strongest allies in my connection to the Spiritual Realm. I send gratitude to them every day. Fairly recently, I was introduced to another spirit guide named Scalion. He is a very advanced guide and escorted me on one of my most intense visions I have ever encountered. I will share that transformative experience with you in the following chapters. We all have the ability to reach out and ask to meet our personal spirit guide. They may come to you in a dream or during a moment of quiet reflection. Be patient; it may take multiple attempts to connect with your guide. It took me many years to fully consciously understand my relationship with my spirit guide, as I did not have all the tools at the time that I am presenting to you now. I felt their presence on many occasions but could not articulate that feeling into knowing until much later in life. Have confidence and do not question your positive responses while attempting to communicate with your guide. Communication with your spirit guide may present in many subtle forms. I will be further discussing how you may access your guide and crossed-over loved ones through many avenues.

Angels and spirit guides have very different and unique roles. I have been shown that there are varying levels of angels. The higher ascended angels have generally never experienced a life on Earth. They surround and protect us from their elevated heavenly station. These are the angels that accompany us during extreme life-threatening events and in Near-Death Experiences. These situations may also be referred to as potential exit points. I will later elaborate on this concept in detail. On another level, we have guardian angels. Most of these angels have had a prominent role during our lifetime on Earth. Our guardian angels may have been grandparents or very close family or friends who have crossed over. Another category of angels involves those who occasionally reincarnate on Earth. These are selfless souls that lead a life of extreme service and sacrifice for the greater good of the collective. I believe Mother Teresa, Princess Diana and Nelson Mandela are examples of these angels on Earth. This does not imply that earthly angels are perfect. They still struggle with assimilating with their earthly body and brain. They are purely on a higher plain of energy than the average soul on Earth. I have been shown that Jesus embodies the highest energy level next to God. Jesus was sent to Earth to reinvigorate our faith and create an awareness of eternal life. The highest level of angels are archangels. They are the most powerful and protective of all angels. They have sat at the side of God since the dawn of time and continue to serve and act as Source's messengers.

All levels of angels are gifts from Source to surround and protect us. They will not interfere if an event is inevitable and predestined to occur, but they will intervene in potential critical moments that will not serve our higher purpose. When you open your heart to these majestic entities, you may feel their loving embrace envelop you at crucial moments in your life.

The next step for our souls in the Afterlife is to prepare for our upcoming Earth life or reincarnation. We once again encounter the Council of Elders, this time for recommendation of potential future lives and advice on which life is best suited for our needs. Our guides accompany us into this phase of planning but are primarily there as support and not active participants. Each Elder or Ascended Master has their unique individual knowledge and strengths, which are instrumental in guiding us to our next life selection. The Elders conduct themselves within the preview of Source. The Highest Power's energy is felt as a constant gentle and loving presence.

My vision, for the pre-selection of choosing our next lifetime, takes place in a grand room with huge screens. I believe that every soul has their own unique experience, but the general process is similar for all souls. The Ascended Masters are positioned in an elevated semicircle formation within a structure that resembles a Greek architectural style. This part of our soul's journey is less intimidating than the first time we met with the Council of Elders during our life review. The screening room displays critical events in each potential life option. We are presented with approximately one to five alternative lives to choose from. There are a multitude of factors that are considered with each life option. A few of these elements are gender, nationality, parents, siblings, life lessons being worked on, balancing karmic agreements, soulmates, triggers and exit points.

All souls reincarnate as both male and female. We tend to gravitate towards our preferred gender throughout the majority of our chosen lives. We are free to choose whatever gender suits our needs for that particular life. One of my visions guided me through approximately twelve of my previous lifetimes. My predominant gender was female in approximately seventy five percent of my life selections. My vision was similar to viewing a slide show in fast-forward motion. We are encouraged to choose any variation of gender that further enhances our earthly lessons. The more challenging the body selection, the greater potential for excelled growth and learning on Earth. There is no judgment in Heaven for any choices we make concerning our body selection, race, religion or sexual orientation.

Within the Council of Elders, there is a hierarchy of junior and senior members. The senior Ascended Masters perform their duties similar to our judges but without judgment. They keep the process progressing at a smooth pace. All Elders have personality strengths, which support our growth in areas we require the most. The Elders have access to the records of all our past lives and can foresee into potential future lives. These documents are contained within the Akashic Records. These logbooks reside within the grand hall that I envisioned. There are record keepers whose soul profession is to control our Book of Life within the Akashic Records. Contained within each individual Book of Life is not only all our past lives but also options for future lives. This divine book is presented in a variety of formats to every soul. Our spirit guides and panel of Elders help us navigate access to our information. We may view it in book form, a movie scene, slide show, 3D images and many intriguing configurations.

While viewing optional future lives, we are able to virtually "try on" specific aspects of that life. We are given glimpses into what each life selection may entail. Our Elders can transport us within a potential future life to see if the fit is comfortable for our needs. We have free will to reject a body or life we are not agreeable to. The process of selecting our future lives is similar to aspects of playing video games. It has always intrigued me why some people have an almost obsessive desire to continually play virtual games in this format. I believe that our soul is triggered to recall aspects of our pre-life selection and how video games are a reflection of that process. Life on Earth is similar to being in the middle of that virtual world. Imagine the player as your Higher Soul Self. The avatar you create and the virtual world of the video game becomes a representation of your earthly life. You are in control of all the decisions made in your virtual reality, but the avatar is not consciously aware of the role of your Higher Soul Self. This realization gives us a new insight into the expression, "the game of life."

I was curious about this fascinating area, so I requested the assistance of my spirit guide to view my Book of Life. After many attempts to contact Aridel through meditation, they escorted me into a building that resembled a Roman structure with huge white pillars at the entrance. I felt like a visitor, yet there was a deep familiarity surrounding my experience. There were stairs leading up into a magnificent hall, but no walls or floors existed. The space appeared to go on to infinity, with columns on either side of this ethereal structure. I felt wonderment and a deep inspirational compulsion to learn. Aridel then presented me with a magnificent grand book. It was unlike any book I have ever seen on Earth and seemed to shimmer and glow with an ancient light. The book was open, but I was unable to decipher any message or information contained within it. Aridel informed me that I was not meant to comprehend the contents at this time. I feel so much gratitude for even being shown my Book of Life and the existence of the Akashic Records.

There is one aspect of soul selection that I found particularly fascinating. When we reincarnate on Earth, we do not bring 100% of our soul energy with us. A moderate percentage of our soul energy remains in Heaven. This may prove to be problematic if we underestimate the percentage required for a very challenging life. Our soul energy that persists in the Spiritual Realm remains with our soul family. We are still able to participate in all heavenly activities but at a more subdued level. Our true home exists in the Heavenly Realm. We are gifted the temporary experience of this earthly life to grow and learn at an accelerated pace. We are sent here to rediscover our Eternal Soul Self by working through challenges and discovering love as the ultimate energy.

Another consideration in choosing a body is to acknowledge the challenges that body possesses. We must merge our soul with the personality and physical limitations of the body we are entering. It is ultimately our choice, but there are times our soul cannot fully appreciate the complexities of that body and brain. We carry our eternal core personality with us across each lifetime, and the body we enter has its own characteristics. We must learn to integrate the duality of our soul with the cloak of another persona. In our pre-birth plan we are aware of this and take it into serious consideration while planning our next life. Evolved beings may purposely take on very challenging bodies to endure hardships that help release collective negative energies on Earth. We are always given free will and are ultimately responsible for choosing our next life.

Some immature souls request a life on Earth before they are ready. These young souls feel invincible and are overly confident. Even when our spiritual superiors advise us against embarking on a life too early or too difficult, we retain our free will. Sadly, some of these immature souls are so ill-prepared for life's challenges, they may die from suicide to return home to their soul family.

When that young soul returns to Heaven, they are not judged or punished. Immediately upon their body's demise, these souls realize the enormity of their actions. These souls may require extra time recuperating to fully appreciate how their actions affected their loved ones on Earth. Circumstances and intentions of the soul are considered in why this decision was made. There is no judgment experienced in the Heavenly Realm during their life review, but they will acutely experience the emotions internalized by loved ones remaining on Earth. Suicide is never part of a pre-life plan, but a soul enters a body with the knowledge that there may be an increased probability that suicide may occur. These souls must fully understand that they squandered the precious gift of an earthly body and life. This is never looked upon as a failure but is considered an opportunity for growth and learning. These souls are always surrounded with forgiveness and love, yet they may require an extended time in the Afterlife to fully recover from their premature exit from the Earthly Realm. I will explore the concept of suicide in greater detail in upcoming chapters.

Choosing our next reincarnation requires coordination with many other souls. Our guide, Elders and soul family work tirelessly in planning how to orchestrate life experiences and the roles each soul takes on. This process may be one of the most challenging and lengthy activities we participate in while in the Afterlife. Every major life event is pre-planned and takes into account many factors. The enormity of this process is beyond our human ability to comprehend. We choose our birth parents, siblings and experiences based on past relationships and the karmic balance we hope to achieve in our future lifetime. I have been shown that the eldest child chooses the parents, and the younger siblings choose their eldest sibling. The siblings are predominantly from our soul group, but one or both parents may be from an adjoining core family. This is all arranged for optimum learning and growth on Earth. Processing our challenges at an accelerated pace and raising the universal energy to create a planet of peace and compassion are primary motivators for reincarnation. We are also excited to experience the earthly pleasures while accepting the potential hardships of that life.

We have now entered the next phase of our soul contract, where we embrace our free will and celebrate the power to influence our critical choices on Earth. In the Afterlife, our perspective encompasses all our objectives without the limitations of our human emotions. We now have the ability to expand our myopic view from our earthly perspective and observe from a much more encompassing lens. Within our human viewpoint, it is difficult to understand why our soul chooses situations where we may suffer and encounter people who will potentially harm us. We now understand that these difficult challenges are for a much greater purpose. They are specifically there for the empowerment and growth of our soul. Our soul expands in love and awareness with every life challenge we overcome. We are now alerted to the concept that this life on Earth is only moments in our soul's journey, and we will have many opportunities in a multitude of lifetimes to fulfill our soul's purpose. Every lesson learned on this Earthly Realm is engrained on our soul for all eternity.

Conversely, once we enter the Earthly Realm, amnesia takes over our consciousness. We would not be able to embrace our earthly lessons if we were consumed with all our past-lifetime memories. Amnesia is a gift that allows us to compartmentalize our intense memories of past lives that we could not process with our earthly emotions all at once. Also, if we were aware of the entire plan of our lives on Earth, we would not fully experience the lessons we had pre-planned to embrace here. Eternal knowledge is optimally obtained through experiencing opposites and internalizing the lessons we require for soul growth. Without amnesia, the process would be similar to taking an open book exam containing all the answers. We would not absorb the information in this format. When our soul learns our life lessons through experience and healing the most intimate aspects of ourselves, these lessons are ingrained on our soul for eternity.

Learning and growth can best be accomplished here, as Earth is the most challenging realm in all the galaxy. There are an infinite number of alternate areas around the Universe for lessons to be learned, but Earth is strongly desired due to the potential for the most expedient growth to occur. Our soul desires the challenge of a life on Earth. We require stimulation and experiences to feel invigorated. Earth is the best realm to provide that, and it does so in spades.

Our dense three-dimensional state on Earth only allows us to experience life in a linear perspective with boundaries strategically placed for learning. This is an essential aspect for optimum growth to occur. Amnesia is a gift that allows us the ability to trigger our soul to return to the state of Divine Love and rediscover our Higher Soul Self. When we fully embrace the knowledge of eternal life, we can begin to understand our purpose in this lifetime. We now realize that we have always had control over every major aspect of our life. Once we accept that we were instrumental in choosing this life with all its challenges, we open ourselves to the energy of the unconditional love of Source. This energy of pure love is a beacon that draws spiritual awareness into our being. Once the portal to the Spiritual Realm is opened, our purpose becomes clearer as the amnesia lifts. We will explore many avenues of how to access the information required to reach this elevated state. Simply embracing the commitment to approach our life with an alternative perspective alerts the Universe towards our intent for spiritual growth. We have opened the door to allow enlightenment and awareness into our consciousness.

By contrast, our soul in the Spiritual Realm has no boundaries. Time is always fluid, and we can travel forward or back at will. Our soul is free to explore through the layers of energy fields or realms without restraint. We may potentially experience a few lives simultaneously in a variety of realms. Our souls are not at the mercy of linear progressive time as we experience on Earth. Spiritual order is maintained through a vibrational frequency that all souls instinctually respect. The closest we can come on Earth to achieve a fraction of this level of travel is during sleep, through hypnosis or in a deep meditative state. Some refer to this as Astral Projection, Astral Travel or Out-of-Body Experiences (OBE). I will explore this concept later in the book in greater detail.

We have now come full circle with our soul's journey. Embrace the amazing and brave soul that you are. Empower yourself with the knowledge that you enthusiastically agreed to return to Earth to challenge your soul to grow and learn in this difficult realm. Now is the time to fulfil your obligations with your soul family that you agreed upon in your soul contract.

The world is a stage and you are living out your own story. Understand that your life is the play you scripted to act out and your soul is the true individual within that character. Your soul is an accumulation of all the characters you have chosen to play in all your lifetimes. With every lesson learned, you are creating greater awareness and enlightenment within yourself and outwards into the Universe. When you embody your soul's purpose, you become a beacon of light. Other souls will be drawn to your light and absorb the love in your soul. This creates a ripple effect that touches the souls of all humanity. Remember, we are all connected to every soul in the Universe, and every soul is connected to Source. Through this imperceptible cord of love, every action and intentional thought is experienced by all. This is your role in the play that is your life. How you perform affects all those surrounding and observing you. You control the narrative.

When we fully embrace the knowledge of eternal life, we can begin to understand our purpose in this lifetime. The challenges we embrace on Earth can lead us to the realization of love being the energetic force that we all strive to become. When we open ourselves up to Divine Love, we create an energetic vortex that draws spiritual awareness into our essence. When we rediscover our Higher Soul Self, we can transform our suffering into being of service to others. This is our greatest opportunity to work towards becoming one of Source's Ascended Masters and to sit within God's inner circle and be of service to all souls.

TRIGGERS AND FREE WILL

When we are preparing for our life on Earth, we place specific signs alerting us to key people or events that are pivotal in our life lessons. These signs are also referred to as triggers. If we listen and observe, we will learn how to recognize many of these signs. Triggers let us know when we are on the correct path or direct us towards an alternative junction when we are veering off course. Triggers alert us to situations and people who are critical in our life journey and are sent to help us recognize our soul's lessons.

When we are in the phase of pre-birth planning, we are able to virtually see every potential major aspect of our next life. All that information is muted once we reincarnate, through the process of amnesia. That is why it is so important to become aware of the vital role triggers have in our lives. We understand that amnesia is necessary for us to internalize the lessons we set out to learn. Triggers are like pre-approved cheat notes that alert us to our intended paths. There are key life events and people, which trigger an internal recognition of our soul's purpose in this lifetime. We are given options, through our free will, on how to achieve these life goals. Our pre-birth plan incorporates free-will choices and triggers within our planned life. When we absorb this truth into our lives today, we empower ourselves to live our most authentic lives possible. Every challenge in life is for a greater purpose. We have chosen every aspect of this life so we may learn the lessons our souls require. By reflecting on recurring themes in our lives, we will become aware of many of our primary objectives. We all come into each lifetime with the intention of focusing on a few specific crucial characteristics we need to heal. Some of these may be patience, empathy, self-worth, compassion, or increased awareness as a spiritual being.

In my pre-life selection I chose my family, my life partner, and significant experiences that direct me in my journey of self-discovery. When I began the process of identifying my purpose, I realized I had struggled with self-love since I was a child. Growing up, I often felt my voice was not heard. I know my parents loved me, but I did not feel worthy of their love. As I went through life, I did not feel worthy of anyone's love. When I objectively reflect on my life, I now understand that conquering low self-worth was a vital aspect of my healing journey.

This greatly influenced who I would become during my lifetime. I was an overachiever, a perfectionist, and required external praise to raise my self-esteem. I attracted people and experiences that reinforced my lack of self-worth and self-love. My life reflected Johnny Lee's song, "Looking for Love in All the Wrong Places." It would take me years to realize that I simply needed to look inside myself to discover the love I was searching for. That path took me on a winding and bumpy road that eventually led me to where I am now.

I found myself a single mother in my thirties, a failed marriage behind me and a future that looked very bleak. I had rejected religion and lost faith as a spiritual being. In desperation I called out to the Universe to help guide me to a place of peace. This journey took me on a roller coaster ride of despair and hope. I began journaling again, which helped me process my emotions. I went to counselling and embraced a healthy lifestyle. I had a long way to go, but now I had a focus in my life.

When I was thirty-seven years old, I experienced a trigger moment from my pre-birth plan. I had no conscious knowledge of what that was at this point in my life, but I sensed that my life was about to radically change. This was the night I met my current husband, Dale. I felt an immediate recognition for this person yet initially rejected the idea of a romantic relationship with him. Dale knew instantly that we were meant to be together. He showered me with love, understanding and patience. I eventually began to accept that I deserved his love, but the road took a long and convoluted path. My soul knew what my logical brain would not allow me to see. The Universe required me to work on my journey of embracing myself as a loving soul and to release my feelings of low self-worth. My greatest fear was that I would not be able to love him as he loved me and that I would hurt him deeply.

Despite all the blocks I erected, fate continually brought us together. We would unintentionally meet up in locations that were not common to either of us and were not planned. Our lives began to intersect and connect in ways beyond our control. Serendipitously, our parents met in Texas on vacation before we even introduced them. They were spending their winter a few feet from each other in a retirement community that catered to people from northern locations. This was all pre-planned independently a year before Dale and I even met. They became lifelong friends from that moment on. I have had multiple confirmations from our crossed-over parents in the Afterlife that they are still partying and enjoying each other's company.

My next trigger moment occurred six months after I met Dale. We had a platonic and comfortable friendship up to this point. I invited him to my home as a friend after a challenging evening at work. He had just finished playing hockey and came over. When I hugged him, the smell of leather triggered a deep awareness within me. We then shared our first romantic kiss together, and I felt a flash of recognition in the core of my being. My heart expanded in a way I had never experienced before. I did not understand why at the time, but I finally accepted an inner knowing that I was meant to be with this person. Dale and I blended our beautiful family together six months later and married the following year. We have had many challenges but have learned and grown together and individually for over twenty-three years.

Only recently, I discovered the significance of all the factors that brought us together. One major realization came when I re-experienced a past life through hypnosis. During this past-life regression, I found myself in the Scottish Highlands in the 1700s. I visualized a handsome muscular man walking over a hill towards me. I felt incredible love and passion towards this person. As he approached, I could smell leather from the leggings he was wearing. This was the same scent I recognized from Dale's leather hockey gloves in this lifetime. I knew immediately that Dale was my soulmate in that life and again in our current life together. I have since discovered a few lifetimes where we were in close personal relationships. Interestingly, the smell of leather was the trigger for me to recognize some of those past lives also. I vividly recalled a previous life where Dale was a World War One pilot and I was a nurse working for the Red Cross. We fell in love very quickly and had a passionate relationship. The scent of the leather jacket he wore as a pilot was the trigger to recognize him in that lifetime also. One of my best friends from nursing school was also present in that lifetime with me. We worked closely together as nurses in combat in that previous life and worked in the same nursing unit for over twenty years in this lifetime.

When you reflect on crucial moments where you made a pivotal decision that changed the trajectory of your life, understand that that is a trigger. Your free will gives you the choice to act on those trigger moments or reject them. This is sometimes referred to as the "fork in the road." Even when we choose the path that leads us down the road that does not serve our higher purpose, we are given many opportunities to return to our intended destination. Since our soul prearranged to work on healing specific characteristics, the Universe will place people and circumstances in our life that alert us to our life goals in future trigger moments. When you are presented with a choice that is critical to your life in the future, take the time to process your intuitive messages. Simply recognizing that trigger moments exist and are pre-planned by you will be an invaluable tool for you to progress in your life journey. These triggers are powerful reminders of the soul contract you created in your pre-life plan that alert you to your life purpose.

Another trigger for me occurred when I graduated from high school. Three friends and I decided to move about 1000 miles away from home. I put my intended life on hold for a year of adventure. This became a pivotal learning experience in my life. I discovered a foundation of strength that shaped the person I was becoming. I began a serious relationship with a caring man who was in the health care field. Eventually, I came to that proverbial fork in the road. If I stayed, I may have never realized my dream of becoming a nurse. Ironically, his passion for medicine reinvigorated my goal for a nursing career. This trigger was the motivating factor in returning home, where I had financial and emotional support. I was accepted into the nursing program, and my aspiration of becoming a Registered Nurse became a reality.

I can acutely recall, with three of my lifelong best friends, experiencing a life-defining trigger moment. When I first encountered my childhood best friend, I knew in an instant we would be forever connected on a deep soul level. We have had many life-altering experiences that have had a vital impact on both of us. I have recently spoken to my dear friend about our first encounter. She mirrored the exact sentiments I experienced when we first met. We clearly recall a feeling of knowing we were safe together and recognized each other's soul in a deep way. This is not our first life together, and I know without a doubt that we are soul sisters and have shared many precious lives together.

During nursing college, I strongly bonded with another dear friend. We continue to be unwavering support for each other and have shared many hardships and joy together. Our relationship has been consistent and solid for over forty years. I have experienced multiple lives with her in a variety of roles. She is the friend I previously spoke of who was present in a past life during World War One. She was also present in my carefree life after the turn of the twentieth century, which I will explore later in more detail.

The moment I met my next best friend, I felt a shift in the energy around us. I believe her beautiful soul was placed in my path at an extremely vulnerable moment for both of us to learn important life lessons. We continue to learn, grow and support each other instinctually when the need is strongest.

Each of these women have contributed to my life in powerful ways. If I had ignored those triggers, my life would not be as full and supported as it is today. I am grateful for all the friends I am blessed to have in my life. All my friendships, both recent and long term, have helped shape the person I am today.

There are so many factors involved in the journey of our soul. Pre-life planning, triggers, synchronicity, soul families, soulmates, life purposes, karma, spirit guides, and awareness of our Spiritual Selves are all critical in understanding our purpose in this lifetime. Become observant to the triggers that are placed in your path every day. We are alerted to them through subtle and direct means. Triggers may come in the form of quiet whispers, dreams or a gentle nudge in the right direction. They may also be so obvious that it is nearly impossible to ignore them.

One of the most crucial factors in alerting us to our trigger moments is through acknowledging a life challenge. The more critical this life lesson is to our healing, the more obvious our trigger moment becomes. This trigger may come in the form of a traumatic incident that alerts us to healing emotions that are holding us back from realizing our full potential. By being aware and alert to these triggers, you are given a vital tool in discovering your life purpose. Do not worry if you feel you have missed a trigger, because you have placed many triggers in your life to achieve the goals you have set for yourself.

SYNCHRONICITY AND SERENDIPITY

I have been directed from Spirit that synchronicity exists in our life to highlight key moments, which alert us to our life plan and create awareness of our spiritual path. There are no coincidences or accidents in life. Remain observant and meet the Universe halfway to receive the messages being sent. Everything has meaning, and the Universe continually provides us with what we need when we are open and aware. Synchronicity presents itself in many forms and works with triggers to direct us on our life path.

The most subtle nudge comes from serendipitous encounters in our daily life. These are moments where we discover something meaningful while seeking something else. We may alter these occurrences by intentionally sending positive intentions into the Universe. This raises the probability of meaningful serendipitous moments manifesting in our lives. The power of sending intentional thought into the Universe is a divine gift that is available for us to activate whenever we choose.

Synchronicity is a tool to help us recognize important messages from our Higher Soul Self and spiritual supports. These messages may present themselves in recurring numbers, patterns or symbols. Pay attention to songs that convey a repetitive theme or music that directly links us to a crossed-over loved one. Instinctually listen to what your heart is conveying through these synchronicities. Do not let fear interfere with the message being sent. This is a gift from the Universe to help balance our spiritual experience with our Earth adventures. Evaluate what is occurring in your life at that time, and contemplate what potential message is being conveyed.

Triggers are the most powerful of all the messages we receive. These are like bolts of lightning directing us to our life path. When synchronistic events occur coupled with trigger moments, pay very close attention to what the Universe is sending you. Even if the message is not clear at the moment the incident occurs, there are still valuable lessons to be learned retrospectively. When we can objectively look back on the incident, we may clearly realize how significant the circumstance was. It is a powerful tool to be aware of how synchronicity, triggers and intuition can all be instrumental in discovering our life purpose.

An example of how these events occur may be a common situation in the lives of many people. There may have been a time when you were anticipating a big promotion but failed to get it. Then, weeks later, your dream job is offered to you that would not have been possible if you had received that promotion. Another scenario may involve an intense relationship where the other person seemingly breaks your heart. Months later you find the love of your life during an activity you chose to distract yourself from your previous relationship. Years later, you find out the person who hurt you is living a life that would not have supported your journey. By reflecting on these incidences in your life, you are empowering yourself with another tool towards recognizing your life purpose. The more familiar you become with the emotions evoked around triggers and synchronicity, the quicker you will be alerted to the critical role these tools have in your life.

Synchronicity may present as a series of events that appear insignificant or even inconvenient at the time. Becoming aware of these factors is another tool to alert you to your life purpose. When you can recognize these signs in the moment, you are empowered to create a more optimistic outcome. You are also being given this gift to allow you to perceive a seemingly adverse experience as an opportunity for a favorable life lesson. Attempt to approach these potential negative experiences with a more positive intention.

Recently, we were in the middle of a long road trip home. We went for breakfast in the hotel and had to wait an extra five minutes for our eggs. This was frustrating at the time, as we wanted to continue on our journey. A few minutes into our trip, we came upon a very recent multiple-vehicle accident. If we had not had to wait for our eggs, we likely would have been involved in this horrible crash. A couple days later, we stopped at a drive-through for coffee. They had to brew a fresh pot, which delayed us once again. Shortly after getting back on the road, a large truck had very recently experienced a tire blow out, and there was debris and thick smoke all over the road. We were merely moments from being in the center of that potentially dangerous situation.

There are synchronistic incidents that occur every day in our lives. They are specifically orchestrated by our pre-birth plan, free will, spiritual supports and our angels who protect us. Even when we experience events that appear catastrophic at the time, understand that there is an underlying purpose to each event. There is a reason for everything, and everything works out exactly as we planned it and how it was meant to be. We don't always get what we think we want, but the Universe orchestrates everything so that we get what we need and what we ensure would occur in our pre-birth plan.

INTUITION

A similar tool to assist us on our life path is intuition. Our intuition is led by our heart and will always guide us up the path to love. Listen to your intuitive inner voice to feel more and think less. Our ego and intellect attempt to divert us from our spiritual journey. Ego creates illusions that blurs the line between coming back to our Spiritual Self and influencing us to live an egocentric existence. It may be very challenging to reject ego-motivated rewards, as they reflect many basic human desires. Simply becoming aware of the strong force ego has in our life empowers us to make decisions from our intimate soul center. Lead with your heart and not your head. Build your intuitive abilities through meditation and prayer. When you focus on love and not fear, you strengthen your intuitive ability to make spiritually-driven choices. When you have a critical decision to make, gather as much information as you can, and then use your intuitive heart center to make the final decision. It is important to understand that our initial authentic intuitive response is the one we should weigh importance on in our decision-making process. Our ego attempts to blur the simplicity of this process with complexity and grandiose illusion.

Incorporate all your gifts of triggers, intuition, prayer and meditation to help guide you to follow your chosen purpose. Our soul is motivated by pure and transparent heart-centered truth. When you realize you are being pulled down a path that does not serve your Higher Self, readjust your trajectory by using all the tools presented. Above all, forgive yourself and use all experiences as a learning venture. We are spiritual beings having a human experience and as such will falter. Use these life lessons towards soul growth and discovering your life purpose. When these events highlight a common theme, understand that this is life reflecting what we need to work on. Another realization that comes from these synchronistic moments is that we have spiritual support in every aspect of our life.

Give gratitude for these events, as they all lead us back to our intended purpose on this Earth. Understand that by approaching these situations with a broader lens, we may see the full potential of these events that may initially appear devastating or merely inconvenient. We do ourselves a disservice by dismissing these events as coincidence. Embrace synchronicity, intuition and intention as additional tools to help you continue on your intended life path and discover your soul purpose. Embrace the concept that all life events occur for a reason and are all part of a divine plan orchestrated by your Higher Soul Self and your soul family in the Heavenly Realm.

INTENTION

Intention is the cornerstone for all aspects of spirituality. When we come from a place of authentic intention, we are rewarded with reciprocal favorable experiences. Intention is a great tool to evaluate how we choose to respond to a life challenge we perceive as being detrimental. If our intention is revenge or hate-motivated, it is in our best interest to reevaluate our next step. Once we are given the tools to approach this situation with an alternative perspective, we may be afforded a more optimistic outcome. If our intention is driven by love and forgiveness, there is a greater probability that we will enjoy a positive higher vibration and a more joyful experience in this lifetime. Even when there is no immediate perceivable result to intentions sent into the Universe, understand that the energy encompassing the intent will be reflected back on us and the collective. When our genuine intentions are sent with love, we may not be consciously aware of the enlightened energy shift we create. Have faith that on a spiritual level, every beautiful intention has a powerful impact on our soul journey and on the positive universal energy shift for the collective.

EXIT POINTS

Another factor we will explore from our pre-birth agenda is exit plans or exit points. Exit points exist as potential avenues to facilitate our return home to Source. This occurs on a deep soul level, and amnesia prevents us from consciously being aware of this concept. Once we have completed our soul contract on Earth, we have the option to choose from approximately three to five exit strategies. These potential exit strategies are orchestrated in consultation with our spirit guides, soul family and the Council of Elders in our pre-birth planning.

I personally have had three distinct opportunities for exiting this earthly plane that I am currently aware of. My first potential exit occurred when I was an inexperienced driver, about seventeen years old. I was driving my siblings home and underestimated the time it took to go through an amber light at a busy intersection. I saw an eighteen-wheeler truck barreling down the highway, straight at us. The next moment I recall, we were on the other side of the intersection, safely intact. We were all in shock but so grateful to be alive. Our guardian angels were definitely surrounding us on that day. It was like they picked us up and placed us out of harm's way. We all felt the power of our spiritual supports in that moment.

My next two potential exits were health related. At age thirty-nine, I was plagued with abdominal pain. A voice in my head relentlessly encouraged me to investigate. I insisted on an ultrasound, despite my physician's reluctance due to my good health and younger age. Finally, after nine months, an ultrasound showed an abnormality on my right ovary. I immediately had surgery, and the oncologist confirmed it was ovarian cancer. Ovarian cancer is referred to as the cancer that whispers, as it is difficult to diagnose at an early stage and mimics many benign conditions. At the time, I was a nurse in a women's health unit that dealt with gynecological issues, including ovarian cancer. I had cared for many courageous women who had passed away from this horrific disease. It was their voices, and those of my spiritual supports, that encouraged me to pursue this. I am eternally grateful to every soul that influenced me to advocate for myself.

At the age of forty-three, I contracted Lyme Disease from an infected wood tick. Within a few months I was in total liver failure. Despite a drastic decline in health, I kept hearing, "You will be fine." My doctors and surgeons were doubtful of my chances of surviving this health crisis. After weeks of getting weaker and my liver enzymes continually rising, a risky surgical procedure was performed. Gradually, my liver began to heal and so did I. I am still dealing with the residual pain and fatigue from that experience. I now know this was all part of my life lesson that I pre-planned for my soul in this lifetime.

My two eldest children both had serious illnesses in their early childhood. My son became hospitalized with a severe respiratory infection at one month old. A few children that winter died of this same condition. My daughter contracted scarlet fever and was also extremely ill. Scarlet fever can lead to a possible long-term or fatal heart condition. We were so blessed that these conceivable exit points were not carried through.

My husband also had defining potential exit plans during his lifetime. His first one was at the age of five. Dale's father was in the military, and their family was stationed at an air force base in a foreign country. Dale and his buddy were exploring the surrounding woods around the base. He discovered an interesting item and brought it to show his dad in the hockey arena. It turned out to be a live bomb. The situation was quickly dealt with, and everyone was safe. Dale distinctly recalls saying to his friend, "Should we pull this pin?" Thank God he did not. I am certain his guardian angels were protecting him from that possible exit point.

Another experience Dale had occurred in California, where he was attending University. He was partying with friends in the surrounding mountains. Dale accidentally fell off a cliff into a shallow body of water over three stories down. Miraculously, he sustained no critical injuries. He had to be airlifted out and has no memory from that moment until he awoke in the hospital. Dale was unquestionably supported and surrounded by his angels during that experience.

On contemplation of your life, you may be able to recall some of your potential exit points. The fact that you are still here confirms that you have not accomplished all you planned in this lifetime. Even when you have completed your pre-life goals, your soul may choose to live on this Earth for a few more years. Time is perceived much differently on Earth compared to the Higher Realms. Take this opportunity to reflect on what your life goals are. Your personal potential exit plans will reinforce the lessons you set out to learn. This is one more tool to bring awareness to your pre-life plan and your intended path.

KARMA AND DHARMA

To help empower ourselves, it is important to understand the meaning of karma. Karma is often misinterpreted as punishment or retribution against an individual we perceive as committing an evil act. In the true spiritual sense, karma is balancing and releasing energy. Karma works on the principle of cause and effect. Intent and actions of an individual (cause) influence the future of that person (effect). Therefore, present karma not only affects us in this life but also in future lives. It may also be the result of past-life actions and decisions.

Dharma is about fulfilling our duty and creating changes in this lifetime. It is a spiritual discipline that guides us to live our best lives through joy, happiness and peace. Dharma is the foundation of life. Change is the catalyst for growth in our lifetime. By discovering and fulfilling our life purpose, we are contributing to the universal greater good. This may be achieved with positive intentions and by being of service to others.

We not only work on achieving karmic balance and release from this lifetime but also from many previous lifetimes. To fully release karma, we must release and heal the underlying fear and emotion. Balancing karma is achieved when all sides of an issue are experienced and resolved. Actions contribute to help balance karma, but the emotional work is the true challenge in achieving karmic release. Divine Healing is one tool to help achieve balance in karmic energy and the release of underlying emotions.

It is necessary to stress that in pre-birth planning we incorporate karmic awareness into this life. We may be working on past karma, where we wronged souls and now must achieve karmic balance and release with these souls. We may also be instrumental in assisting members of our soul family balance and release their karma. As advanced souls, we may also be bravely taking on extreme challenges to advance the betterment of the collective universal energy. Releasing karma does not always require great suffering, but it does necessitate awareness and willingness to process painful emotions. It is possible to instantly release karma; it does not have to become a lifelong exercise. One of the greatest challenges in releasing karma is understanding that fear and ego are our greatest barriers. Karma is not a punishment and primarily works to achieve balance in the Universe.

I will share with you a very personal experience I had regarding karma. This process took time and energy but resulted in profound clarity on my soul journey. Through counselling, soul-searching and reliving a past-life experience through hypnosis, I became aware of how important karma is to emotional healing. I will explore the concept of past-life experiences through hypnotic regression and other avenues that facilitate understanding karma in greater depth in the following chapters.

My first past-life regression brought me to an isolated farming community in the 1800s. My family successfully farmed our land until tragedy struck. My father passed away, and I was left to care for my ailing mother. I resented her for my life of sacrifice and misery and died an angry old woman. I did not achieve many of my pre-planned goals in that lifetime. I created karma that would later require healing in a future life.

In my present life, I was given another opportunity to balance my karma. My father passed away and I once again became the main caregiver for my mom. She had dementia when my dad crossed over, but her symptoms greatly exacerbated after his passing. I also took on the daunting task of caring for my aunt who had advanced dementia. I had to work hard at processing the anger and frustration of my overwhelming responsibilities. Thankfully, I have released the crushing and distressing emotions attached to this recurring scenario in my existence. Through this experience, I have learned compassion, patience and love on an elevated level. This has been validated through confirmation from my father and spiritual supports. My journey took years to achieve the lessons I set out to learn in my pre-birth plan.

Another realization surfaced for me during this karmic journey with my mother. As I peeled away each layer of emotion, deeper engrained feelings began to reveal themselves. I have always sensed a feeling of guilt around the circumstances of my birth. I was born surrounded by anxiety and trauma. My mom had a miscarriage prior to my conception and remained anxious and cautious for the entire pregnancy with me. Understandably, she feared also losing me to another pregnancy loss. The emotions around any pregnancy are also experienced by the unborn child. During my birth, my mom hemorrhaged and came close to dying. I believe that when there is a difficult delivery, the pre-born soul is expressing a reluctance to come into that life. I feel my Higher Self realized that this was going to be a very challenging lifetime.

Through many years of intense soul-searching, I have come to realize the full impact of my pre-birth plan with my mom. During the birthing process, there was a release of karmic obligation. I believe my mother's karmic commitment to me was partially absolved through her traumatic delivery. I now realize to fully balance my karmic obligation to my mom, I had to release emotions that had attached from this lifetime as well as from past lifetimes. I processed the guilt I felt because of my challenging entrance into this world. I released the anger and shame I had internalized from my previous life and from this life in being resentful as her caregiver. The transformative energy shift I experienced through this process was life-altering. My father sent me a message from the Heavenly Realm that I was exponentially growing in compassion, patience and unconditional love. My mom and I worked on karmic balance our entire lives. I know in my heart that we achieved that in the most forgiving and loving manner. Whether the person you are seeking karmic balance with is mentally incapacitated or even crossed over, you can achieve karmic release through beautiful intentions and Divine Healing.

By embracing the role of karma and incorporating the process of forgiveness, I discovered one of my soul's purposes. I now have the tools to deal with similar emotions when they surface during future events. I no longer see myself as a victim and I feel empowered and awakened by this experience. I am also confident that this incident is now embraced by my soul for all eternity. The imprint of learning these valuable lessons will follow me into all my future lives. I will never have to go through this critical learning experience at this level again. This is one example of how karma enters our lives to help us recognize our souls' plans and creates the perfect circumstances to heal trauma attached to our souls.

DISCOVERING OUR SOUL'S PURPOSE THROUGH LIFE CHALLENGES

Our soul's journey began long before we were born and will continue eternally after we leave this Earth. In the Afterlife, our soul created pre-determined agreements with other souls to fulfill many key life lessons. We chose our body, our family and every critical aspect of our life's path. Our core lessons were pre-ordained by our Soul Self, but we were also given free will once we came to live our earthly experience.

Currently we are a diverse blend of souls who have been specifically chosen to embark on a journey of great change and awareness in society. We are a balanced mix of experienced advanced souls and young ambitious souls. Many of these souls have chosen extremely challenging life scenarios to achieve optimum growth. With great change must come great sacrifice.

Our souls are on a journey to be one with the Highest Power's pure love. Our souls recognize that as we learn our lessons on Earth, we greatly accelerate our progression towards being in the inner circle of Source. This is one of our souls' main motivators for living this difficult life on Earth. When we surrender to the belief that there is a divine plan and we have control within that plan, we are on our way to our spiritual purpose. Being aware of our truth is an important step in discovering our intended path in this lifetime.

If our lives continued on a repetitive neutral course, we would not be motivated to resolve a situation that challenges us to heal and grow. These life events influence us to embark on our intended life journey. Through our pre-life plan, we create experiences in our lives that help us learn and progress. We attract situations and people who help fulfill our spiritual learning. Working through many of these traumatic events may be a lifelong process. Simply alerting the Universe of our willingness to heal will alter the trajectory of our path in an enlightened and positive direction. The more knowledge and tools we accumulate empowers us to progress towards a more peace-filled existence.

From a karmic perspective, the soul may be choosing to correct unresolved choices from a previous life. This is definitely not a punishment, but a desire for karmic release coming directly from the soul. It is important to note that we are not necessarily making up for past negative karma if we have a challenging life. Many times, these ambitious lives are chosen for accelerated growth. We may also be very advanced souls who chose this life circumstance to elevate positive energy for the collective.

Feelings of anger from any challenging life situation is normal. Anger requires processing for emotional healing to occur. The circumstances surrounding these sentiments should not be the primary focus. The most important lesson here is to acknowledge, process and release the emotions that are underneath the pain. Behind anger is fear. When we repress anger and fear, it may emerge in many destructive forms. Depression, addiction, aggressive behavior, self-destructive behaviors, victim mentality, manifestation of mental or physical illnesses are all possible results of emotions subconsciously being repressed as a defense mechanism. Exploring these adverse feelings, allowing them to be acknowledged, processing them and finally releasing these sentiments will contribute to finding peace in your life.

As one emotion emerges, there are likely deeper feelings buried underneath. Be patient and kind with yourself. Trust the process. Enlist all positive support and healthy avenues you require for healing.

The lessons we need to learn are contained within the situation and are reflected back to us through the people we encounter. Sometimes the most horrific experiences hold the key to our greatest healing. Healing occurs when we work through the emotions that emerge from the experience. As difficult as this is, our soul chose this life event to occur. It is within our control to decide how long we choose to remain in a victim-conscious state. This was a pre-ordained scenario for soul growth and advancement; it was not meant for us to sit in shame. Our soul is love and our ego is fear. Our most profound lessons in life are experienced through opposites. To know love, we have endured rejection; to feel joy, we have known sadness; to embrace spiritual freedom, we have processed being released from a victim mentality. This leads to forgiveness of ourselves and those who we previously believed victimized us. When we heal our soul, we are contributing to healing the soul of the Universe. We are on the journey of remembering who we are and why we are here. This brings us full circle to rediscovering our Higher Soul Self and realizing our purpose in this lifetime.

We will now explore a variety of life challenges that are part of our human journey. The answers are contained within the experience, and I will give you the tools to focus on the intended lesson in many of our critical life events. I will approach each challenge from a human perspective while understanding that, from a spiritual point of view, there are no victims or perpetrators. These events were pre-planned by all parties for our soul's learning and growth. In our pre-life planning, we understand that this life is a moment in time. We are privy to the entire big picture without the burden of earthly emotions. Our soul has a very different perspective on the myopic life we are living on Earth.

There is unique and valuable information that benefits everyone within each life scenario I will introduce. Allow yourself the gift of remaining open to this enlightened perspective on your healing journey. With every circumstance presented, there is an abundance of tools and knowledge for us to consider. I share my truth and personal experiences within every life situation presented. Each situation encompasses the potential aspects of forgiveness, peace and love. Another benefit from realizing the journey of others is to absorb empathy and compassion. These lessons enhance our ability to discover our intended life purpose and spiritual path. By embracing the messages presented in each life scenario, you are greatly contributing to substantial universal growth and an elevated positive world vibration.

GRIEF

The first life challenge we will tackle is an emotion that everyone experiences in their lifetime. Grief presents itself as a variety of emotions within many life-altering scenarios. It is important to be aware of the phases of bereavement and the tools necessary to process the emotions that arise during critical life events. We can readily identify grief with the loss of a loved one. We do not always recognize grief as clearly with other traumatic life incidents. Grief can result from any loss in life. This may include divorce, job loss, financial ruin, loss of innocence, loss of control and any situation where a devastating loss is felt.

In pre-life planning, our soul creates triggers for us to recognize an emotion that requires healing. One trigger is the emotions released by bereavement. Fear and anger are often primary sentiments that accompany grief. Grief and fear vibrate at the lowest energy level of all our emotions and often paralyze us into inaction. It is imperative to recognize that by working through heartbreaking loss, we are creating one of the greatest opportunities for growth and healing.

Acknowledge the emotions resulting from grief, hold them in a protective embrace and release them into the Universe. When we can alter our perspective of adversity, we are gifting ourselves the clarity for change. When we purge barriers of intense loss, we compel the Universe to grant us the tools required to fulfill our soul's mission. When you allow yourself to embrace grief, you are exponentially empowering yourself on your healing journey. This helps you recognize a key element in the path to your soul purose. By processing the emotions connected to your loss, you are fulfilling a crucial life objective and creating an opening to rediscover self.

Elisabeth Kübler-Ross recognized grief decades ago and bravely created a step-by-step method to process our emotions around death and dying. This concept was foreign to most people in 1969. We have learned so much in the last 50 years regarding emotional healing around the demise of our loved ones and any loss in life. It is helpful to understand that this is an individual journey and we all experience grief in our unique way. Through my life path and messages from the Heavenly Realm, I have created a more personal spiritually guided approach to recognize the grieving process. You can apply this course of action to any loss in life or to any personal experience that triggers grief.

Denial and Shock

When a loved one has crossed over, we are numb and do not believe that death has occurred. Denial may also occur when you experience a divorce, loss of innocence or any major loss in your life. Shock, which often accompanies denial, is a physiological response that creates a buffer to the catastrophic emotions that will slowly emerge once shock fades. Denial is a defense mechanism that affords us time to begin to process our loss.

Anger

Anger is generally the next emotion to emerge and is a normal response to grief. Allow the anger, rage and all the complicated emotions come to the forefront and be processed. When we repress anger, it may have devastating personal repercussions. We may feel anger towards our deceased loved ones or lash out at those left behind. Alcohol and drug abuse are never part of the healing process and only postpone the inevitable emotional journey. It is important to truly feel the anger. Be aware that the anger will most likely reappear a few times in what seems like an endless cycle. Approach anger as a catalyst to begin the processing of devastating emotions. Anger may be that tangible anchor you need to use to become aware of your healing process. When you are able to release the anger, it will eventually dissipate.

The Revolving Cycle of Bargaining

In this stage, we may call out to the Universe or God to take us instead of our loved one. We ask and repeatedly question the "what ifs" and "if onlys." Be aware that it may be difficult to exit the revolving messages that persist in our mind during this phase of grief. It is very important to break the cycle of bargaining so that we may progress on our healing journey. When your grief is a result of divorce or similar losses in your life, understand that living in perpetual remorse is stagnating your healing journey. Be aware that projecting devastating scenarios in your mind around potential future events is also a form of debilitating stagnation in the grief process. Attempt to ground yourself in the moment and not reside in a haze of guilt and regret from the past. Remind yourself that our soul is immortal and we orchestrated all these events in our pre-birth plan with our soul family.

Depression and Complicated Grief

Situational depression is a natural response to a catastrophic loss in life. You may also experience extreme sadness, emptiness, helplessness or despondency at this stage. Everything becomes overwhelming, and you may find yourself withdrawing from life. During this stage of grief, you may need to reach out and accept help from support groups, professionals or friends and family who can help you process your pain. If you contemplate suicide during any phase of grief, it is imperative to reach out for professional help or crisis intervention. Another scenario where you may require the assistance of a professional is when debilitating grief manifests as prolonged complicated grief. It is critical to work through depression, so you are open to the final stages of releasing grief.

Acceptance of a New Reality

Accepting our loss is not about forgetting our loved ones. Acceptance is realizing that they no longer exist in physical form but remain with us in our hearts and souls forever. Every day brings us closer to reuniting with our loved ones in the Afterlife. We do have to readjust to this new reality, as their passing has left a void in our life. We can work towards rearranging the empty space our loved ones' demise has left. This will take time and patience. A crucial aspect of acceptance is processing the emotions that are triggered from grief. We are releasing the stagnating impact of grief, not erasing our loved ones from our life. The process is similar for every loss experienced. The main difference is the intensity experienced by that loss and how we choose to perceive and release our pain associated with the emotions elicited from our grief.

Finding Meaning in our Loss

At this stage, we can return to the process of Divine Healing to help guide us in this phase of recovery. Create a narrative where you are empowered to embrace this life-changing event with an enlightened perspective. The lessons we embrace from our loved ones' transition into the Afterlife, or with any great loss we experience, may be the catalyst required to discover our life purpose. We are also encouraged to recognize loss through divorce or any life circumstance that triggers grief. The process of healing is similar in many of our life's challenges. Embrace the lessons we set out to learn by healing our pain and moving through the debilitating emotions this experience has created. This was all part of our pre-birth plan and the primary reason for our journey on this Earth. It is transformative to find purpose in every experience that creates a critical emotion within ourselves.

Grief as a Catalyst for Healing

The grief process does not occur in a linear sequence. There is no formula to follow that immediatly alleviates the excruciating pain of loss. We must feel the emotions and work through each sentiment to continually move forward on our healing path. We may experience each state of grief and return to previous stages multiple times. We do not have to experience each phase to process our emotions. These recommendations are merely a guide to help us recognize the deep emotions that we may experience on our healing journey.

A negative repercussion of not processing our emotions is that we may become paralyzed in a state of complicated grief. This is a deep grief that is not addressed and may last years or a lifetime. It is a direct result of the denial of emotions stemming from unresolved prolonged grief.

Do not get discouraged while processing grief. We progress at our own pace and in our own unique way. There is no time limit on grief, as long as you are moving forward on your healing path. Grief is a normal response to loss and presents an opportunity to open our hearts to the continuing love we have for ourselves and our loved ones. If we do not release the debilitating emotions resulting from grief, it potentially blocks us from experiencing the full impact of our loved ones' continued support from the Afterlife. Our lives are forever altered and we will always feel the loss that our loved ones' transition has created. As the intensity of grief lessens over time, our love continues to grow and strengthen. Empower yourself with the understanding that when you remember your crossed-over loved one with more joy in your heart than pain, you are progressing on a forward path to healing.

It may be challenging to assist others during their grieving journey. Being present and listening are the most important gifts you can give them. Giving advice or offering platitudes is not well-received at this stage. Be mindful that this is their grief and we do not know exactly how they feel. Simply offering a shoulder to cry on or an ear to listen is invaluable support. Many people do not know what to say and become uncomfortable around grieving people. Remain alert to what the grieving person requires from you. Offer to perform specific tasks and do not be afraid to speak about their crossed-over loved ones. We can keep our loved ones in our hearts by talking about the positive and honest memories we have of them. We will miss them for our entire lives, so there is no harm in speaking about them even years later. Grief is expressed uniquely by every individual. Do not judge others for how they choose to grieve. If you observe their actions going in the direction of destructive behaviors, then that is one circumstance you may need to intervene in. Gently and lovingly acknowledge your concern. Encourage them to seek professional help, and support them through this critical period of intense loss. If you are the one engaging in harmful coping behaviors, seek help and guidance as you would for any dear friend. Reaching out for help is a sign of strength and not weakness. There are many options available for aiding you in your healing journey. It is important for you to understand that it is ultimately your path to work through the emotions elicited from any loss in life. Do not forget that you are always surrounded by loving energies supporting you every step of the way.

One element of grief that many deny involves the emotions of guilt and regret. There may also be feelings of anger, betrayal, abandonment, fear and a myriad of other emotions that create raw pain on a level that may not have been experienced before. These feelings can emerge at any point in the grieving process. Guilt is experienced by many people, but it does not serve a higher purpose. Remember, guilt is anger turned inwards and is an emotion that decreases our vibration and stagnates our healing journey. Your loved one's passing was predestined and planned by them. All circumstances around their passing were meant to be. If you were not present, it is because they chose that. If you had to make the decision for the conclusion of their life, they support that. Your brave soul agreed to help your loved one's crossing, at their request and with your consent, during pre-life planning. By embracing the lessons you need to learn due to their passing, you are honoring your loved ones with the most beautiful and profound gift. You will always miss their physical presence, but work to change the perspective of your role in their transition to the Heavenly Realm.

It is fascinating to comprehend how our soul is in charge of our last moments on Earth. This is a strong message I have received, both on a spiritual level and on a human level, by being present when souls crossed over from their bodies' demise. Our souls may leave their body well before that vessel ceases to function. Our soul has the ability to exit from our earthly body prior to a violent or painful death. We are in charge around every aspect of the final stages of our earthly existence. It is important to fully embrace this truth for us to begin our healing journey and release any guilt surrounding their return home. This truth also greatly decreases the fear surrounding our own earthly demise and empowers us to embrace our ultimate control during the end stages of life.

Relinquish the guilt you feel around believing you could have done anything to prevent this. If you feel that you contributed to their demise by not insisting they see a doctor, checking on them too late or any number of circumstances, understand that the outcome that occurred was meant to occur. If you feel guilty about not being present at the moment of their last breath, accept that this was pre-planned and orchestrated by your loved one. You were not meant to be present for numerous reasons. I have witnessed this during many deaths in my nursing career. The family would maintain a constant vigil, yet their loved one chose to cross over when their family members stepped out for just a brief moment. If you were not present at the exact time of death of your loved one's physical body, be reassured that their soul was and is surrounding you in an embrace of pure love energy. Take a moment to experience this gift and release any distressing emotions around the circumstances of your loved one's earthly demise. Even if you were miles away, your loved one has the ability to transcend space and time to be with you. If you were the brave soul who had to make the final decision to end your loved one's suffering, forgive yourself. In every sense there is nothing to forgive. You took on this brave task in your pre-birth plan with your loved one. They now sit in gratitude and great love for your role in their return home. Your loved ones have relinquished all feelings of anger, pain, resentment and any adverse earthly emotion attached to their demise or their earthly existence. They bring only love and compassion into the Heavenly Realm. They forgive all because now they understand that this was pre-planned by them to learn and progress in their soul journey as well as yours. There is truly nothing to forgive.

People who have crossed over and experienced an NDE consistently express an overwhelming desire to continue on their journey to their forever home in Heaven. There is much reluctance in returning back to their earthly existence. Take heart that your loved ones are exactly where they planned to be and are meant to be. We are greatly loved and appreciated for fulfilling the role we pre-planned with our crossed-over family members and friends on their return to their heavenly home.

The energy that grief and guilt require may become all consuming. Release the guilt so you are free to continue on your healing journey. As tragic as death appears, every death that occurs was meant to happen. When grief lifts, you may be able to objectively view their crossing from a renewed perspective. We do not move on from loving the souls of our departed. We move through the pain and grief and move forward with the love and support that continually surround us from our loved one's spiritual energy.

Our crossed-over loved ones do not want us to live in a state of perpetual depression and prolonged complicated grief over their passing. They want us to feel joy and happiness so that they may experience those emotions through us. Feel empowered to celebrate your loved ones in many meaningful ways. Honour them by living a healthy and joyous life. They love to be present when we think of them or celebrate them in any way. When we are aware of our loved ones popping into our consciousness, know that this is their soul communicating with us. Be open to the loving message they are sending us at that moment. Release the doubt and ego to allow their love and compassion to fill the empty space their crossing has left in our heart. They forgive all and encourage you to live your best life possible. Do not worry, they are not interested in observing our intimate moments. Their main concern is for our health and well-being. Celebrate every day, because we are that much closer to seeing our loved ones again. The symbolic cord that connects every soul is never severed. We always maintain a spiritual link to our loved ones. Love is an energy that knows no boundaries. It is interesting to note that many times, when our most beloved life partners cross over, they will send us a new partner to share our life with on Earth. When love is experienced on such an intense level, it only expands the probability for love to continually enter into our lives. We are also alerted to rediscovering our roles in this lifetime and become awakened to our souls' journeys here and in the Afterlife. In this sense, grief may be the catalyst that alerts us to the priorities and lessons we have been denying up to this point in our existence.

You are not alone in this monumental task of healing. On the spiritual side, you have your guides and crossed-over loved ones for support. The Higher Realm is not some elusive place thousands of miles away. The souls of our loved ones and the love of Source are always within us and surround us at all times. Even in deep grief, we can become aware of our soul supports. In this Earthly Realm, there are counselors, friends, prayer or support groups, yoga, breathing and meditation techniques and any healthy support you choose.

It is normal to go through the stages of grief in many of our life's challenges. When we experience loss in any form, we may symbolically undergo the death of that part of us. This may include the loss of innocence, financial loss, divorce, loss of self-esteem or any number of losses in our life. When grief begins to lift, attempt to approach this life experience with a new perspective. Explore what this loss is teaching you. The lesson is contained within every situation. Grief becomes the trigger to remind us of what requires healing in this lifetime. By applying our tools of knowledge of the Afterlife, Divine Healing and working through our painful emotions, we are enlightened to embrace our intended path.

It may be comforting to realize that when we learn our lessons in this life, we will not have to repeat them in future lives. Imprinted on our souls for eternity are our ingrained life lessons, love of self, love for others and Source's purest love for all. What we gain from each challenge in life, we gain for eternity.

MISCARRIAGE AND LOSS OF A CHILD

The loss of a child is the most devastating event in the human experience. There are no words or actions that can relieve the immediate pain that this situation creates. Time may eventually soften the intensity of emotions, but closure is a word I choose not to associate with any critical loss. Grief may become a lifelong emotion, but I hope I can offer an alternative perspective on how to approach the grieving process.

Every soul is precious and loved. The loss of any child who left us too soon is grieved enormously. We feel love for our babies from the moment we are aware of their existence. We plan a future and an entire life with them in our hearts and minds. They instantly become beloved members of our family.

Each soul's experience is unique and was pre-planned long before coming to this Earthly Realm. There are many factors involved in designing our experiences on Earth. The mom, dad, baby and extended family were all instrumental in this plan in the Heavenly Realm. There is no deeper love than that of a parent and child on this Earth. This is the closest we come to Source's great love for us in Heaven. The soul of the baby or child is so grateful for experiencing that incredible earthly love, regardless of how brief the time is. This includes the love they absorb in utero before our babies are even born. In the pre-birth planning with the mom and dad, it was decided this experience was necessary to benefit all participants. For the parents, it may have been to process grief, work through a karma agreement or to deal with and release other intense emotions. From the perspective of the soul of the baby, they may not have been prepared to live a full earthly life. This young soul may have been very early in their development as a spiritual being. This soul may have wanted to experience the love of a mother and father but was not yet ready to participate in an entire life on Earth. It takes much courage and strength to experience an earthly life, as it is the most challenging but effective means of learning and growing for a soul. The parents also gain in this aspect by understanding unconditional love in this miraculous form. All participants involved agreed to experience this event during the pre-birth soul plan.

There are many women and men who feel guilt associated with the loss of their child. Holding guilt is harmful and destructive. Guilt is an emotion that serves no greater purpose if it is repressed and not dealt with. Allow the guilt to surface, and process all the emotions that emerge. There is nothing anyone could have done to change the outcome of this painful experience. This was all pre-planned to help strengthen your soul for this life and future lives you have planned with your precious soul family member.

If we are able to view this crisis with an altered perspective, hopefully we can fully appreciate what we set out to learn. By working through the deep sadness and grief, we are learning to cope with these emotions at a heightened level. We are building tools which assist us in dealing with situations that elicit similar emotions throughout this and future lives.

It is important to understand grief, so we are able to process and learn from our experiences. When we grieve the loss of a child, we grieve our dreams and the altered future without that child. It is important we work through any feelings of guilt and self-blame. We can easily get stuck in the emotions that do not serve a greater good. It is imperative to release those emotions that do not fill us with love and compassion. We are doing a disservice to our children who have crossed over if we become stuck in our pain. A life was created, and we became parents the moment our baby was assigned a soul. We will be reunited in Heaven and will be intertwined with that soul for all eternity. You are their forever parents at the most intense level. They have been, and will always be, a precious member of your soul family.

There are many scenarios that may play out that involve the journey of this innocent soul. They may enter into the body of a future child you are blessed with in this lifetime. Their soul may enter a child whom you are very close to in the future. This may be a nephew, foster or adoptive child or a close friend's child. Our soul group from the Heavenly Realm does not require biological connection to be a member of our eternal divine family. Remain open and alert to close relationships in the future. If you experience a connection with someone so intensely that it is difficult to comprehend, understand that this may be a member of your soul family. Personally, I experienced that feeling with my son-in-law. He is my soul son and I cherish the relationship and deep spiritual love that we share.

A selfless gift is to honor our children who have crossed over by living a joy filled life. Their souls are living through us now. Do not feel guilty for loving present or future children or for embracing all the beauty the world has to offer. They want happiness for us and to experience life and love through us.

These innocent souls are now in the loving arms of our Creator. They have returned home, where we will soon join them. Every day brings us closer to our reunion with our loved ones in the Afterlife. For them, this is only a moment in time. When we sit in deep grief, time seems to stop for us. Releasing these paralyzing emotions allows us to continue on our soul journey so we may embrace the lessons we set out to learn with our crossed-over loved ones. They are always supportive and proud of where we are on this life journey. Our children and the souls of all our soul family hold us in a loving embrace. This is especially felt in times of healing.

When we remember our soul family, they are automatically with us. When we feel their presence, do not question that they are by our side and in our heart. In Heaven, communication is through telepathy. We have the ability to communicate with our loved ones by speaking with them in our minds or out loud. Even though our children cross over at a young earthly age, their souls in the Heavenly Realm are wise and are able to communicate clearly. This is the language of love.

I have been blessed with a gift of being able to communicate with souls who have crossed over. As a nurse in high-risk obstetrics, I have experienced assisting the souls of babies in their transition to the Heavenly Realm. I am also grateful for having the opportunity to help parents on their healing journey. I am extremely honored to have visits from some of the souls who have crossed over. They will often come in the arms of a crossed-over grandparent on the other side of the veil. These souls may also present as young adults. Our souls are energy and do not adhere to the age they crossed over at. Regardless of the earthly age of our children who cross over, we are always able to connect with their soul energy. All communication is through telepathic love energy. All souls are able to receive and send love from their heavenly home.

As individual as each soul is, the message they express is similar. They are grateful for the love they experienced, even for a short time. For them, time is inconsequential. The love they internalize lasts for all eternity. It is the quality of love they felt and not the duration of time that is important. They also reassure me that they left all the pain and unfavorable experiences on Earth. They only experience a heartfelt and powerful love in God's embrace and forever carry the love we have for them and them for us.

Every person experiences their own unique encounter with grief. My miscarriage occurred in the 1980s. Discussing and speaking about loss was discouraged, as society was so uncomfortable with death and dying. My miscarriage occurred after the birth of my daughter. The sense of loss was overwhelming and devastating. I had assisted many couples in dealing with their loss, so I felt I should have known how to deal with my own pain. I clearly did not. I quickly became pregnant with my son and buried all my unresolved emotions from my loss. I was told to "get over it," and I thought I had.

A few years later, I was presented with an opportunity to be in a program supporting families who had experienced miscarriages. As an R.N., nursing women and families through their loss was a major aspect of my profession. Unfortunately, in the 1980s and 1990s there was little follow-up support. Our innovative program established the first burial plot for miscarried and stillborn infants. We encouraged parents to view and name their children and to fully grieve their loss. Astoundingly, this was not a common practice at this time. We initiated a counselling program to facilitate healing and support parents during this critical time in their lives. I also participated in a curriculum to educate medical students and members of the supportive staff in validating women and couples who suffered this great loss. I was very proud of the work we did, and I know it was beneficial to many.

The Universe brought these opportunities in my life for a specific reason. Through being of service to others, I was able to finally grieve my personal loss. There is no time limit on processing and working through grief. This became a pivotal opportunity to continue on my healing journey. Repressed feelings of unworthiness and low self-worth also emerged. These were complicated underlying emotions that would take years to unravel and finally release.

Another profound experience regarding the crossing over of young souls began early in my childhood. My mother had a miscarriage with her first child, which I was not aware of until I was in my teens. Speaking about miscarriage or death in general was greatly discouraged at that time. Denying and repressing feelings was a normal way of dealing with any emotional issue for many generations. Keep in mind, this was a different time in our history, and my parents did the best they could with the knowledge they had at the time.

I was the eldest of three children, all a year apart. My mother struggled emotionally with raising the three of us in an isolated community. My dad was an R.C.M.P. (Royal Canadian Mounted Police) officer and had to work long hard hours to provide for us. I felt a huge responsibility to help my mom with the younger kids. I absorbed a lot of her pain and despair subconsciously at the time.

There were many times I felt lonely and afraid, but I had a deep sense of being protected and supported. This became evident during a field trip in first grade. I recall telling a friend, sitting next to me on the bus, that I had an older brother named Daniel. My mom was a chaperone on this bus trip and, unknown to me, overheard the conversation with my friend. When we returned home, my mom confronted me and accused me of making up stories. At that age, I was unable to articulate my abilities and connection with souls that others could not see or hear. I tried explaining to my mom how I knew Daniel and that he often came to me when I needed him. My mom did not understand, and we never spoke of him again. Daniel eventually faded from my life at that time.

Years later, after my father crossed over to the Heavenly Realm, he would come to me often during meditation. Dad frequently brought a baby wrapped lovingly in his arms. He presented this baby to me with pure love, joy and pride. In the background, I would hear a Bible song very familiar to me from my childhood. This song referred to a young man named Daniel who had such a strong faith, he was willing to be thrown into the lion's den to prove God's love for him. I recall singing this song frequently as a child. The baby then appeared as a young man who looked very much like my father. He came across as confident and caring. I began to recognize his soul from when I was very young. He confirmed that he was Daniel, my crossed-over older brother from my mom's miscarriage. He assured me that I did not make him up all those years ago and that he has always remained by my side in times of need.

Daniel then spoke of our pre-life plan we had made together before either of us came to Earth in this lifetime. We both agreed that the eldest would require great strength and compassion for the life ahead. He knew he was not ready to take on this responsibility. Daniel also decided to come before me so he could help me from the Heavenly Realm. Daniel informed me that his role was primarily to assist Mom with her emotional challenges in the future. He had to have her experience the pain of losing a child for her to fully appreciate the love for her future children. I truly believe that this experience was essential for my mom to survive many emotional challenges in this lifetime.

As Daniel faded from my vision, I heard the Elton John song, "Daniel." For me, this song represents a meaningful relationship with an older and wiser brother. This brother made sacrifices so his family could experience a better life. This song resonated strongly with me in my teen years and still does today.

My mom recently listened to my experiences of Daniel with an open heart. Due to her dementia, I was not expecting a coherent response. She looked clearly into my eyes and whispered, "Daniel, my son." I am so grateful for that brief moment of clarity with my mom. We are all a product of our generation and past. My parents' growth in this lifetime is remarkable, and I am honored to have been a part of their souls' journeys.

By altering our perspective on grief and loss, we can accelerate our growth towards love and peace. Our children will forever be a part of our heart and beloved members of our soul family. We are never separated in spirit from them and will continue to live many lives together. This earthly life we are experiencing now is only moments in the Heavenly Realm. Our crossed-over loved ones, and especially the souls of our little children, want us to live a joy-filled life so they may experience that happiness through us. Every day brings us closer to being reunited with them. They are embraced in Source's great glory and are basking in the eternal love we have for them.

ABORTION

Our society is extremely divided on the issue of abortion. It has become both a moral and political issue. Certain religions also have very rigid ideals regarding abortion.

Unless we are the ones making the decision for abortion, we do not know the circumstances around why that choice was made. Judgment and anger do not serve a higher purpose...ever. Judgment of others, or self, is not a healthy road to go down. We do not know what anyone else is going through. Uncover the feelings this brings up, work through those emotions and strive for compassion and forgiveness of yourself and others.

Once a child is conceived, a soul is chosen to merge with that baby's body and brain. Especially during the first and second trimesters, the soul has the option of leaving whenever that soul chooses. The soul remains close to the baby but does not have to fully merge until the birth of that baby.

When a decision is made for an abortion to occur, the soul can decide to enter into another baby's body. The soul may also decide to wait and enter as a future child to the same mother. This has all been previously decided in the pre-birth plan by all parties involved.

Abortion is a very personal and difficult choice. After that decision has been made, take time to process all the emotions that come up for you. Forgiving yourself and healing your pain will allow you to live an emotionally healthy life in the future. This event was pre-planned between you and your child long before you came to live this life. It is important to stress that we always have free will once we begin our existence on Earth. Honour yourself and your child by dealing with and processing all the emotions that arise for you. This is your gift for your loved one and the primary reason for this experience.

This is extremely difficult for the souls who enter into this pre-life contract. I pray for love, understanding and compassion to all involved in this often-painful situation. I believe Source has a very special place for the souls of those precious babies. They are held closely in the loving arms of our Creator, as are all our beautiful children who have left this Earth too soon.

SUICIDE

Throughout life, we are bombarded with conflicting messages. Media, society, family, church and peers all contribute to perpetuating these injurious communications. We lose sight of understanding that other people's opinions are often misguided. We may eventually begin to internalize many painful experiences and communications. It becomes a challenge to eliminate these false beliefs from our mind and, more importantly, from our soul.

Sadly, there are times when a person cannot reject or process these distressing messages. They become so wrapped up in their pain that suicide becomes an option as a way out. A soul may have taken on the challenge of a mental illness, a mental health condition or an addiction as part of their pre-life plan. These souls often take on an extreme life circumstance to advance their soul family's progression on Earth or to clear recurring karma for the collective. Every person who dies by suicide does so for many individual reasons. Regardless of the rationale, it is not our job to judge or condemn. From a soul's perspective, they may have been too young and inexperienced to endure the rigors of an earthly life. Sometimes our souls do not bring an adequate amount of energy to sustain life's challenges. Our soul often underestimates the percentage of energy required on this Earthly Realm. Remember, our soul leaves a significant amount of their energy in Heaven to pursue their soul commitments.

Suicide is never part of the pre-birth plan, but some souls are more inclined to die by suicide as an exit strategy. A soul enters a body knowing that suicidal tendencies may be part of the blueprint. In the Heavenly Realm, that soul may feel empowered to overcome the pull towards suicide as an exit point. Free will can override good intentions on the Earthly Realm.

Source always accepts every soul into Heaven with love, compassion and forgiveness. There is never any judgment or punishment for a soul in the Afterlife. On the soul's part, there is often confusion and regret immediately upon crossing over. In the next realm, the soul may then choose a peaceful area that allows them time to reflect and heal from their untimely exit. The soul understands that they made a hasty decision to prematurely end the gift of this body. They now comprehend that their soul still has to resolve the burdensome emotions that remain a part of their essence. The death of a body does not eliminate the emotions attached to our soul. They will bring those same challenges into their next reincarnation on Earth and will have to work on releasing them once again. These souls are bathed in love and forgiveness but must consider and understand the decisions they made. When they feel ready, the soul can rejoin their soul family in the Heavenly Realm to continue to learn and grow in love.

During our life review in Heaven, every soul must internalize the emotions they inflicted on others due to their intentions, words and actions while on Earth. Source does not judge our souls, but our soul deeply feels the emotions experienced by our loved ones and everyone we encountered in our life. The souls of individuals who have died by suicide take full responsibility for their actions. Those left behind often experience feelings of guilt, anger, remorse and confusion. The souls of those who died by suicide do not want their loved ones on Earth to take on any responsibility or burden from their decisions.

Every suicide that could have been prevented was prevented. This is not a platitude, and I have been reassured that this is a deep spiritual truth. I have been shown that the Universe, in conjunction with our guardian angels, attempts to intervene when there is an opportunity to create change. When there is an opening for an alternative action, the Universe provides that option. If the Universe understands the situation as inevitable, the suicide will occur. When we witness loved ones going through emotional pain, we may attempt to intervene. We can encourage them to express thoughts of depression, suicidal ideology, hopelessness or any emotion they are feeling. It is important to listen without judgment and do not attempt to insert your opinions or advice. Tell them you love them and do not promise you will keep their threats around suicide a secret. We can then suggest and direct them towards professional support. There are critical questions you may ask a loved one if you are concerned with their mental health. You may directly ask if, in the last few weeks, have they wished they were dead, have felt their family is better off without them, have had any thoughts of killing themselves, or have tried to kill themselves and have a plan to end their life. If they refuse to answer or reply yes to any of these questions, strongly encourage and assist them in reaching out for professional help as soon as possible. There are crisis centers, crisis phone lines, and mobile crisis units that are available for immediate response to support people experiencing an acute mental health episode. Occasionally, despite all our good intentions and effort, the inevitable occurs. Ultimately, we have little control over the factors involved when a loved one dies by suicide.

 One of the only elements we can control around suicide is how we respond to the event. Grief is a normal reaction to every loved one's crossing over. When suicide occurs, there may be an immense release of intense emotions that are directly and indirectly associated with the grieving process. Working through these emotions is complicated and painful. Guilt, shame and blame have the ability to paralyze us into inaction and prevent us from processing our emotions in a healthy way. It is imperative to work through and release all emotions that arise from this devastating event. Only then can you begin to understand this loss as the learning experience it was meant to be. I will stress once again that suicide is not directly part of the pre-birth plan, but all souls are aware of the potential for suicide to occur through free will.

Engage in any healthy avenue you choose to heal during this process. There are support groups, counselling, journaling, prayer, meditation and many other options. You will forever miss the presence of your loved ones on Earth, but they are always with you in spirit. Your life is radically altered, but the intensity of your loss will gradually soften over time.

There will eventually come a point in time where you will predominantly recall your loved ones with favorable memories and love. When that day comes, realize that your healing is on a forward path. To fully heal, you must release the image of your loved ones' last moments on Earth. They want us to remember them for the beautiful souls they are and not for the tragic circumstances of their demise. The souls of those who have crossed over are aware of and feel our emotions. What a great opportunity to give your loved ones and yourself the gift of forgiveness. Forgiveness for yourself and your loved one is the ultimate act of love. It will not only set your soul free but also the soul of your loved one living in the embrace of Source.

There are many reasons why people die by suicide. Death with dignity is an option for individuals who are physically or mentally suffering or terminally ill. Under these circumstances, they may choose to take their own life or arrange for a medically assisted transition. The primary motivation is to alleviate pain for themselves and for others, physically and emotionally. The intention of any earthly action is an important factor in our soul's journey in the Afterlife. Many countries are legalizing medical assistance in dying with strict criteria in place. When these souls cross over, their unique circumstances are considered as they enter the Heavenly Realm. Their soul's transition is generally very smooth and follows a course that is similar to a natural death of the body.

We all chose to be on Earth at this exact time. In our pre-life planning, we focused on specific challenges we needed to work through. We collaborated with our soul group on a plan that would benefit every member of our soul family. There are times when one or two souls take on the majority of difficult potential life experiences. They do this for many reasons. It may be to accelerate the growth of others in their soul family. These souls may be very advanced and take on major hardships for healing the collective. Every soul who chooses a life on Earth is aware of what that experience will entail.

When we reside in the Heavenly Realm, we are able to view the entire big picture of our existence. We understand that each life is only a moment in our soul's journey. When we are able to lift the veil of amnesia on Earth, we are empowered to enlighten ourselves on our life's purpose. By fully accepting this renewed perspective, we are given the tools towards spiritual and emotional healing.

Our soul's mission on Earth is to work through our pain and emotions that do not serve a higher purpose. Forgiveness for yourself and your loved ones who die by suicide is a critical step. Releasing the shame and guilt and any other emotions that stagnate your healing are essential for learning and growth. Honour your crossed-over loved one for all the hardships they embraced so you could be alerted to what your soul required in this lifetime. Remember, they chose this life path along with everyone involved so that healing can occur.

Our loved ones are now in the loving embrace of Source. When you are able to begin releasing the pain of your loss, you are freeing their soul to continue on their healing journey, as well as yours. Your loved ones remain present in your life, just on an elevated energy level. You will soon be reunited with them in that realm. You will continue to participate in many lives together with your loved one and all your soul family in countless future experiences.

CANCER AND CRITICAL ILLNESS

Cancer: immediately, this word evokes strong emotions of fear, anger and loss. It has the power to bring our world crashing down around us. In an instant, it can alter the entire trajectory of our lives. I have experienced the ramifications of this word since I was a child. I have had many family members and friends cross over from this horrific disease. I am a cancer survivor. In society, cancer and critical illnesses surround each of us in crucial ways.

Cancer took my kind maternal grandfather in my youth. That began a continual theme of loss to this dreaded disease for our entire family. In 2016, my beloved father crossed over to his eternal home in Heaven. During my father's journey with stomach cancer, I had been exploring our family genealogy. We discovered that dad's grandfather Michael had also passed away from stomach cancer. This discovery was new to all of us. I instantly became aware of a deep spiritual connection with my great-grandfather and namesake. This realization gave me a sense of deep comfort. There were many times I have since felt my great-grandfather's and my father's souls blend together. I will explore that when the time presents itself for me to know what that connection is.

I miss the physical aspect of holding my dad and his hugs every day, but what I have gained from his transition is great spiritual awareness. From the Heavenly Realm and his elevated perspective, my dad was instrumental in creating a portal for me to have access to the Afterlife. My psychic and mediumship abilities heightened to a level that astounded me. My dad reassured me that this was his path for a multitude of reasons. His crossing over from cancer was predestined and planned long before he began this life on Earth. My father informed me that he had to cross over so that his family could fulfill the lessons we required on our life journeys. Dad reassured me that he would best serve his supportive role with my mom from Heaven. He also assists me with encouragement and confidence in sharing healing messages with the world through my writing and through the strengthening of my divine abilities.

From a human perspective, cancer is cruel and creates unimaginable pain in our lives. If we are able to alter our perspective on this disease and other critical illnesses, we may be alerted to what we need to learn in this lifetime. Illness may be the catalyst for immense growth. We can modify the impact and path of disease before it enters our life and also after we are diagnosed. If we are empowered to take our control back, we may drastically alter the outcome of every challenging experience in our lifetime.

It is important to be aware of all our options for healing. From the Western Medicine viewpoint, patients are treated for the disease they present with from a scientific context. This discipline affords us the options for treatment, surgery, medications and the expertise of many skilled physicians and surgeons. In Naturopathic Medicine, healing is approached with a holistic and Eastern Medicine foundation. My brother, a Naturopathic doctor, focuses on healing the whole person. He investigates the core issues underneath a person's symptoms while considering mind, body and spirit. His dedication and passion are an inspiration to his patients, friends and family. I have had many opportunities to experience all these modalities in my time on this Earth and can now share that knowledge with others.

In life, we are presented with repetitive and similar experiences to alert us to lessons we need to learn. As a young nurse, I began to notice patterns occurring among my patients with gynecological cancers. The primary site of these cancers originated from the female reproductive organs. This was not a coincidence. I also noted that the majority of these women were caregivers who sacrificed their needs over those of family and friends. They abandoned their well-being to help others and prioritized everyone but themselves. During the last stages of their lives, I spoke to many women and their families about this subject. Another common theme among these women was that they were reluctant to advocate for themselves. They were conditioned to give their power away to someone else without fully realizing what that meant for their personal quality of life. Near the end of their life journeys, many of these women expressed to me lessons they had learned. An important message was for everyone to first look after our own well-being and to stand up for what we believe in. We teach people how to treat us, so insist on being treated with respect and compassion. Only when we heal ourselves are we able to help others heal. I took this wisdom to heart.

At the age of thirty-nine, I noticed an unusual pain in my lower right abdomen. It was challenging to try and convince my doctors to order further tests, because they claimed I was too young and healthy to have serious issues. I could hear my previous patients' voices encouraging me throughout this journey. After months of advocating for myself and abnormal ultrasound results in hand, the oncologist agreed that exploration was necessary. The surgeons removed my right ovary, and I was diagnosed with early-stage ovarian cancer. During this time, I kept hearing, "You will be okay." Later that year, a good friend crossed over to the Heavenly Realm from the same cancer that I had been diagnosed with. In her gentle and loving manner, she helped empower me to advocate for myself and other women to take our power back.

This occurred in the early phase of my spiritual journey. I instinctually tapped into the messages from my patients I had cared for. Up until that point, I had numerous characteristics in common with many of these women. I frequently put the needs of others before my own. I had low self-esteem and felt unworthy. I felt my opinion was not fully heard or understood. My experience with cancer allowed me to begin to process some of those repressed emotions. I acknowledged my feelings and finally started dealing with them. A definite pattern began to emerge to alert me to the need for healing around my low self-love.

At this time, I was still in the early stages of becoming aware of my Higher Soul Self. My knowledge of my soul's journey was just becoming a part of my consciousness. I required all these life situations for my personal clarity. Upon reflection, I am curious to know whether I would have had to experience all these critical life events had I learned my life purpose sooner. My sincere hope is that with the knowledge and tools presented, you will be able to recognize your soul's lessons in a less intense and clearer enlightened path. I remain grateful for every experience that has led me to this place in my life, especially if it empowers others to become alerted to their purpose in a less extreme way.

When you reflect on your life, be open to recognize recurring patterns that alert you to what emotions require healing and to issues you need to resolve in this lifetime. These are all triggers for discovering your path to your soul purpose.

During my cancer journey, I was discovering my personal self-worth and how to trust my instincts and inner voice. I was learning to love myself and realized that my voice held validity and truth. In this sense, cancer became the trigger to alert me to what required healing in this lifetime. I truly believe that I can now view my cancer journey as a gift that prompted me to begin resolving underlying emotional challenges that kept recurring in my life.

I have witnessed cancer and chronic illnesses become a manifestation of emotional trauma in many circumstances. There are a multitude of contributing factors to why disease exists in this world. Emotional health affects our physical health in direct and indirect ways. Having this knowledge is another tool to living a healthy existence. Processing and releasing adverse emotions are strong factors in the potential prevention of many illnesses. When we are emotionally stressed, we create a state of fight or flight within our bodies. That creates a brisk response in the activation of our protector cells. That intense response may cause an environment to prompt your body to produce an abundance of cell growth and create inflammation. This may lead to arthritis, autoimmune diseases, cancer and a multitude of other life-altering conditions. When we use this knowledge to help support our decisions to get emotionally healthy, we are strengthening our resolve for optimum overall health.

If you are currently living with any form of unwellness, work diligently on approaching it with an alternative perspective. There is an astounding amount of anecdotal evidence that supports the power of positive intentions and prayer. Even if you are skeptical, you have nothing to lose by choosing an optimistic approach to healing. When we use this knowledge to help support our decisions to get emotionally healthy, we are strengthening our resolve to overall better health. We are functioning at our best when we can balance physical, emotional and spiritual well-being. An important psychological aspect is to relinquish the victim mentality. Repetitively asking yourself "Why me?" serves no higher purpose and paralyzes you into inaction. It is time for you to take your power back and embrace a positive attitude to every aspect of your life. You can continue living as you are, or you can radically change the outcome of your experience in this lifetime. At the very least, you will be exposed to a new method of dealing with challenges and potentially resolve buried emotions that have prevented you from living your best life. To learn and grow, acknowledge the perception adjustment presented to you so that you may view this experience in a new light. This is your soul's pre-life plan playing out. It requires soul-searching and Divine Healing to help you discover the lessons you need to learn from this experience.

When we are initially given the diagnosis of cancer or a serious illness, we are understandably in shock and denial. Allow yourself time to process the emotions that come up. You are only doing yourself a disservice by burying the emotions that are destructive in your healing journey. When you are able to process, release and heal your emotional and spiritual wounds, you will empower yourself to help heal the physical aspects of your illness.

Although I continued on my healing journey after experiencing cancer, I did not fully embrace all the lessons my soul had pre-arranged to learn in this lifetime. I had slipped back into living a chaotic life and ignored my personal well-being once again. The Universe sent me a strong wakeup call when, at forty-three years old, I became critically ill after contracting Lyme Disease. Prior to my illness, I was leading a life that was not sustainable. We were raising four teenagers at the time. In addition, our foster sons had disabilities that required constant monitoring and supervision. Dale was working full-time and I was an R.N. on an intensely challenging critical care unit. Our two wonderful dogs added love and pandemonium to our busy lives. My husband was active in coaching and loved playing hockey and golf himself. My only escape was going to the gym when the kids were at school and before I went to work. Sleep and relaxation were last on my list, and self-care was almost nonexistent. Even my psychic and spiritual connections were shut down. I was exhausted! That was when Lyme Disease brought a sudden halt to the life I had been living and stopped me abruptly in my tracks.

Six months after my initial infection, I was hospitalized with liver failure. I was told twice by my specialists that I would most likely not survive this critical illness. Again, I heard deep in my soul that everything would be okay. After weeks of progressively worsening symptoms, my surgeon performed an experimental surgical procedure. I began to improve, but the healing process was going to be a long and excruciating journey.

I am still living with the pain and debilitating fatigue of chronic Lyme Disease, which now presents as an autoimmune condition. I am also battling the internal damage caused by my liver failure. My most significant challenge through this life experience is to maintain a positive attitude and not slide into a victim mentality.

The support of family and friends has been an essential aspect of my recovery. I pursue a variety of medical interventions, primarily in Naturopathic Medicine for optimum healing. I care for my mental health through counselling and exercise. Practicing meditation and prayer affords me the ability to maintain a strong spiritual connection. I honestly believe that Lyme Disease was a gift that sent me on a path of emotional and spiritual enlightenment and immense growth. I work on acknowledging, processing and releasing adverse feelings that have encumbered my ability to discover my true essence. I actively pursue avenues of growth in all aspects of my life. When I make decisions that I interpret as a mistake, I now realize that every misstep is an opportunity. I have empowered myself with self-love and self-worth. This has enabled me to send love into the world from a soul level in a way that does not compromise my health or well-being. The most powerful lesson I learned was that by healing myself first, I am able to send an authentic higher vibrational love into the Universe. This creates an ideal environment for others to absorb that love and continue their journey of soul healing and discover their life purpose. This is a gift of transformative healing from the core of my being.

When we stray from following our pre-birth plan, our soul alerts us in sometimes extreme ways. Cancer and critical illnesses are strong triggers for awareness of our life purpose. For myself, cancer was my initial signal to warn me to return to my life plan. I had just enough spiritual awakening at that time to remind my soul I was veering off course. Unfortunately, I pushed that knowledge to the side once again and became critically ill with Lyme Disease. As with many messages in my life, it took a boulder to alert me to the path I required to discover my true essence. After years of faltering, I finally began to truly listen and understand my soul's intention.

During much reflection and prayer, I now understand that cancer and critical illnesses can be viewed through many perspectives. My father chose cancer as part of his exit strategy in his pre-birth plan. On a soul level, he understood that he would not be able to care for Mom in the way she would eventually require. I also believe that my dad was aware, on a spiritual level, of how Covid would shut down the world and create an atmosphere where he could not thrive. Dad was extremely socially active and Covid, in conjunction with the isolation of caring for Mom, would have created an insurmountable challenge for him. Dad was instrumental in orchestrating Mom's care from the Afterlife. I clearly see that he caringly created an opening in an appropriate and safe personal care home setting at the perfect time. My dad's crossing has also allowed the rest of our family to embrace our lessons on a spiritual level. He has created a passageway for many of us to heal our repressed life-defining emotions and become aware of our intended life plans.

When you are healed, your soul will carry self-love and forgiveness within you forever. Not only are you healing yourself, but the positive energy within will radiate to heal others. Your higher vibrations will resonate into the Universe. The authentic energy you exude attracts universal positive energy and surrounds you and the collective in light and love. This is the divine result of all soul work.

Since these experiences, I have been shown that there is a spiritual connection regarding cancer and critical illnesses. As difficult as this concept is to fully comprehend, it enables us to transcend the fear regarding this life-changing diagnosis. When we are able to accept that cancer and critical illnesses are pre-planned choices, we are able to take our power back. Remove the fear by working on the emotions that emerge from this critical incident. Remember that our souls continue on, and that this life is a brief moment in our eternal spiritual journeys. This is an opportunity to create an everlasting enlightened imprint on your soul. It is never too late to impact your true inner essence.

I have noted that cancer and critical illnesses present as potential crucial triggers when all other life strategies have failed. We receive many messages throughout our life to alert us to our life goals and challenges. When we continually ignore those messages, the Universe sends us a trigger that we cannot deny. Cancer and critical illnesses may be that crucial incentive that prompts us to release emotions that hinder our soul growth and motivate us to discover our life purpose.

If the inevitable result of illness is to return home to God as my father did, finding peace and acceptance will benefit you in your transition. Speak openly about your fears to those you love and trust. You are still in control of so much of this process. Allow yourself to work through the inevitable demise of this physical body. By dealing with each stage as it arises, you will expedite the process of healing in preparation for your next journey. By accepting that the death of this body is imminent, you can take control and express your desires for your last act on Earth. Embrace the faith and truth that your soul will live on forever. Surround yourself with people who support your beliefs. Speak about whatever comes up for you. You may want to give or receive forgiveness. Most importantly, forgive yourself for any residual pain from the past. Honour each emotion as it emerges, in any order or in any healthy format you choose.

You can write up a health care directive for any end-of-life requests you desire. Feel empowered to express control about comfort measures, medications and medical interventions around your care. Explore the option of being an organ donor and giving the ultimate gift of life to a fellow soul on this earthly realm. You can be involved in the planning of any aspect of your will, funeral or wishes you may want followed through once you have crossed over. Remember, you are in control of all these decisions when you choose to be. Through meditation or prayer, set the stage for your transition into Heaven. Envision who you want to greet you and what that experience will look like once you cross over. Dream big; you are worthy of this divine gift. Relinquish the fear surrounding the Afterlife, so you may experience a smooth transition to your Eternal Home. Enter into Heaven with joy and love in your heart and soul. All is forgiven, and we are all welcomed into the Afterlife with open arms, an absence of judgment and only pure joy and Divine Love.

CHALLENGES OF BEING A CAREGIVER

Being a caregiver to a person with physical or intellectual disabilities, a person with developmental disabilities, or a person with a severe mental health condition creates an opening for great spiritual growth. Approaching this challenge with an enlightened spirit is helpful in understanding the opportunity for immense learning and love on an elevated level. By altering our perspective, we can view this life situation as a pre-planned karmic choice.

I have learned that there are many potential life lessons woven within the experience of being a caregiver. The opportunity to resolve the feelings of judgment, impatience, abandonment and many other emotions is presented in this role. There are also many opportunities for karmic balance while caring for a person with disabilities.

My husband and I have cared for young adults and adults with developmental and intellectual disabilities for over twenty-three years. It has been a journey of transformative revelations for our entire family. I have admired my husband's patience and knowledge of how to deal with each individual in the most authentic and compassionate way. I had to learn many important lessons through self-reflection and intense soul searching. When I started exploring why I was challenged at times, I realized unresolved emotions and insecurities were being reflected back on me. I was able to then work through those emotions and become a more understanding and compassionate person. The elevated love energy I internalized while caring for people who are vulnerable in our society became a personal transformative experience. I am so thankful for every person in our lives who influenced us all to become better human beings and who have taught us invaluable lessons about ourselves and others.

I am also the primary caregiver to my mom. She has had dementia for over ten years. My dad was her main caregiver until he crossed over in 2016. Initially her disease progressed gradually, but it accelerated aggressively after dad passed away. I became overwhelmed and resentful that I had to care for my mother… again.

As I discussed in the karma section of my story, I was shown a previous life where I was a caregiver to my mom in the 1800s. In that lifetime, I did not learn my life lessons. I died an angry and bitter old lady. I believe that in my pre-birth plan for my present lifetime, I ensured that my soul would have another opportunity to learn and grow. Karma was presenting me with an ideal situation to work on my emotional issues that were highlighted around being a caregiver. Experiencing, processing and dealing with my unresolved emotions afforded me karmic release.

When my heart opened up, I continued to learn valuable lessons from my mom. I admired her ability to live only in the moment. She did not experience any guilt or remorse that held her in the past. She did not fear or worry about the future. My mom still has her moments of extreme confusion, but with patience and love we are able to help her find her place of peace. Daily I strive for that peaceful state of being. I remind myself often to live for right now, embrace the beauty around me and simply breathe. I am having a human experience, so there are still times when I am exhausted and impatient. I noticed that when I became frustrated with my mom, she responded by being anxious and appearing more confused. My adverse energy directly affected her energy.

I could feel her vibration lower, sometimes within moments of bringing my detrimental attitude into her space.

I decided to meditate before visiting my mom. I would allow my low energy emotions to emerge, acknowledge and process their presence and peacefully send them into the Universe. I could then approach my mom with an authentic feeling of love and compassion. My mom reflected a serene and peaceful response and appeared clearer in her thought process, even if for a brief moment.

Another strong emotion that emerged from this experience was judgment. I judged myself for dealing poorly at times with my mom. I projected my resentful feelings towards family members for not contributing as much as I did. I was angry at my mom for not trying harder to get better. I even resented my deceased father for dying and leaving me to be the primary caregiver of my mom. Obviously irrational fear was also infringing on my thought process.

Throughout this journey, I began to realize that my strong emotion towards others was a reflection of the judgment I imposed on myself. I was projecting the feeling I was denying within myself onto loved ones. After much painful self-reflection, I was able to release the judgment within myself and towards others. I further opened my heart to compassion and forgiveness for my mom, my family and most importantly for myself. I am human, and there are still times I get frustrated and sad. I allow myself those natural responses, but I am able to quickly process my impassioned feelings that arise and work through them. When I feel my frustration begin to emerge, I use the process of instant Divine Forgiveness. I count back from five and acknowledge the feelings that come up. I honor those feelings and release them. This process takes seconds and works well in the moment. If I require further processing, I do that when I have time for a more in-depth self-reflection.

As I began to resolve my most immediate emotions, I became aware of a growing underlying fear. I have a multigenerational history of dementia in my family. My grandfather, three aunts and my mother have experienced Alzheimer's or various forms of dementia. This disease is a recurring theme in my life, and there are times I feel like I am drowning in its clutches. I was adamant I did not want my husband and children caring for me if I also developed dementia. I had decided I would choose medical assistance in dying if I became incapacitated with severe mental deterioration. Again, I had to do major soul-searching. I realized my fear was based on my feelings of being unworthy of love. In the past, I have felt that caring for others and giving of myself were the only ways someone could love me. I know now that I am worthy of love. I also understand that an expression of love is allowing others to care for me. I accept that if this is part of our pre-life plan together, I need to be open to fulfill my role.

Even after resolving many emotions around being a caregiver, one prominent emotion remained. That emotion was sadness. I felt sad for my mom, that she had to live the rest of her life without the ability to remember her past and was even becoming unaware of the here and now. That was when my dad came to me in a vision. He gave me the most beautiful and comforting message. Dad reassured me that Mom is not suffering. He confirmed that when we reincarnate on Earth, we do not bring our entire soul energy with us. Dad also informed me that the majority of Mom's soul energy is back with him in Heaven. As decreased mental capacity increases on Earth, a greater percentage of soul energy re-emerges with our Higher Soul Self in the Afterlife.

Now when I look into Mom's eyes and see further decreasing awareness of this lifetime, I can change my perspective on what this means. I now know that my mom's soul is primarily with my dad in the Afterlife. They are enjoying each other and all the other loved ones that have transitioned to the Heavenly Realm. My mom occasionally speaks of being on a trip with her parents and husband or travelling somewhere with her friends. I love when she tells me these stories now, as I am convinced that she is actually experiencing them in the Heavenly Realm. This was also confirmed by my mother-in-law, who has also crossed over. She came to my husband in a visit within a dream and informed him that "There is a place set for Muriel at the banquet table." I know my mom joins them there frequently to celebrate in Heaven and that a majority of her soul now resides in the Afterlife with her beloved husband and her loved ones on the other side of the veil.

Another reassurance that I have received lately is quite astounding. When my father communicates with me from the Heavenly Realm, he will often bring my mother's soul energy with him. My mom does not come through as clearly or solidly as my dad, but her energy is still present in the most loving and reassuring capacity.

My dad asked me to share this message with other families so they may also find comfort. Every person who has diminished mental capabilities has a smaller percentage of their soul remaining in their earthly bodies. The greatest portion of their soul is living a wonderful life with their soul family and friends who have crossed over. We all have the capability to live parallel lives here and in the Afterlife. This does not diminish them as a person but allows their soul to continue growing and learning both here on this Earthly Realm and in the Heavenly Realm. Another reason our loved one remains on Earth is to facilitate us in learning our lessons. These brave souls selflessly agreed to come to Earth for the greater good of the collective. My dad gifted me with the knowledge that my mom is still here to create opportunities for all of us to embrace our lessons from our soul contract.

Another aspect of being a caregiver is to realize the time when we are encouraged to surrender our role in our loved one's direct care. When an opportunity presents itself to place our loved one into a personal care home or an alternative living arrangement, understand that this was always part of the plan. Relinquishing your role as primary caregiver will expose many extreme emotions. Fear, guilt and feelings of failure may emerge. Allow yourself healing time to release these emotions. This event was pre-planned by you and your loved ones for optimum growth and learning. The transition period will be challenging but necessary for life lessons to be processed. Release the guilt and work through all your emotions. Our loved ones, on a soul level, want us to live a joyous life. Our loved ones do not want us to live a life of great sacrifice and want us to know our lessons will be learned wherever they reside.

My father then left me with an image that will be imprinted on my soul forever. I witnessed Mom and Dad embraced in a loving dance together, which created an ethereal light that radiated from their inner core. I experienced an infusion of such intense love; it was difficult to fully comprehend from my human perspective. I will remain forever grateful for this divine gift from my father.

RELATIONSHIPS

Relationships are a complicated and exciting part of the human experience. Relationships are one of our greatest sources of joy and can contribute to the most intense pain a person can endure. For us to be successful in this aspect of life, we should be open to altering our perspective on the purpose of relationships. When we view a union with another as a means to fulfill what is lacking within us, we are entering a path of potential emptiness and disappointment. If we are open to the concept of a relationship being a trigger to heal what is creating pain from within ourselves, we open our reality to the true meaning of these interactions.

As we get more intimate with someone, we become closer to what requires healing within ourselves. As we allow ourselves to open up, many of our repressed emotions will emerge to the forefront. Since we have never fully dealt with these emotions, we project them onto our loved ones. At the time, this feels safer and less threatening to us but is counterproductive to healing our core issues. When we feel ourselves losing control towards another person, a part of us is projecting an unresolved adverse emotion from within ourselves. We may find ourselves in situations where our anger explodes out of control when the circumstance does not warrant that extreme reaction. We may lash out at others with an intense emotion we do not understand or comprehend. We are now caught in a vicious cycle of fear and pain. If we do not break the cycle of fear and pain at this time, it will continue in all facets of our lives. For healing to occur, it is imperative to jump off this merry-go-round and restructure our healing journeys.

All these factors are critical reasons why we choose life partners, friends and experiences. Our soul chooses people in our lives who reflect what needs to be healed within ourselves. On that basis, we may eventually dislike the qualities of that partner whom we were once attracted to. Ultimately, those emotions that are so raw within ourselves are revealed and reflected back in the partners we choose.

In the past, we have been drawn to people, and them to us, who reflect the unaddressed pain we are carrying around. We had a lower vibrational energy that attracted similar people with lower vibrations. Be aware that this creates a situation where we are coming from a very vulnerable place in our heart. Recognize the people who have been placed in your path for healing versus the emotional vampires. The emotional vampires are people who suck all our energy, and encounters with them leave us exhausted. We are attracting these people unknowingly due to our lower vibrational energy and the message we are projecting out into the world.

Throughout my life, I have encountered a few emotional vampires. Due to my low self-esteem and self-worth, I projected a desperate and decreased vibrational energy. I was a beacon for people who required extracting the energy from others to empower themselves. In one particular relationship, I learned valuable lessons in life and became aware of how this encounter was predestined.

This person entered my life when I was extremely vulnerable. They also had issues of low self-worth. As our friendship grew, they became more demanding of my time and energy. We had many fun and exciting experiences together, which was the bond that kept us connected. I slowly came to realize that I could not sustain this friendship due to the energy it required to maintain it.

We had become codependent on each other, which was destructive to both of us.

I now understand that this relationship served a multitude of life lessons. They were in my life to reflect my own insecurities so that I could deal with them. Once I was able to process and release some of those emotions, our friendship eventually faded. I would not have recognized the signals for healing if that relationship was less intense. I am forgiving and grateful towards this person today. They were an important aspect in the progression of my healing journey. I realize now that this was a trigger to help me recognize the emotions that needed healing within me.

Be cautious who you allow in your inner circle. Recognize a situation that was pre-planned to alert you to what you need to heal within yourself. Do not stagnate in the negative cycle of giving your power away. Remain vigilant to what requires healing within you and promptly move on. Most importantly, filter out the emotional vampires so you may discover other healthy opportunities to heal.

When we choose not to do the work, we repeat the same destructive behavioral patterns. We blindly enter a relationship because that is what we know and that is the message we are sending out into the Universe. We are emitting a lower vibrational energy, which in turn attracts a situation or person who also has a similar lower energy. Wrapped up in our lower vibration, we may also project a victim mentality. We attract those who are more likely to victimize us, as this is what we are projecting into the Universe. We are searching for others to fulfill the emptiness and hurt we feel. We now know that the pain can only be healed by ourselves. We will continue to project our unhealed emotions onto others until we heal ourselves. Without awareness and self-healing, we will repeat the same pattern. One trigger to alert us is to observe a trait that irritates us about our partner. Honestly search within yourself to recognize that this may be a characteristic about you that requires addressing.

This is a critical moment to recognize that these relationships are in our lives for a very specific reason. We have chosen this person in this scenario so we can heal the pain that is attached to our soul. If we choose to bury our emotions in this situation once again, similar life events and people will re-emerge that raise the same emotions that require healing within us. If we can become aware that this person was placed in our life for us to understand what needs to be healed within ourselves, we can move forward with confidence in resolving this conflict.

At this point, people often leave the relationship that challenges them. Sometimes this is necessary for personal safety or mental health reasons. Attempt to objectively assess whether you may grow and learn within this relationship or if healing will occur more effectively outside of it. Your main objective now is to work through your unresolved emotional pain. It is not a coincidence when we choose the same type of person repeatedly in our relationships. The reason this occurs is because we are not healing our inner emotions and are therefore perpetuating a pattern of selecting partners who mirror our unresolved feelings. When we are aware of this vicious cycle, we become empowered to heal ourselves and drastically decrease the likelihood of entering into a relationship that disappoints us once again.

Through processing our emotions that have held us back, we are becoming aware of the life we were intended to live. Once we free our souls from the emotional prison we have previously held them in, we are open to exploring healthy relationships and friendships. While initially embracing this new adventure, feelings of fear and anxiety may appear. This is our ego making us question ourselves. View this as another opportunity to process the emotions that arise and release them.

While healing, you may find that you are attracted to people you would never have considered previously. Step away for a moment and objectively assess the qualities this person has that are drawing you in. Keep repeating positive self-affirming messages.

Ensure that this new person is reflecting back those positive messages. This may be new territory for you. Your ego may try to interfere and send communications that you do not deserve this genuine experience. Use your emerging self-confidence and empowerment to view this potential relationship in an entirely new light. Continue to work through any past or present emotions that emerge. The process of Divine Healing is a tool you can access for the rest of your life. You will feel more comfortable and at ease using this method of healing and awareness every time you put it into practice.

Step out of your pain to fully embrace the lessons you have set for yourself. Use your newly acquired skills and objectivity when entering into this current relationship or friendship. Ask yourself what you are going to learn and grow from in this experience. Be patient and do not rush the process. Allow this relationship to organically reveal itself to you.

If we pre-planned this relationship to be an important learning experience in the Heavenly Realm, then this situation will play out to reveal what we need to learn from it here on Earth. If it was meant to be, it will happen. If it does not, then be grateful you can discover a relationship in the future that will reinforce the amazing person you are. You now have the tools and knowledge to recognize the potential outcomes of the experiences life is presenting to you.

My life journey reflects this scenario in many ways. Traditionally, I had always chosen men who had a "bad boy" image, and I saw a challenge in trying to fix them. I now know that it was my unresolved emotions I was projecting onto them that required fixing. When my current husband came into my life, I was just beginning another phase of self-discovery and spiritual awareness. Dale was different from any man I had ever dated. I repeatedly told my friends that "he is not my type." It was six months before I allowed him to fully become a part of my life. He was patient, kind and loving throughout the entire process.

During that time, I became more self-confident and started healing my inner soul. This was completely new territory for me. I saw how Dale viewed me as a reflection of how I was beginning to view myself. In retrospect, I understand all this now, but at the time this concept was foreign to me. Once I accepted that I was worthy of love and happiness, my life took on an entirely different trajectory. This was not a fairytale, and we did not sail smoothly into the sunset. Our life together was hard work and extremely challenging blending a family of seven that grew to nine. It was also a time of supreme growth and awareness. I can honestly say that the journey was necessary and predestined for us to arrive at this exact place. I understand now that we are soulmates. Traditionally, society views soulmates as this perfect union steeped in romance and passion. In actuality, true soulmates are the partners who alert us to what requires the most critical healing within ourselves. I have also been shown that, as a soulmate, our job is to respectfully challenge and create experiences to discover what is necessary for healing within ourselves and each other. This can often lead to situations that initially feel disheartening and frustrating. With this knowledge, I am now able to approach our challenges with a clearer understanding of the purpose of our interactions. We are at a time in our lives where we support and love each other because of the solid foundation we have built. I am eternally grateful that we found each other in this lifetime to fulfill some of our pre-planned life goals. It has been a bumpy ride, and I foresee more bumps to come. I know that we have the tools and foundation to continue that journey together. One of my sincere hopes is to alert you, through my experiences, towards the path you may take to enhance your self-love and discover a future successful relationship.

Once you have reached that place in your journey where you feel equipped to enter a new relationship, my heartfelt advice is to proceed with caution. Work diligently on not resorting to old patterns that do not serve you. Always continue on your own personal healing path. Do not abandon the work you are doing on yourself; you are continually growing and learning. Step back and objectively assess this new relationship or friendship. Watch for triggers, both negative and positive. Listen to your inner knowing voice (intuition) and accept the messages you receive. Allow your loved ones, here and in the Afterlife, to help guide you to a healthy decision. Honestly permit yourself to feel the true emotions that come up for you. Learn to distinguish between ego and the pure loving messages from your soul. Ego-driven fear will be bathed in negativity, self-doubt and create a lowering of energy. Conversely, your soul message comes from a place of love and emits a higher energy vibration and feels empowering. Use all the knowledge and tools you have acquired. Again, this is a lifelong process. You will achieve success, and you will falter. This is not failure but an opportunity for further growth. Every relationship is a building block to your next life experience. Do not live in regret or shame; be thankful for every relationship that has got you to this point. Approach every experience with an open heart and the knowledge that you now have the power. If you are in a relationship where you feel abused, unworthy, afraid, demeaned or are in any danger, get out immediately. When your soul pre-planned this relationship, any form of abuse was not part of the equation. The lesson is to learn from this past experience by processing the emotions that emerge, releasing them and moving on. Do not waste your precious energy sitting in a place of regret, anger, fear, guilt or shame. Embrace the lessons you learned and the empowerment you now have in yourself. Replace fear with love and trust the process. You are in charge of your destiny.

With these newly discovered tools of awareness and recognition of the repetitive patterns in your chosen relationships, you are given the gift to alert you to what requires healing. Work diligently on resolving your feelings of low self-worth or other significant emotions that emerge for you. Embrace these feelings and release them into the Universe. When you commit to doing the challenging work, the Universe is alerted to your effort. You will be rewarded with an increase in positive people and situations placed within your path. I have found that every conflicting experience I work through becomes less challenging and less time consuming. The process flows smoother and requires less effort every time I embrace Divine Healing. Inevitably, other challenges will be present in your life. Working through each challenge is the reason for our existence on Earth. With each hurdle we successfully face, we come closer to discovering our true self and life purpose.

DYSFUNCTIONAL RELATIONSHIPS

All relationships are complicated, but abusive and dysfunctional relationships are on another level of intensity. Most people do not enter a relationship with the expectation of being emotionally or physically abused. Often a pattern emerges where people subconsciously enter into dysfunctional relationships. When we are in a cycle of choosing relationships that contain a high probability of dysfunction, we are sometimes caught in a pattern that has elements of addiction attached to our choices.

There are a multitude of factors that explain why we repetitively choose to enter into dysfunctional relationships. Our upbringing and childhood experience are a dominant cause for many of the decisions we make as adults. If we were raised in an abusive home, we often perpetuate the role of abuser or victim. When we are a survivor of childhood abuse, we carry many unresolved emotions that affect every decision we make as an adult. You may not be consciously aware of many specific incidents, but the underlying emotions leave an imprint on your soul. A family dynamic may appear healthy to the outside world, but the unresolved detrimental emotions from childhood are deeply ingrained into our psyche.

People who have experienced chaotic and abusive childhoods are at high risk of entering dysfunctional relationships. Feelings of low self-worth and insecurities are often a result of this type of childhood. As an adult, a partner who is controlling and possessive is often chosen. This is seen as love because it is familiar territory for that person. Eventually, the controlling behavior that once felt grounding and secure now feels confining and abusive. We initially choose these partners to help heal the pain we see in them. In actuality, we are subconsciously projecting the pain from within ourselves that requires healing. When both partners feel their needs are not being met, this potentially sets up an opportunity for a dysfunctional or abusive relationship.

If both parties can recognize this as a trigger for healing at this stage, the relationship may become healthier. Unfortunately, this does not often occur simultaneously. If you choose to individually deal with your emotional healing, recognize this as a healthy alternative. If at any time the relationship becomes abusive, remove yourself immediately. It is never part of a pre-life plan to be in an abusive relationship for healing to occur.

My personal experience with this scenario occurred during my first marriage to my ex-partner. We were caught in a cycle of dysfunction which contributed to my already low self-worth. As with so many unhealthy relationships, there is unresolved trauma at the core of our behaviors. Unknowingly, we were drawn to each other because we recognized the pain that we subconsciously understood needed healing within ourselves. I buffered the internal anguish with food and hid my emotions so deep where they wouldn't be exposed and raw. We spiraled down the rabbit hole of devastating suffering and further buried our pain, which led to the demise of our marriage.

Through counseling and much soul-searching, I now know that my connection with my ex-partner was part of a pre-ordained soul contract. We were both in that exact situation to trigger our need for healing. I am aware of this now, but at the time I was blind to the implications of that experience. I can honestly say that today I forgive myself and my ex-partner for all the pain and suffering we caused each other. This relationship was the catalyst for me to focus on my spiritual journey. I am eternally grateful for my beautiful children as a result of that relationship and the lessons I am learning with them every day. I am thankful for the friendship my ex-partner and I have now, especially for our children and grandchildren. I send forgiveness and gratitude to the Universe on a soul level for every experience that has contributed to my life today.

There is also the spiritual aspect we must consider in why we enter relationships that have the potential for becoming abusive. In our pre-life plan we incorporated many learning opportunities within every relationship. Sometimes we are overly ambitious or have not brought enough soul energy down with us to deal with the planned challenges. We may have had prior life experiences with this soul that require karmic balance and release to occur. Abuse is never part of a pre-birth plan. Our enthusiasm in the Heavenly Realm for tackling a difficult relationship may have underestimated the influence of free will.

We enter relationships with the expectation of receiving and giving love and compassion. We may inadvertently try to fix or change that person to fulfill an emptiness we feel inside ourselves. We do not enter a relationship knowing that physical or emotional abuse is inevitable. When abuse occurs, we often blame ourselves for choosing the relationship. Due to our past and present experiences, we carry unresolved emotions deep within our soul. We internalize fear and pain that resonate low frequencies. We draw in people and experiences that reflect a complimentary frequency to ours. If we have been victimized in our life, we unknowingly attract potentially abusive partners who are attracted to our victim vibration. Out of the trauma we have endured, we are drawn to experiences and people with common energies. It is what we know and what we feel on a deeply ingrained level. Regardless of the circumstances, these underlying factors are powerful motivators for perpetuating the subconscious decision to enter into dysfunctional or abusive relationships.

Most importantly, when you find yourself in any type of abusive relationship, your priority is to remove yourself immediately from that situation. Once you have safely accomplished that action, you can begin your healing journey. For you to break this pattern of dysfunctional relationships, you must heal the ingrained emotional trauma that has occurred. Be aware there may be entrenched ancestral pain and suffering at the root of subconscious behaviors. Forgive yourself and take the time you require to learn and grow from these experiences. Recognize the feelings that arise, process the emotions that do not serve you and release them into the Universe. If you do not address these repressed overburdening emotions from a lifetime of pain, you will continually repeat this destructive cycle. Through Divine Healing, you can also help heal generations of past pain that you have carried in your soul. If you choose not to heal the debilitating emotions that arise, similar people and events will enter into your world to reflect the emotions that are crying out to be healed within you. Relinquish the desire to change others. You can only control how you respond to others' actions and how you choose to heal yourself. It is within your power to alter original trauma and create peace in your life. With the knowledge and tools presented here, it is possible to break the cycle of abusive relationships.

Dysfunctional and codependent relationships are common triggers to alert us towards the need for emotional healing. You now have the opportunity to acknowledge the unresolved emotions attached to your soul. Process these exhausting debilitating feelings in any healthy format available. There is counseling, books, journaling, support groups and many other resources available. You may use Divine Healing in conjunction with any healthy avenue that assists in processing and releasing these repressed emotions.

We place subtle and sometimes not-so-subtle triggers for us to recognize the goals of our pre-birth plan once we arrive on Earth. Slow down and listen to your spiritual supports who are there to help you recall your life's purpose. Be alert to that inner knowing of what your plan is. You will instinctively know when you are on the right path. This will transpire as a sensation that is difficult to deny. You will eventually accept that every challenging life experience is a gift for growth and learning. Every experience is an opportunity, not a punishment. There are no mistakes or failures. Childhood does not define the course of your life; free will even trumps aspects of your pre-life plan. Your purpose will become clearer as you progress in your healing journey. You will begin to embrace forgiveness for yourself and towards others.

    This is a great opportunity to alter your perspective on any past relationship or friendship that you previously viewed as unsuccessful. Reframe this experience as being a critical event that alerted you to the emotions that required healing within yourself. Do not dwell in regret, shame or blame. Eliminate the "should haves" and embrace every relationship as the learning experience it was always meant to be. Realize this as the trigger you require to accelerate your healing growth. All emotional work entails faith and perseverance. Empower yourself with knowledge, strength and the tools to discover your life's purpose.

ADDICTIONS

Addictions are an overwhelming aspect of our society. Various forms of addiction affect many people on this planet, either directly or indirectly. Addictions may include drugs, alcohol, gambling, sex, food, work, shopping, hoarding, smoking, pornography or many other behaviors that dictate our life choices.

There are specific characteristics that define what an addiction is. First, there is an uncontrollable urge or desire to perform a specific action. Your craving for this action becomes all-consuming in your life. You ignore the consequences of this action to the detriment of your well-being and the well-being of others. The final characteristic of an addiction is the complete loss of control over seeking to gratify this action.

Do not hesitate to pursue assistance if you experience any of these signs of addiction. People often experience multiple addictions at the same time. When the core emotions are not healed while attempting to eliminate the primary addiction, another addiction may develop to replace the initial one. There is a high probability that the first addiction will recur, and then you have multiple addictions to heal.

Emotional trauma, mental illness, genetic and environmental factors, and severe or chronic stress are commonly at the root of addictive behavior. Often, there is a critical event or emotion buried deep in the subconscious mind. It may be too distressing to deal with the feelings incurred from this event, so you seek to buffer the pain with your addiction. There are numerous triggers that may exacerbate your behavior. Some of those factors include associating with people who share your addiction, being unable to cope with daily stressors such as sleep deprivation, chronic pain, or emotions that remain unhealed. Every time the perceived threat begins to surface, a choice is made to dull it with your addictive behavior.

It is difficult to comprehend why a soul would choose addiction in their pre-life plan from our earthly perspective. These souls are daring and fearless. They have chosen a profound scenario to learn and grow from the lessons they are mastering in this lifetime. The process for awareness of our life's purpose is similar in all challenges presented to us during our lifetime. Addiction has an extra layer of healing to overcome before progression of lessons can be accomplished. The stigma attached to addictions in our society must be addressed. It is vital to abandon judgment on anyone who is battling with an addiction. When society can view addiction as a trigger that alerts us to what requires healing, we are given an alternative perspective to the true purpose of addictive behaviors. It is time to stop isolating and alienating people with addictive characteristics. We are encouraged to be sensitive around how we label people with addictions. We are all individuals with multiple unique qualities. Attempt to refer to any person who has an addiction as someone with an addiction and not a person who is their addiction. Our job is to accept and support every person on this Earth and to assist them on their healing journey.

There are many aspects of healing that are essential for your recovery. This begins with a conscious decision to take your power back and relinquish the victim mentality. Realize that the road to recovery requires you to process and release the emotions that have paralyzed you from living the life you were intended to live. When your repressed emotions begin to surface, allow the process for healing to occur. Do not give your power away by attempting to bury those emotions once again. Use any healthy avenue to assist you on your healing journey. This may require inpatient recovery programs or intensive outpatient counselling. In addition, support groups or twelve-step programs are helpful tools to support sobriety. Reaching out to friends and family for their assistance may also be an option. It is important to note that when you give your power away to your addiction, you may be strengthening the hold your addiction has over you and alienating yourself from potential supports. Find strength in your faith, and accept that you are always loved and supported by a Higher Power. Your most important priority is to stay strong in your sobriety. Sobriety is the path of enlightenment towards realizing your life's intended journey.

Realize that, through resolving addictive behavior, this is how you chose to heal your pain in your pre-life plan. Your soul requires this extreme experience for your learning and growth. It may involve past karma, previous life events or issues from this lifetime. Regardless of the origins of your trauma, the process of resolving and releasing buried emotions is the main goal for this life experience. There are many options available for you to now live your best life possible. You are fulfilling your life's goals and empowered to be of service to others on discovering their life path through sobriety.

SEXUAL IDENTITY AND ORIENTATION

We are all souls with both masculine and feminine energies. In the Heavenly Realm, we are not defined by gender. We are gender neutral. Our souls experience earthly lives in both male and female bodies. As souls, we are often more comfortable experiencing life in our preferred gender the majority of the time. During one of my visions, I saw myself in dozens of lifetimes. It was presented in a format similar to fast-forwarding through a series of still pictures. I observed that about seventy-five percent of my lives were as a female. Interestingly, I felt a vibrational energy within each of these images that was familiar and comforting.

A soul chooses their next life for very specific reasons. They choose their gender, sexual orientation and gender identity to best reflect what they need to learn on Earth. There is absolutely no judgment from Source. The only judgment comes from the society that soul chose to reincarnate in. There are a multitude of factors souls consider prior to reincarnating.

When planning our next life, we take into consideration all of our previous lives. A soul who has had negative experiences in a female body may be reluctant to return as a woman. The soul's memory of being abused, raped or tortured as a female may still carry trauma from those lives. This soul mainly identifies as woman but is reluctant to occupy a female body in their next lifetime. They may choose a male body, but the imprint of predominantly female characteristics remains. Their dominant female soul may be drawn to a male body with primarily female traits and mannerisms. There may still be a sexual desire towards males, or they may also be attracted to both sexes. There is no judgment in the Heavenly Realm either way.

Another scenario may be that a soul experienced a previous life where they chose to be an assertive and driven male. That soul may have diverged from their original intent and become aggressive and ego-driven in their lifetime. That soul may decide to occupy a female body in their next reincarnation. They will still carry residual energy from their previous life but hope to experience a gentler and kinder life as a woman. A soul may also make the choice to live a life outside the "norms" of society purely for the experience and lessons that lifestyle creates. There is no judgment from Source on any of these scenarios. The main motivation is to experience life in a way that affords optimum growth and learning.

When we can open our hearts to this truth, we are given a great insight into how gender identification awareness is so predominant in society today. As souls, we are gender neutral. We only adapt to specific genders when we assimilate into our earthbound bodies. At this time in our universal experience, we are enlightened souls who are working on becoming aware of our Higher Soul Selves. This glimmer of awareness may contribute to the consciousness experienced by many people as to why they are limited and confined in this body. As enlightened souls, the veil is lifting on our pre-birth plan. Our soul understands that the body we chose may not have been our best option for growth. We are blessed to live in a time where we are able to choose any version of ourselves that we feel empowered to become. We may have misjudged our ability to adapt to this chosen gender once we came to Earth. There should be no shame when someone realizes this and has the ability to experience life as their authentic self. As a society, we are encouraged to accept those that feel they chose the gender that does not support their true spirit in their pre-life plan or those that do not conform to the social norms of the time. There is no harm to society when someone chooses to alter their gender identity. It is imperative to release all judgment and allow every soul to live out their genuine life plan.

Every choice we make in our pre-birth plan ultimately brings us to a similar path. We are choosing a life journey that best reflects our personal goals for learning and growth. When a soul chooses a life outside of the norms of society, they are courageously choosing a life with the potential for immense growth. The soul may be choosing a challenging life experience to learn self-love and acceptance. It is not right or wrong, good or bad. It just is. We are not exclusively our sexual identity; it is just one part of us. This was an important aspect in planning our life on this Earth, so in every sense that soul was born with their sexual identity as an integral characteristic of themselves.

Our youngest son chose a life outside of the heterosexual experience as part of his pre-birth plan. This was evident even when he was a young child. It is part of his essence, as much as his sweet spirit and uniqueness that we all love in him. His identity involves all aspects of his personality, and each characteristic is as important as the others. At the heart of life, we all want to love and be loved. Who we choose to love should be a personal choice with no judgment from the outside world.

Those who project anger and hate towards others for any reason are still on their journey of self-discovery. When we judge others, we are reflecting emotions onto others that require healing within ourselves. Release the fear so love and compassion can occupy that space within you. Send out love and acceptance to all, and you will be rewarded with peace in your soul.

As a family, we support and love our youngest son openly and proudly. Initially, his dad had a difficult time understanding the concept of homosexuality. His love for his son never wavered; Dale just had to process his logical thinking around the situation. Dale was respectful and open to understanding all aspects of a lifestyle he was unfamiliar with. I believe that if we all approach any aspect of life without fear and only love in our hearts, our world energy would become a positive place to learn and grow. This non-judgmental attitude has to originate from both sides of the community for true healing to occur. We must learn to accept and respect all sides of a person's journey and be patient when someone is seeking clarification from a place of love and not fear or hate. I am proud of our entire family for how we have embraced any new experience openly and inclusively with love and compassion.

Individually and as a family, we are achieving karmic balance. By processing the emotions that arise, we are experiencing karmic release. Questioning or knowing what occurred in a previous life for this particular karma to be addressed is not necessary. Karma, in this sense, is merely the vehicle required to alert us to which emotions need healing in each individual and for the greater good of the collective. Seizing the opportunity for positive change towards self-love and universal love and acceptance of everyone is the lesson we need to embrace.

Every experience is a great opportunity for growth and learning. The more challenging the experience, the greater the potential for growth to occur. Source gifted us free will and an infinite number of choices for our learning on Earth. Our Creator celebrates each individual for all the decisions made in their pre-birth plan. There is absolutely no judgment or negativity associated with the choice of sexual orientation or gender identity. It is time to accept and celebrate the brave souls who choose a less conventional way of life and to embrace and love everyone for who they are and the journey they are on.

DEPRESSION AND MENTAL HEALTH AWARENESS

Depression and mental health awareness are being acknowledged with greater understanding and acceptance today. Historically, people with mental illnesses were isolated or imprisoned. Society misinterpreted mental unwellness as something to fear and chose to institutionalize or kill people who acted outside the norms of the time.

Souls who choose mental health challenges in their pre-birth planning are extremely resilient and highly motivated. Every soul chooses life experiences that best suit their goals of learning and healing. Mental health challenges present a potentially transformative opportunity for awareness of growth through opposites and extremes.

For healing to occur, as with any life challenge, we must first connect with our deeply buried emotions. Depression and mental illness may greatly interfere with our mind's ability to even begin our journey of healing. It is very difficult to steady the mind and work through the blockage that depression and mental illness create. There is also the societal influence that still exists, which has a negative impact on many mental health issues. These scenarios create a perfect storm, whereby the person dealing with these challenges buries their emotions even deeper. The underlying feelings then become even more arduous to deal with.

Depression creates a cycle of fear and anxiety, where a hyperfocus on the fear and anxiety may create worsening depression. These emotions may be rooted in many different experiences. It is not necessary to be aware of the exact cause of your depression or mental illness, as the main focus should be dealing with the feelings that require healing. Labeling or diagnosing is not imperative to begin your healing journey. I encourage you to enlist any healthy avenue to support you on this challenging task. These deeply ingrained emotions may be from previous lives that you may not be consciously aware of. It may be a comfort to embrace the realization that your soul chose this experience to help you recognize your life purpose. Use this knowledge to strengthen your resolve to process all your emotions that block your ability to discover your soul's path. Many times, healing requires a drastic life experience or an extreme life condition to be able to release stubbornly blocked emotions. By dealing with those emotions in this lifetime, you may be removing plaque on your soul that has been accumulating for many lifetimes. It may also be newly acquired from recent pain and suffering in this life. The goal remains the same: healing and freedom from these restrictive adverse emotions. When you are able to release the fear and anxiety, you may begin to break the cycle of deepening and recurring depression.

There is an important aspect to releasing depleting emotions that do not serve us that I will share with you. Discovering this realization was a long and sometimes painful process for me. When we sit in the depths of depression, it is extremely difficult to break out of the myopic view we have created. I personally understand that these emotions have been entrenched in our being for so long that there is hesitation in releasing them. There is a part of ourselves that is afraid to know who we are without these feelings that serve only to hold us back from a life of joy. Depression and mental unwellness have developed a dysfunctional relationship within ourselves, which we believe we can't break away from.

Subconsciously and out of fear, these stagnating emotions create a situation where we become so immobilized that it feels nearly impossible to crawl out of the pit we are in. Having this knowledge is imperative to understand another aspect of ourselves. With knowledge comes power. We have engaged in coping mechanisms that have kept us merely surviving in this lifetime. It is time to release all those emotions that do not serve us anymore. When we release our feelings of unworthiness, seeing ourselves as unlovable, or living in shame, there may be a space that needs to be filled. Work on filling that part of you with forgiveness, acceptance and love. You now have the power to fill that space with any authentic emotion you choose. Celebrate how strong you are becoming while beginning your healing journey. Send your message to the Universe that you are committed to create change, and the Universe will reward you with positive energy to continue on your journey.

There are many factors that explain why we are living the life we are. Understand there may be a part of you that is afraid to break out of the fear that holds you back from living your best life. Realize that the fear may be a result of experiencing debilitating messages and situations in your life and how you were conditioned to survive in that chaos. These coping mechanisms became ingrained in your being and were internalized as survival mechanisms. Now is the time to break free of these emotional chains. Use any healthy means that best suit your process. A great start may be through Divine Healing to initiate your healing journey. Use every support system available, such as counseling, group therapy, inpatient or outpatient programs and any resource you are comfortable with.

Learn how to calm your mind so you can work from a place within your heart and soul. Connect with those emotions that have been repressed by focusing on where in your body that emotion emanates from. These emotions have ingrained themselves into your being at a deep cellular level. Sit in your peace and allow the emotions that emerge to come to the forefront. The feeling may be attached to an image or memory. It may also be independent of any circumstance or event. You are encouraged to release the debilitating energy created from those emotions to begin your healing journey. When emotion is held within, we give it the power to grow like a cancer on our souls.

With depression and mental illness, there is the added challenge of stilling the mind so that you can gain access to your center for healing. This may require assistance from a professional. Research and discover which modality and method resonates within to support you. Trust that your instincts and inner voice will lead you to your best option for healing. The most critical initial step is to talk about your pain and depression. Allow loved ones to help support you through this process. You are never alone, especially in the spiritual sense. Be prepared that this may be a lifelong process that requires perseverance and dedication to root out depleting emotions. As humans, this is our reason for being on Earth. Alter your perspective and realize this condition is a gift of awareness for your life purpose. This is not a punishment but merely a process for learning and growing.

One option to help you on your journey may include finding a psychologist or psychotherapist who uses hypnotherapy as part of their practice. The hypnotherapist gently guides your brain from a beta state (fully awake) to an alpha state (first level of hypnosis or resting state) to possibly a theta state (deeper hypnosis or meditative state). Hypnotherapy bypasses the "busy" part of our brain to access the brain center where healing and awareness can occur. When in a hypnotic state, you are in control at all times. I felt rested and rejuvenated after my hypnotherapy session. Hypnotherapy can be a tool for healing issues from childhood until present. If you choose, it may also guide you to past-life trauma that occurred and has not been resolved. Not all therapists are trained in past-life regression, so you must do your research if that is the path you choose to take. By accessing and calming that area of your brain that has previously created a blockage for you, hypnotherapy may expedite your healing journey. Traditional therapy is always a healthy option for dealing with depression and mental health issues. You have the power to choose the best-suited path for your personal healing journey.

Meditation is another tool for calming your brain to access the emotions that require healing. You can take workshops or courses on a variety of meditation methods. The internet offers many options on how to meditate. I will present a method of meditation in a future chapter that I have found beneficial. Again, do your research and practice the therapy that resonates for you. Concentrate on what you can control in your life. Reframe your state of mind. It is beneficial to work on this every day. Even when the external world seems out of control, find that inner place of peace that you have created. Fill that space with forgiveness, compassion and love. You may not be able to control the outside world, but you can control how you respond to it. Work on creating a new perspective on life. Come from a place of kindness and love, not fear. Control what you can control and let the rest go.

Your soul is who you are at the core of your spiritual essence. Your soul knows that you are able to heal from all the challenges in your life. Take one step at a time, and forgive yourself for any setbacks. This is a marathon, not a sprint. Be patient with yourself. Allow yourself to evolve through every experience, including depression and mental illness. This is incredibly challenging and requires awareness and willingness to work through great hurdles. When you become overwhelmed, return to that safe place within that is surrounding you with love, compassion and forgiveness. This is your energy center where you can rejuvenate and find the strength to continue on your journey of life.

There is also the physiological aspect of healing that is important to become aware of. When we repeat negative messaging, our neuropathways in our brain become entrenched in that narration. When we think a negative thought, that pathway lights up to send that message down a negative road. We have the power to create an alternative fork in the road simply by repeating positive self-messages and internal affirmative thoughts. Eventually, that old road becomes inaccessible, and the new positive pathway is illuminated for easier access. This is another tool we can use on the road to emotional wellness.

During my lifetime, I have been affected by depression and mental health issues. Depression has infiltrated its way into both my spiritual and personal experience. I have felt the pain of losing friends to suicide who were living with depression and mental health issues. I have experienced my own darkness with depression. I am witness to the battle of loved ones fighting to manage their mental health every day. I empathically feel the emotions of family and friends who are currently on the erratic rollercoaster of depression and anxiety. I have spiritually assisted souls cross over into the Heavenly Realm when their earthly bodies cease to function after they died from suicide. Anxiety and depression are very prevalent in our society today. Most of us have witnessed or experienced some level of mental health issues in our lifetime.

My personal journey with depression initially manifested as Seasonal Affective Disorder (SAD). I also experienced postpartum depression, especially after my second child was born. At that time, I was in an abusive marriage, which only exacerbated the intensity of my depression. I realized I needed help when I found myself 90 miles from my home in my car and had no recollection of how I had arrived there. Thirty years ago, resources were very limited and difficult to access in any form of therapeutic support. There was also the added negative stigma from society around any mental health issue.

I felt so much shame, pain and guilt at this time. I was counseling patients and friends through similar issues, but I felt too unworthy to accept help for myself. Finally, I sought out a counselor I could eventually trust and began my long journey towards mental wellness. I built up the strength to leave my marriage and worked diligently on maintaining a positive self-image. I eventually released the shame and guilt, but the pain and fear were stubbornly attached to my soul. That part of my journey took many more years to resolve. I knew I was on a healing path when the dark clouds of my daily existence began to lift. I now surround myself in white light and love every day through meditation, positive self-affirmations and support from loved ones on both sides of the veil. Meditation looks different for every person. Meditation is one tool that helps to keep me grounded in the here and now. I spend minutes to hours every day in meditation. My husband meditates while practicing on the golf course. I meditate in nature or a quiet space in our home. There is no wrong way to meditate, and it is a beneficial method of grounding and discovering inner peace. I will later share my practice of meditation with you in the following chapters.

My mom suffered with depression throughout most of my early childhood. Sixty years ago, depression was never mentioned or acknowledged. As the eldest child, I internalized much of my mom's pain and felt a heavy responsibility to keep her happy. I did this by taking on physical responsibilities around the care of my younger siblings and attempted to emotionally keep peace in the family. I had created the idea in my mind that if I couldn't keep my mom happy, she would abandon us. I can recall this greatly ingrained fear from around the age of three. As in many families, unresolved emotional trauma may create generational depression and mental anxiety. I had repressed and buried the emotions of my childhood into every fiber of my being. It has taken years of intense introspection, awareness and hard work to release all the lingering adverse emotions of my past. I am still working on that trauma to this day. I hold no blame for my mom or anyone else in my past. We have all done the best we can under the circumstances and knowledge we had at the time. I now know that this was part of my soul contract that I signed up for with my mom in our pre-birth plan. I am truly grateful for every experience that alerted me to fulfill my life purpose.

Much more painful than dealing with my own depression is witnessing my son's mental health journey. He has not dealt with his buried emotional trauma, which resides in his soul. As a child, he witnessed physical and emotional abuse and has repressed the resulting emotions from those experiences. He has superficially dealt with his issues through occasional counseling and intermittent medications. Anger and fear prevent him from digging deeper. He uses work and many distractions that keep him occupied as a diversion from dealing with his feelings. I can sometimes see the fear and detachment in his eyes and feel that from his soul. He must embrace the truth that he is worth the work it will take for him to heal. The healing begins by acknowledging the pain and fear, which often erupts as anger. For many people, anger may be the predominant tangible emotion that they desperately cling onto. The other emotions have become muted in their lives due to the pain they have experienced. It is imperative to then allow those feelings of pain and fear to surface and work to release them in a healthy manner. We surround our son with love and understanding, but he must choose his own path to healing on his timeline.

There is another aspect of depression and mental unwellness I would like to explore. I feel I must include this because it is what I have been shown. Use this information any way you choose. You may want to sit with it and objectively process it at any point.

I had glimpses of three previous lives my son has had. I feel I have been shown these specific lives because they relate to his life today in a revealing way. All three instances were centered around being a strong and invincible warrior in his previous lives. The first life I saw him in was during medieval times. He was proudly sitting on top of a horse in full metal gear. The horse was protected with metal around its face and body. My son had a club in one hand and a ball with spikes connected to a chain in the other hand. The next life I saw him in was as a Mayan warrior. He wore a cloth covering his lower body and his chest was bare. It appeared like he had tattoos or a neck covering on the upper part of his body. He was participating in a war dance, where he was in a crouched position. My son carried a long spear in one hand and a shield in the other. In the third life where I encountered my son, we were living in the Scottish Lowlands in the 1400s. In my vision, I was able to recognize members from my current lifetime and from another lifetime we had experienced in Scotland in the 1700s. During that life in the 1400s, we were residing in a building made of local materials and were very isolated. Our life was serene and loving until war erupted. My husband (who is Dale today) and my sons went to battle against those who wanted to take away our peaceful way of life. They were all dressed in plaid kilts with leather leggings and boots. They carried crude shields and clubs or knives.

Today my son works as a professional in the justice department. He is a leader in his career and holds himself to a very high standard. He has a natural and amazing gift of creating beauty out of wood. His process involves using ancient techniques for the preservation of the wood he works with. My son was always highly motivated to be the best in every aspect of his life and is extremely competitive. At one point he became a bodybuilder and grew enormously with a passion that was all-consuming. There was also a time he researched and became interested in Mayan dance. I believe that my son's soul is struggling to find a balance in this modern world with his past-life experiences. This is also reflected in his fascination with fighting ancient and current war games online with his friends and recreating them in person. He is in battle within himself, fighting to adjust to today's moral code. In his past lives he was a fiercely independent warrior who led lives of free will and violence. His desire to be a loving husband and father in this lifetime clashes severely with his previous lives. I see this as being partially responsible and influential in his battle with depression today.

I am so proud to share with you a continuation of my son's story. Since I began writing my book, my son has embarked on a healing journey that has amazed me. He has been working extremely hard on resolving past trauma and creating a new narrative for his life today. He has been able to begin to forgive people and situations from his past and most importantly has embraced self-forgiveness. My son has a long journey ahead of him, and he works daily on releasing the emotions of anger and pain that no longer serve him. I am confident that he will make great strides in this lifetime to achieve the goals of his pre-life plan. His journey continues to be a roller coaster ride of extreme emotions and challenging life situations, but I am hopeful that he will find joy and happiness in this lifetime. When I began writing my book, I said if one person benefits from reading my words, all my work would be worth it. Knowing that my son was motivated by my message fills me with so much gratitude and peace. My sincere hope is that many others can begin their healing journey with the information, tools and most importantly the love that I am sharing with you.

As I mentioned previously, I have been shown that our current interest in specific historical events or places that resonate with us potentially reflect elements of past lives. We may experience this through déjà vu or while in a dream or deep meditative state. Déjà vu incidents may be triggered from memories of our pre-life planning or memories from past lives. We all have the ability to explore aspects of our past lives. Reflect on times in history that fascinate you. A past-life memory may be alerted when you visit a place you have never been to, yet it feels like home. Recalling themes from books and movies that keep drawing you in may trigger glimpses into past lives. I have also been shown that the lives we recall or those memories that resonate within us are the lives that are significant for our healing today. By exploring themes from past lives or from our current life, we are accumulating another tool to discover our life goals. I will be discussing the concept of past lives in great detail in the following chapters, and I promise it will be a captivating journey.

We are all on our own individual path, but we are definitely not alone. Every soul is connected to every other soul, and all souls are connected to the Highest Source. Take strength from this knowledge. We have signed up for a challenging life. The more intense our experiences, the higher probability of learning the important lessons we set out to discover. With great sacrifice comes greater potential for substantial rewards.

With knowledge, faith, altering our perspective and a willingness to put in the work, we are committing to a life where freedom of spirit can prevail. There is a reason for all these challenges on Earth, and this knowledge assists us on our healing journey. Simply sending our intent to heal into the Universe will activate a shift in our consciousness. Use these valuable tools to enable your soul to recognize its pre-birth plan and discover your way back to your authentic Higher Soul Self.

RAPE AND SEXUAL ASSAULT

In experiencing acts of rape, sexual assault, extreme abuse and other atrocities of human behavior, we are the chosen souls who carry the potential for paramount learning and healing. When we bravely process the emotions raised by these experiences, we accelerate our spiritual awareness and our path to discovering who we are on a deep soul level. Through the most critical experiences, humankind receives our greatest rewards. The more extreme the life event, the higher the potential for a greater impactful result there is. When we work through the pain, our true passion for life often emerges.

As humans, we endure many difficult life events. Rape and sexual assaults are especially heinous. As a society, we find it very difficult to even speak about these acts. This creates more shame and isolation for those who are dealing with these experiences. That is one of my main motivations for speaking on this subject. This will be an uncomfortable topic for many, but the lessons we can absorb may be profound. I can only speak on issues that have touched my heart. Personally, this will be a very emotional aspect of my journey that I am sharing with you.

We chose experiences, in our pre-life plan, that potentially balance and release karma from our past lifetimes that are stubbornly clinging to our soul. This does not mean we were the perpetrators in a previous life. There are hundreds of previous life scenarios that contributed to the decision on how we chose to live out this life. We may be the brave souls who are taking on extreme life challenges to benefit other members of our soul family to progress on their journey. We also plan events that set the foundation for many lifetimes to come. When we work on our emotions today, we are not only freeing ourselves to live our best life now but also for many future lives.

It is extremely difficult for us to comprehend why our soul would choose such a horrendous life experience. When our souls are in the pre-birth planning stages, they view life on Earth with an objective and impartial attitude. They do not internalize all the emotions that are an integral aspect of our earthly lives. Our soul understands that this lifetime is one of many and is part of a greater whole. Our souls choose these extreme life events as a means to a more profound learning and growing experience.

Our soul may underestimate our ability to deal with challenges once we are on Earth. We may also miscalculate the amount of energy required for a particularly harsh life. Our soul does not feel the emotions with the same intensity as our earthly heart experiences. This knowledge of our soul's motivation will hopefully create a foundation for our healing journey.

The process of healing after experiencing rape or sexual assault will be lengthy and extremely challenging. Surround yourself with trusted and supportive loving people. Seek out professionals, workshops, friends, family and others with similar experiences to be members of your support system. Create a foundation of self-love and compassion. Understand that you are not the shame, the betrayed trust or the victim mentality. You have the power to overcome and heal.

When we repress and deny our painful emotions, we give away our power and give the perpetrator control. We can begin to heal by holding space for these emotions, acknowledging each one that comes up and releasing all that does not serve us. We are not ever responsible for the cruel acts forced upon us. Leave all the blame and shame on the shoulders of those who have harmed you. This now becomes their path that they have taken on to learn the lessons they require. Release the emotions of anger, self-loathing and despair. When we bury pain, we create an opening for our emotions to erode our true selves. Allow all emotions to freely emerge, process them and release them into the Universe. There is an enormous power within nature. She will absorb our pain and disperse it wherever the residual energy serves a purpose. I have been shown that some of that energy enters into our perpetrators. This enables them to absorb some of our pain, so they have an opportunity to learn and grow. This empathic route is accomplished so subtly that, as humans, we are not consciously aware that this is occurring. This is karma, not punishment. In our pre-birth plan our souls orchestrated these experiences with all the souls involved. Use this awareness to empower yourself to an enlightened understanding of your life's plan.

Honour yourselves for the brave and beautiful souls that you are. Embrace the unconditional love from Source that eternally radiates from within us. We are God's innocent children, and no earthly experience can take that away from us. The inner child reflects the deepest part of our being that requires healing. Wrap your inner child with love and compassion. One of our most powerful tools for healing is our ability to create unconditional love for ourselves. When we live in forgiveness and love for ourselves, we can send forgiveness and love into the Universe. We can begin this process through Divine Healing on a deep soul level. With perseverance, we can accomplish incredible growth, awareness and achievement. Emerging from our healing, we may discover underlying messages that guide us to our soul's purpose. With every self-discovery, we are elevating our vibrational level. When we vibrate at a higher frequency, we increase the likelihood of positive energy experiences. When we sit in a lower vibration, by holding our pain and anger in, we attract situations with equally low vibrations. We are also vulnerable to attracting people who replicate similar devastating life events that may reoccur in our lives. We are at greater risk for another sexual assault to occur. We often go through life without ever becoming aware of these destructive cycles. When we walk through life in a victim mentality, we attract those who are more likely to victimize us. When we shed the emotions that imprison us in a low vibration, we increase the likelihood of joyful life experiences.

One of my greatest wishes is to enlighten you on how to break the adverse repetitive patterns in our lives. As I have expressed, I have traditionally felt that my feelings and opinions were not acknowledged or heard. As I went through young-adulthood, I chose partners who reflected my feelings of unworthiness. During a time of great vulnerability, I was raped. This incident compounded my feelings of low self-esteem and unworthiness while adding emotions of shame, guilt and self-loathing. I lacked the support or knowledge to begin my healing journey. I looked for affirmation in situations with men that reinforced my damaging beliefs of myself at the time. I was in a very low place and had no idea how I would climb out of the hell I perceived I was in. I felt I was being pursued by a dark angry cloud that infiltrated my emotional, physical and spiritual self. There were few readily available healing resources at that time, and I felt completely alone in my journey.

It took me a very long time to be able to admit to the rape, the abuse in my marriage and the subsequent emotional trauma I had endured. Through my decreased vibration, life kept sending me situations and people who reinforced my debilitatating feelings about myself. I was operating at a very low energetic vibration and existed in a depressed state of mental imprisonment. I finally began counseling, enlisted the support of friends and family and began my journey towards spiritual awareness. There were many hurdles and times I felt like I was moving in slow motion. I would be able to verbalize the times I was violated, but the emotions would surface independent of the disclosure of the event. I realized I would react with anger at situations that did not warrant such a strong emotional response. Eventually, I was able to connect the incident with the appropriate emotions. I then allowed each emotion to emerge, sat with it and processed the feeling as it surfaced. This experience was like peeling away the layers of an onion, with each section being an emotion I needed to expose and release. It took years of counseling, self-healing and hard work before the clouds permanently lifted.

There are many stages to heal from a deep soul level. Even though I began my healing journey decades ago, I am still exploring continual methods of learning and growing. I have been successful at peeling back the complicated layers of emotions, but recently I chose to address my deeply rooted core issues. I chose to forgive those who have caused me pain and anguish in this lifetime. This was like jumping over the highest hurdle at the end of a grueling race. Through the process of Divine Healing, I was able to forgive and release the emotions closest to my heart that were holding me back. The most important aspect of forgiveness is that this is for your benefit, and how you choose to forgive is in your power. You never have to confront those who caused you pain. Divine Healing works on a soul level. This method works even when you are dealing with people who have crossed over to the Heavenly Realm. I initially chose those who had the least emotional impact and slowly worked up to those who deeply devastated my soul. Most importantly, trust the process and be patient with your progress. This is a lifelong exercise, where you will hopefully find peace and love throughout the journey.

It was an arduous challenge to discover my deep core issues. That voyage eventually brought me to a place of self-love and forgiveness at a soul level. To this day, I still work on residual emotions from a lifetime of insecurities and self-doubt. When those feelings surface now, the intensity is significantly muted, and the process of forgiveness flows smoothly. I have released the unfavorable energy in my life. That means I choose enlightened people and experiences to reflect the feelings of love and acceptance for who I am. Life is not perfect, nor do I aspire to any level of perfection. My growth is with living and learning. I am empowered to embrace the positive experiences and inner joy that surround me. I have the tools to live my truth and process challenges that will inevitably occur in this life and many lifetimes to come. I strongly believe that these difficult life events created an opportunity for profound learning and growth. By experiencing the extreme emotions of despair, guilt and shame, I was presented with the opportunity to grow in self-love, self-worth and forgiveness. As I stated previously, I sometimes require a strong message to learn from the experience. My soul knew I required extreme triggers to alert myself to what needed healing for my life lessons to be embraced. I feel that without these intense experiences, I may have lived a life without purpose, consumed with self-loathing and despair.

The emotions that arise from being violated and abused are complex and individual. There is no judgment—except within ourselves—around how we deal with residual emotions from being abused. If we continue in a victim mentality, we are at a higher risk of attracting incidents and individuals who reflect our state of mind. When our vibrational energy is very low, it attracts experiences that reflect our low vibrational state. The result of not processing our adverse sentiments may infiltrate into every aspect of our lives. Our trust in humanity can be lost or greatly altered if we do not find the strength to take our power back.

As a result of repressed detrimental emotions due to being violated, individuals are at high-risk of developing unhealthy attitudes around their own sexuality and intimacy. There may be distrust of intimate partners, and the boundaries around sexual behavior may become blurred. A tool to help you recognize if you are entering an unhealthy situation is to listen to your inner voice and how your body language responds to the situation. Assess what messages you are receiving. Are you feeling threatened, angry or getting a gut reaction that something is not right? Step back, proceed slowly and objectively assess this potential new relationship with confidence. Do not ignore the red flags; this is your intuition sending you warnings to proceed with caution. If you feel the need to change crucial aspects of this person's characteristics or feel threatened in any capacity, walk away. The only person you can change or control is you. Listen to all these cues and remove yourself immediately from any situation you feel endangered by.

Using every tool you feel comfortable with is imperative in helping you reach your goals. There is counseling, support groups, prayer, meditation, restorative yoga, journaling and many other healthy options. Seek support from your trusted family and friends. Take comfort in embracing the unconditional love of Source, loved ones who have crossed over and your spirit guides. It is imperative to request assisstance from those in the Heavenly Realm. They will not interfere unless we give them permission to assist us in our healing journey and life events. There are many roads that lead to achieving your final goal of forgiveness, compassion and self-love. Untangling the complexity of your emotions will take time and effort. Every baby step brings you closer to the emotional freedom that is a crucial aspect to this journey. When healing begins, you are raising your vibrational level. This in turn attracts authentic life experiences and people into your life. When this work is done at a soul level, it will not only last for this life but for all lifetimes to come. You are on your way to rediscovering your inner essence and who you are at a deep spiritual level. This process empowers you to discover your life's purpose and eternal soul plan.

EVIL ACTS

Understanding why there is evil in the world is a difficult concept to grasp. It is challenging to comprehend that evil must be experienced to know good. Where does evil come from? What purpose does it serve? I have been shown the answers to these questions through my spiritual guides and through messages from a Higher Power. I have been exposed to evil in the human sense and also through spiritual experiences.

While planning our next reincarnation on Earth, a soul would not deliberately plan a life of evil. When a soul is choosing a body to enter, they will be aware of the possibility for violence or anger within that body. Our motivated and sometimes overly optimistic soul may see that challenging life as a potential for overturning the negative into a positive. The soul may overestimate their abilities or underestimate the soul energy required to influence the unfavorable characteristics of that particular body. Every soul has a unique and individual experience and motivation. When a damaged or immature soul enters a body with an underdeveloped brain, there is a higher probability that evil may prevail.

A soul has the potential of being contaminated by their physical body and may require intensive purifying upon entrance into the Afterlife. When going through a life review in Heaven, intent is closely examined. There are many circumstances where we pre-arrange challenging life situations with our soul family. This situation can be misunderstood as an evil act on this Earthly

Realm. There is a strong distinction between wrongdoing without malice and intentional evil actions. In the Afterlife, intention greatly affects the path of the soul on its journey.

During the life review in Heaven, souls emotionally experience the pain they inflicted onto others in the Earthly Realm. Souls are not judged by Source or their spirit guides, but they intensely critique themselves. Souls exponentially absorb the pain and suffering that they caused others on Earth. These souls may choose to self-isolate for prolonged periods of time before they go through the process of cleansing and re-entry with their soul family. A truly evil soul, one with malicious intent, may undergo a restructuring of energy of their soul before their next reincarnation. This can only be sanctioned by the Highest Power and only under extreme circumstances. I view this process as being similar to removing plaque from a clogged artery. The plaque is removed from the damaged soul and an intense restructuring of energy occurs. Scar tissue retains some memory in the restructured soul, so the soul will be less inclined to repeat evil acts.

The ones who are evil will have to be accountable for every evil act they perpetrated. They will exponentially experience the pain and terror they inflicted on others in the Earthly Realm. There is no Hell, except for the hell they place themselves in for their deeds on Earth. If they perceive they will be met in a hellish place, that is where they will reside. This is not a permanent state, and these souls may request release from their self-inflicted hellish environment at any time. These souls can repent and grow, but the work is extremely excruciating and requires much time and effort.

These souls are forgiven on a divine level, but they by no means are given a free pass to the higher degrees of light and love. These evil souls will reside in the darker and murkier depths of the spectrum of heavenly levels. Only truly evil souls reside here, and even they are given opportunities to work their way back to the light. Source never abandons any soul, no matter how evil their actions may have been. This place is very different from the description of Hell presented by many religions. These low-energy souls are not able to have any power over the higher energy levels. They must work their way up the levels of light and must earn each step with painstaking lessons and intention.

It may be a comfort for families left on Earth to gain this knowledge. There are many situations where we feel our loved ones who have crossed over at the hands of an evil act have not received their due justice. There are many crimes that remain unsolved or under-punished in society's view. What the perpetrator experiences on Earth is only a fraction of what their soul will have to endure in the Afterlife.

A damaged soul who holds no evil intent may request to return to Earth as soon as possible. This soul is given opportunities to address karmic debts and to work on lessons they have not fully conquered in past lives. For karmic balance to be achieved, we must be able to internalize and acknowledge all sides of an issue. To release karma requires deeper resolution and relinquishing emotions connected to that experience. All aspects of the event must be balanced and resolved. A soul that wishes to balance karma may choose a body that has a great probability for being abused or victimized. This by no means implies that people who live difficult lives now have previously lived evil lives. These people may choose a body or mind that has devastating dysfunctional conditions. Again, there are a multitude of reasons why souls choose extremely challenging lives and bodies. Many times, it is the very advanced soul who chooses these conditions so they may have opportunities to create positive change for the greater good of the collective. I believe Stephen Hawking was one of those amazing souls.

People are often angry at God for allowing or orchestrating these evil occurrences. In actuality, God does not allow or prevent any earthly action. Humans create evil through free will. As a society, we have some responsibility in the prevalence of behavior that does not serve the greater good. Bullying, taunting and cruelty begin in early childhood. Not all parents correct this injurious behavior as soon as it begins. Many of the victimized children are not supported and helped through processing their pain. There are an infinite number of situations that contribute to the evil that exists in this world. We are acutely aware of many circumstances of evil acts perpetrated on the human race. We cannot control the actions of others; we only have the ability to regulate how we respond to the atrocities that occur every day. On social media, cruelty and anger towards strangers and vulnerable people is tolerated. Compassion has given way to ridicule and hate. There are people starving all over the world, yet some choose gluttony and excess of material goods to dominate their life. These are all acts of the human race and free will, not punishment from God.

When all this pain is internalized, there is a likelihood that people will repress their trauma. These deeply buried emotions may surface as anger, depression and possibly eventual violence. As a society, we are discouraged from releasing our emotions in a healthy manner. Males are taught to hold in their feelings and to never cry or show "weakness." Females are told to internalize their pain for the greater good of society. These archaic attitudes have been gradually transforming over recent decades. We are encouraging our children to express their feelings openly and honestly. We are showering our children in love, kindness and compassion. We are beginning to encourage our boys and men to release their emotions and teaching them that crying is a strength and not a weakness. We are allowing our girls and women to speak their truth and supporting them when they do. As a society, we are a work in progress. We have a long way to go, but there is a palpable shift towards genuine change.

Set within our pre-life plans are a variety of experiences that encourage us to deal with our unresolved emotions. Our soul is pure in its intentions, but as humans it often takes extreme events for us to learn. It is possible to change and grow through favorable experiences, but most of our growth occurs when we process our adverse emotions and experiences. We must be open spiritually to accept this knowledge and have the courage to work through our pain. At a soul level, we have all pre-planned our lives in a way that brings the most benefit and growth in this lifetime. When we set out to accomplish these goals, we may have overestimated our ability to cope with these challenges. When we experience a traumatic event and bury the emotions that emerge, we are inviting similar events in the future that elicit those same unfavorable emotions. The Universe will continually put in our path what requires healing until we have done the work to find peace. This is sometimes referred to as the Boomerang Effect. When we internalize negative emotions, we emit lower vibrational energy that attracts other adverse experiences. Our lower vibration attracts circumstances that mirror these debilitating emotions so that we are given many opportunities to heal them. With this knowledge, we can begin to change our perspective on why there is evil in this world. We have the power to alter evil and hate by sending love and forgiveness into the Universe. Breaking this cycle will help break the prevalence of evil behavior.

    Loving oneself is the foundation for all growth in the cycle of life on Earth. We have much more control in overcoming the hate and evil in this world than we realize. By releasing our inner pain and debilitating emotions, we allow for forgiveness and love. When we are able to send compassion and forgiveness into the Universe, we are helping to heal the collective. This is experienced on a soul level and must carry an authentic and heartfelt message. Pain and anger, once resolved, have the ability to emit healing power, which can overcome evil.

    There is so much out of our control in this world. Focus on what you can control and how you respond to the evil that exists. Empower yourselves by dealing with the stubborn emotions that have been buried inside each one of you. Recognize that this is the path for growing personally and for humanity. It is important to acknowledge evil as a trigger to alert us on our healing journey. If we embrace the plan of healing from a soul level, we could shift the Earth's consciousness to learn from a place of love and compassion instead of pain and suffering. We are the impassioned souls who have been given this divine opportunity to change the world, one soul at a time.

COVID

Covid, like cancer, is a word that instantly brings fear and anxiety into our being. We are immediately hurled into a heightened state of conflicting emotions. Our minds and bodies interpret this as a fight or flight scenario. We become entrenched with a constant perceived threat surrounding us at all times.

Just like everyone on Earth, I have been impacted by Covid in many challenging ways. Dale and I both contracted Covid early on in this pandemic and a second time two years later. I question the motive of the messaging from the media and government. I sense an underlying malicious intent from the powerful and wealthy. The fear and anxiety this has created is palpable on a worldwide level. Covid has taken the lives of many loved and cherished friends and family. This is especially experienced by the marginalized communities and is exposing many cracks in the foundation of our social structure. The repercussions of how our society is processing Covid will be felt for decades to come. Mental health issues, suicide and physical after-effects of living under this heightened stress are already affecting us in far greater numbers. I struggle with how families are being torn apart and the divisiveness that opposing views create. Covid has generated ideal circumstances for our repressed emotions to come flooding to the surface.

Previous generations have had world wars, famines and catastrophic events marring their period in history. For the majority of us, we have lived in a world relatively free of extreme universal atrocities that directly affected all. Covid is our generation's collective challenge.

Once again, the Universe is creating an ideal situation for us to learn and grow on a global level never witnessed as a collective in our recent history. We must rise above the fear we are experiencing as a united front. This is a deliberate series of events to create the ideal circumstances for healing to occur. It is in our power to view Covid as a great opportunity and convert our fear into learning and growth. This will take a radical attitude adjustment and much effort from each individual. Covid is potentially the catalyst required to change our world energy to a more love-centered approach. We can overcome the negativity by sending love and forgiveness to all. It is in our power to view Covid as a great opportunity or to remain in a bubble of fear and anxiety. Use all the tools and support you require to move forward in this once-in-a- lifetime event.

By altering our perspective on Covid, we can begin to acknowledge this event with a less threatening and more enlightened viewpoint. Concentrate on what you can control within your own lives to help alleviate some of the anxiety being experienced. We cannot control many of the developments occurring in the world, but we have full control over our response to them. We can empower ourselves by taking the necessary precautions, but be aware of how much energy you are putting into these actions. This can quickly become an obsessive activity that only adds to our anxiety, not detracts from it.

Many people theorize on the origin of this virus, on Big Pharma's role or on how vaccines and the government play a part. Empower yourself with knowledge but try not to get preoccupied with this line of thinking. It is more productive to focus our energy on healing emotionally. Covid has presented us with an opportunity for growth on a worldwide level. Refrain from suppressing the emotions that arise at this time, as this is energy-depleting. By healing ourselves, we are contributing to mending humanity. Through healing, we are lessening the negative long-term impact this virus has on the Universe.

Attempt to approach Covid with an alternative perspective. I have been shown that Covid was a pre-planned universal trigger to alert us to what requires healing for the planet to survive and flourish. We have all been given the opportunity for self-reflection and to discover our life purpose. Earth has begun to repair and mend from the scars we inflict on her. It is within our power to heal ourselves and contribute to strengthening the collective. The Universe is sending us a direct and impactful message. If we choose to once again not heal from this worldwide event, we will be presented with another opportunity in the future. If we are not alerted by subtler events, then the Universe has no choice. This is not a punishment but an opportunity for invigorating the collective on a universal stage.

Fear has insinuated itself into the psyche of many people today. Our fear is in response to an understandable threat, but know that our hearts are not opened by alarm and anger. Behind anger there is always fear. When dread enters our being, we become vulnerable and anxious. When despair consumes us, we are responding to our own vulnerability. This is challenging to understand and to be willing to defeat this level of apprehension. We now have the opportunity and tools to work through the fear and get to a place of forgiveness, love and understanding.

Another challenge we face is accepting that growth does not come from what others do to us but by how we respond to their actions. It is in our best interest to work towards acknowledging, processing and releasing the adverse emotions that others elicit within us due to their actions or as a result of life events. Spiritual growth is not about us changing others but about creating genuine change within ourselves. By forgiving and loving ourselves, we may find forgiveness and love for others. It is important to work through the fear to truly experience peace and trust. We must undergo the negative to fully appreciate the positive. There is no growth in neutrality. Once we release the fear and anger and allow forgiveness and love into our soul, we create a higher vibrational energy within and around us. That, in turn, flows out into the Universe and helps to heal and raise the positive vibration of humanity.

As a society, the stress and isolation around Covid has brought up emotions that many of us have kept dormant for years and potentially many generations. We are feeling vulnerable, lonely, fearful, anxious, isolated, sadness and despair. If we were to collectively heal these emotions during this time, our optimistic energy could shift the trajectory of the Universe. We could begin to overcome the greed, selfishness, prejudice, divisiveness, injustice and hate in the world. Love conquers all. This is not a platitude but a truth. There is power in numbers. When we work together for the common good, our strength multiplies exponentially. We now have the power to embrace the concept of Covid being a great opportunity for enlightened awareness and change.

For societal and individual growth to occur, we are encouraged to change our perspective on what Covid signifies in our lives. Attempt to view this through your soul lens while witnessing the big picture from your pre-birth planning vantage point. A few years prior to Covid, many people with intuitive abilities began to feel a universal shift in energy. Personally, I experienced inexplicable vertigo and sensations of being off-balance throughout 2019. I felt an awareness of impending doom deep in my core that I had never encountered previously. This energy shift also incorporated a universal awakening to the plight of many social injustices that were previously suppressed.

Feminine energy of both males and females and energy of the repressed and under-represented people of this Earth are on the rise. The traditional masculine energy is being challenged by many who feel they have no choice but to take their power back. This is very threatening to those who have held power for many centuries. Feminine energy originates from the heart, whereas masculine energy is predominantly brain-dominant. For us to survive this monumental shift in world energy, we are encouraged to come from a place of increasing heart-centered feminine energy and less from a masculine brain energy. Think less; feel more. This shift is very intentional. The intent is for many of these aggressive energies to alter their consciousness to a more loving and heart-centered approach.

We can also understand this energy through the principles of Ancient Chinese Philosophy. Traditionally, yin refers to a more feminine energy and yang a male dominant energy. Yin and yang together create a perfect balance within the Universe. Every individual is a combination of yin and yang, feminine and masculine energies. This is a monumental opportunity for achieving a more balanced energy in the world.

There is also a remarkable shift among the youth of recent generations. There is an opening of spiritual awareness and heart-centered learning and acceptance. We are coming to the realization that monetary gain and wealth are ego-motivated goals and are not spiritually beneficial for ourselves or the collective. Our focus is shifting to embrace soul growth, which is driven by love and acceptance towards all of humanity. Spiritual growth does not have to occur through fear and pain. As our society grows and accepts this spiritual awareness, we are able to embrace our reason for being through love, forgiveness and a newfound understanding. We are slowly becoming a more open and empathic society. There is still much work to be done, but we have been presented with an incredible opportunity for us to achieve this task.

If we choose to not do the work of healing, we must also be aware that this shift could result in a less optimistic outcome. Daily, we are experiencing a world where our human rights are taken away and our individuality and freedoms are being challenged and slowly eroded. We are witnessing death at an alarming rate, especially among our elderly and most vulnerable populations. Some of the wealthy are accumulating more wealth and power, often through nefarious means. Putting our complete trust in these powerful authority figures is potentially leading us down a dark path. We should always remember who we are at a soul level. Research, read and learn so you can decide what is best for you and your fellow humans. This is most effectively resolved through love and forgiveness, not judgment, anger or violence. We must trust our inner instinctual voice and intuition to discover what resonates as our truth. If we do not, we may find ourselves in a drastically changed world that does not serve the greater good. If we choose not to heal, fear may lead us down a slippery slope to a hole that becomes very difficult to crawl out of in this lifetime. The solution is attainable and clear; we must commit to the process and empower ourselves with the tools and knowledge needed to accomplish the eventual goal of peace, love and forgiveness.

There is a palpable shift in our world energy today. We have been presented with an opportunity to experience a heightened vibrational state rarely available before. It is in our power and control to accept and enter into this higher energy level or continue in the lower stagnating dimension we currently live in. There is no punishment or judgment in the Afterlife for either choice we make on Earth. It is in our power to enact on embracing or remaining in any energy state.

Again, this is a perfect opportunity for healing to occur. We can choose to either empower ourselves by healing individually and collectively, or we can passively be an observer to the changes taking place. Whichever route we decide, as individuals and as a society, I believe we will discover a more peace-filled and loving existence. As individuals, we have the ability and strength within us to change the energy of the Universe. We are much more powerful than we ever realized. When we send our beautiful intentions into the world, they join forces with everyone else's uplifting vibrational energy. This vastly increases our collective energy. When you throw a pebble into the water, you can see the ripples created. When ten people throw pebbles into the water, the ripples expand one hundredfold. This analogy helps us understand the impact of one individual and the immense potential power of many.

Hindsight is 20/20. My husband created a new meaning for this old saying early on in this Covid experience. When we reflect back on the year 2020, we will gauge our life in terms of before and after. Within each individual, we have the power and ability to create a positive and enlightened storyline of life after 2020. We have been given an incredible opportunity for growth and awareness of our spirituality and life purpose. We have all planned to be on this Earth at this exact moment in time. We have prepared ourselves for this event. It is up to us to transform this time into the awakening it was meant to be. Now go change the world.

MARGINALIZED SOULS

I would love to speak about the marginalized people of the world so I can bring this situation to the forefront of our awareness. I can only express my knowledge from a spiritual perspective and from previous-life memories. I cannot give a firsthand account of the experiences of our Indigenous people, the African-American people or of many groups of human beings who are being marginalized in our world today. These include groups excluded due to their race, religion, age, physical ability, mental capacity, gender identity, sexual orientation, language and those of unequal power due to social, political, economic and cultural disadvantages. My only intention is to honor all souls for the journey they are on and to give hope around the circumstances that surround everyone today.

For healing to occur, we must address the truth that we are all equal and accepted in Source's loving embrace. We all chose these bodies and experiences in our pre-life plan for our personal growth and for collective healing. There is a powerful component in choosing to become a member of a marginalized community in your pre-life planning. In doing so, you are aware of a strong generational motivation for healing. You are not only catapulted into a challenging individual situation but also retain the pain and devastation of ancestral atrocities.

Once again, Divine Healing gives you the opportunity and means to begin to heal not only yourself but also centuries of oppression and pain. First, acknowledge the amazing soul you are for taking on this extreme challenge. Replace all the adverse emotions with favorable sentiments that are revealed during your healing journey. Abandon the victim mentality to free up your soul for love and forgiveness. Entrust yourself with knowledge and strength to embrace your soul purpose. Allow forgiveness and love to soothe your soul from generations of pain and suffering. Empower yourself with the awareness that your soul took on this monumental challenge. Understandably, the most crucial aspect of this process is forgiving those who perpetrated these horrific actions against you and generations before you. As you resolve personal core issues, you are freeing your soul from ancestral pain and atrocities from many lifetimes and from previous generations. The work you are doing is also ensuring that future generations will not be burdened with ancestral detrimental energies. You will not only have released past and present pain and suffering, but you are also creating a clear path for your soul and the souls of future generations to advance to a higher level of enlightenment and universal growth. What a beautiful gift to yourself, past generations, future souls, and humanity.

What we are doing now is not working. The division between the mainstream and the marginalized is widening. We must radically change our approach for reconciliation to occur. We have nothing to lose and everything to gain through the process of Divine Healing. If we consciously worked on this as a united front, our perceived enemies would be powerless to resist. When each individual takes on the challenge of releasing pain, anger, hurt, shame, guilt or unworthiness into the Universe, we are creating a tsunami of tangible change, personally and for the collective.

There is a palpable shift in the universal consciousness that is threatening the powerful of the world. As a society, we must take advantage of this critical opportunity to transfer the power away from the privileged few to create balance and a harmonious existence for all. We have the ability to begin this journey today.

Through healing, forgiveness and love, we are creating a powerful transference in universal energy. We are all Source's children who have been blessed with the knowledge and tools to accomplish this divine mission. We are truly "One in Love."

THE CYCLE OF GROWTH THROUGH OUR LIFE CHALLENGES

What we experience in the world around us and emotionally within us is a reflection of unhealed trauma and beliefs we carry in our souls. When true healing occurs, there is a shift in our perception of external events and an internal sense of well-being. This optimistic projection into the Universe reflects an increased occurrence of uplifting experiences and attitudes within us and around us.

When we are deeply entrenched in our daily existence, it is very difficult to step away from our perceived reality for even a moment. When we objectively view our life and honestly see the whole picture, we will find distinct patterns that emerge. Bravely acknowledge how multiple human experiences and events in this lifetime reflect emotions that require healing. When the healing is not achieved, similar events eliciting those core feelings recur throughout our life. For greater clarity, focus on specific events that highlight unresolved emotional sufferings. As these sentiments become evident, we can concentrate on healing them in a direct and forthright manner. Our life purpose begins to take shape through this awareness of resolving emotional trauma.

Work on allowing these persistent feelings the ability to rise to the forefront of your awareness. Process these sentiments in a healthy format that suits your needs the most effectively. You are opening a space within your soul where forgiveness, love and compassion can reside. When your life purpose begins to manifest itself, you become closer to discovering your individual identity. This process occurs uniquely for each person and transpires so subtly that it may be difficult to recognize. Through creating a clear plan and discovering your purpose, your personal identity will begin to emerge.

Understand that by ignoring these injurious feelings, you are potentially manifesting a life of anxiety with fear and an existence without purpose or direction. Another possible result of repressing detrimental emotions is an increased likelihood of a myriad of mental and physical conditions that do not serve you in any healthy way. We are now clearly aware that by not healing emotions, life will continually present circumstances that bring forward the sentiments that require healing for a greater quality of life. Only by dealing with these feelings are we able to create an opening for peace and tranquility in our hearts. It will also decrease the probability of having to endure distressing events from continually recurring in our lives. With every personal challenge that we conquer, there is a probable increased incidence of a less stressful and a more joyful existence.

During the initial stages of this process, we may find the intensity of our emotions increase. This is a normal response to working through buried feelings. We must feel the impact of retrieving painful emotions to experience the freedom of releasing these sentiments into the Universe. In time, our vibrational energy will rise and attract other increased authentic energies and experiences. We may also release karma that has plagued us for a prolonged period of time.

Another promising benefit of working through our traumatic emotions is having the energy to focus on our spiritual awareness and growth. Our pre-life plan manifests itself with gradual clarity. As enlightened spiritual beings, we may become of service to others.

Our renewed energy and motivation allows us to achieve other life goals. On a spiritual level, we are on our way to discovering that love is a state of being. It is our true essence. The purpose of our existence is to come back to self and therefore return to love. This love is Divine Love, which is a state of consciousness and is on an elevated level to the emotional love we experience on Earth.

As humans, we all make decisions and choices we are not proud of. In the Afterlife we will have to process how these actions made others feel. This is all accomplished through our life review. This is not a punishment but an avenue for growing and learning. It is imperative to understand that since we have presently gained this knowledge, it will greatly benefit us to incorporate this awareness into our daily lives. Now that we know better, we must work on doing better and being better. We are not meant to be perfect. We will stumble and fall. It is in our power to learn and grow from each experience. It is how we respond to and learn from every life challenge that is honored in our life review. Ultimately, the power resides in every one of us to be the best versions of ourselves in this lifetime.

Simply sending our renewed intent into the world will initiate a pattern of genuine experiences and favorable results. This may be accomplished in any format you choose. People use prayer, internal intentions, creative writing, songs, art and any means imaginable to convey these inspired aspirations. What we project into the world matters immensely. Intention is one of our most powerful and accessible tools. When we internalize enlightened messages and send them into the Universe, we increase the likelihood of positive experiences reflecting back on us. Even if you remain skeptical regarding some of the concepts presented, understand that simply embracing the process of a love-centered approach may radically alter your life to a more promising outcome.

In the Afterlife, our transition into Heaven may become a smoother and more pleasant voyage. We can celebrate our accomplishments and convey less judgment on ourselves in our life review. In the Afterlife, our soul will advance in our personal journey so that we are freed to assist less advanced souls in accomplishing their goals. Our souls will be one step closer to being in the inner circle of Source. We are on our way to becoming the Ascended Masters who sit in Divine Love to enlighten the souls of many. It is at this stage that our reincarnations may become less frequent or cease altogether if we choose. We are in service with the Highest Power and enveloped in love and compassion beyond anything felt on Earth.

    I am grateful for every experience that allows me to grow, including those that are traumatic and painful. When we can fully embrace and trust this truth, we are on the path to finding our life purpose. We learn our greatest lessons through our own encounters, but we can also learn through other people's experiences. By being mindful and empathetic towards our fellow human beings, our hearts can absorb awareness through their journeys. By observing the experiences of others, we may learn how to recognize and resolve our own life challenges. This does not mean you should only passively observe others on their personal adventures. This is merely one more tool for you to use on your healing journey.

    There is a life lesson analogy I will use to demonstrate how we learn lessons on Earth. This is a metaphorical analogy to help us understand how our pre-birth plan incorporates many facets of learning and awareness. A parent will continually tell a child not to touch a hot stove. The child's natural curiosity and need for learning on their own motivates the child to touch the stove. The experience leaves them with pain and a valuable lesson. When we are in our pre-life planning, we are aware of potential situations that will bring us hardship. When we come to Earth, we choose to experience those situations for our individual learning, even though we understand on a deep soul level that suffering may result. When we are aware of this process, we may diminish the pain of our experience by observing others. We will still exercise our free will, but we can now enter with a cautionary memory of how to approach a situation with awareness. The following are examples of how we may recognize some of our challenges through the life situations of others.

A loved one close to me experiences events and emotions that challenge her on a regular basis. During her childhood, she was raised in a loving family with issues that are common to many. Her father's alcoholism contributed to her feelings of low self-esteem and insecurities. During her lifetime, many experiences reflected these emotions and caused them to re-emerge. She chose to marry someone who reinforced her internal emotional wounds. It is human nature to gravitate towards people and situations that are familiar to us, despite the possibility we are recreating past trauma. We make choices based on the fear of the unknown and are inclined to choose what is commonplace to us.

Regardless of how busy we are, the Universe will continually bring us situations to motivate us to heal our unresolved emotions. My friend's buried feelings emerged with an overwhelming intensity due to a seemingly ordinary incident. A mouse got into their home and became an all-consuming worry for my loved one. She could not sleep or eat until the mouse was caught and removed. I felt her helplessness, hopelessness and out-of-control feelings within her. Even once the mouse was long gone and all traces of the mouse were non-existent, she stated, "I will never get over this." In reality, it is not the mouse she will "never get over," but the intensity of the emotions brought forward because of this incident. The mouse is no longer a threat, but her unresolved emotions are demanding attention. Many emotions around the instability of childhood came rushing back. She felt out of control and overwhelmed. She is now aware of the emotions that require healing and is dealing with them at her own pace. This process should be approached with compassion and forgiveness. This is a marathon, not a sprint.

In another life circumstance, a family member endured a childhood immersed in parental addictions, insecurities, abandonment and fear. To the outside world, he appears a seemingly confident person. Internally, he struggles daily with underlying fear and being out of control in many aspects of his life. This partially manifests as Obsessive-Compulsive Disorder (OCD) that threatens his mental wellness on a daily basis.

In society, OCD is on the rise at an alarming rate. It may often be the result of unresolved underlying negative emotions and trauma that have been suppressed for many years. Once obsessive-compulsive behaviors entrench their strong hold into our lives, it may become difficult to rid ourselves of their negative consequences. For healing to occur, it is important to acknowledge the underlying emotions that drive these compulsions. The process is similar in any life challenge, but every individual chooses their own path towards healing. Divine Healing, acknowledging and releasing unresolved painful emotions and allowing love and gratitude into our core essence may be the foundation for healing to begin.

My loved one is working on this in his unique and authentic way. He is embracing his traditional spiritual awakenings into his healing journey. He is also incorporating conventional therapy in resolving past trauma. This will likely become a lifelong journey. Every step towards healing creates an opportunity for peace and love to be embraced by his Spiritual Self. Each internalized positive experience will strengthen his acceptance of being a loved and important being in the Universe.

During my lifetime, my need for perfection resulted in OCD tendencies. When we feel out of control with our internal emotions, we sometimes overcompensate by obsessively attempting to control our external environment. This manifested in behaviors that did not serve me in any way and only added to my anxiety. The exhaustion from hiding these rituals and the time invested into the repetitive behaviors left me with little energy for self-care.

With each conflicting inner emotion I worked on releasing, my obsessive-compulsive behavior lessened. Once I transferred that energy into healing, I discovered the repetitive behaviors held no power or compulsion over me. The emotional freedom I experienced allowed me to focus on further healing my soul. I would like to stress that this took many years to achieve this level of peace within myself. I incorporated professional counseling and a concrete plan to discover how these behaviors no longer served me in a productive way. Prior to my healing journey, I did not have the tools available to me that I am sharing with you. I am hopeful that with this awareness, your soul is triggered to begin your journey of healing. Today I am free from all my past obsessive-compulsive behaviors. Although my obsessive tendencies have been released, I am motivated to work daily on healing all aspects of my Soul Self. This is one more positive result of spiritual healing and discovering our souls' journeys and life purposes.

I will pivot to a more lighthearted account of how growth works through life experiences. This analogy is introduced here to help us understand how life repeatedly presents similar opportunities for our growth in this lifetime. Recently, I was observing my husband make his morning shake. He had added a new protein powder that seemed to produce an expansion of his ingredients. During this process, he became frustrated with the increased time it took to mix and clean up the mess he created. I suggested he use a larger container or fewer ingredients. He ignored my advice and continued the same pattern, resulting in the same outcome. His ego and pride prevented him from seeing the big picture.

We can apply this similar awareness to how we repeatedly choose relationships and life circumstances that consistently bring us frustration and pain. As discussed, we choose people and situations that reflect what requires healing within ourselves. If we do not do the work to identify and heal those qualities internally, they will continue to repeat throughout our lives. When we blame others for the messy situations that keep recurring, we are setting ourselves up for this experience to continually replicate in our lives. The same repetitive behavior results in the same outcome. Until we are able to heal and change our core ego-centered self, this pattern will continue. We are encouraged to step out of the myopic view we have placed ourselves in. We are then motivated to replace ego with confidence and awareness. Even altering one aspect of this process may create tangible change. We can then celebrate a relationship that fills us with love instead of pain—or a protein shake that fills us with nutrition instead of frustration.

A dear friend of mine experienced how life events continually kept occurring until she was able to recognize and deal with the underlying emotions that were paralyzing her growth. Her childhood was filled with multiple moves and instability. There were secrets and deception surrounding her early years into young adulthood. She was emotionally pulled between divorced parents and experienced a very tumultuous upbringing.

She left home in her late teens and created a life for herself. When she married, she chose a man who she thought needed rescuing. They created a life of financial and physical stability but emotional volatility. She put all of her energy into maintaining a stable life and home. She lost herself and achieved perceived control through her external environment. Her profession involved helping to heal vulnerable people's emotional trauma. Many of her client's emotions reflected her feelings that desperately needed healing. She repressed her own emotions even deeper and lived in a state of anxiety and fear. This caused her physical, emotional and spiritual exhaustion and burnout.

On an intellectual level, she is now aware of all these factors contributing to where her life is today. She realizes how her resistance in dealing with her emotions has influenced the family dynamic. She understands that many life experiences have carried messages which exposed deep emotional trauma that required healing. She is currently working diligently on releasing the emotions and healing the wounds that have plagued her during this lifetime. Her family is adjusting to a new dynamic, and the road to healing will be challenging and difficult. With forgiveness, compassion and maintaining an open heart, they will hopefully enjoy a more harmonious future.

    We are all capable of healing past and present emotional trauma. For this to occur, we must release blame from those we feel have contributed to our injurious emotions and experiences. Understand that when we blame God, fate, people or circumstances for our challenges, we are putting up blocks to deal with our pain. This only increases the inevitable likelihood for increased detrimental experiences in our lives and delays our willingness to recognize our life goals.

    Divine Healing may be beneficial to fully embrace the release of adverse emotions. Send the Universe a message of your intent to alleviate distressing feelings. By activating that awareness, a recognizable shift in our consciousness will occur. This is the soul enabling us to remember our objective to mend from our pre-birth plan. Healing begins the moment we mobilize the purpose of our journey. Be aware of all the triggers placed by our souls to help assist us on our path to healing. Once again, allow these emotions to emerge, and process the pain trapped deep in your being. Then work diligently at releasing the debilitating effects of these repressed traumatic feelings. This allows space in our hearts for healing to occur and enables us to embrace the beautiful soul we are at the core of our being.

HEALING THROUGH OUR LIFE CHALLENGES

> Anything that annoys you is teaching you patience.
> Anyone who abandons you is teaching you how to stand up on your own two feet.
> Anything that angers you is teaching you forgiveness and compassion.
> Anything that has power over you is teaching you how to take your power back.
> Anything you hate is teaching you unconditional love.
> Anything that you fear is teaching you courage to overcome your fear.
> Anything you can't control is teaching you how to let go.
> Jackson Kiddard

The time for healing is right now. When an event or person leaves a negative imprint on your soul, there is no expiration date for dealing with the emotions attached to that experience. It is interesting to note that around thirty years of age, we are often triggered to explore our spiritual awareness and to search for our purpose in this lifetime. Even if you are nearing the last stages of your earthly life, discovering your Spiritual Soul Self and the path to healing can begin today. Become alert to every opportunity to embrace an enlightened aspect as a part of your life plan. There is no age limit or life circumstance that prevents you from continuing on your healing journey. You are worth every effort it takes to process and release the adverse emotions that have held you back from fully embracing the loving soul you are. This not only allows you to live a more peace-filled life today, but the lessons learned are imprinted on your soul for eternity.

We are accumulating many tools for the growth of our soul in this lifetime. Healing false beliefs is an important aspect of our awareness. When we tell ourselves that we are not worthy or are unlovable, we attract experiences that reflect those sentiments. To begin to change that scenario, we must first change the message that we consistently tell ourselves. Practice daily self-affirming messages—"I am worthy," or "I am lovable,"—and any positive sentiments you feel comfortable with. Even the action of flipping the switch is a great first step. Initially, this may feel awkward and disingenuous. With repetition and a renewed perspective, you will begin to believe and feel these genuine affirmations. Again, what we project, others will reflect. Intention of all thoughts is extremely powerful. You will begin to attract experiences that reflect your inner authentic narrative. This will, in turn, reinforce how loved and worthy you are. You will become aware that what you internally embrace is reflected in your daily life. This attracts higher vibrational experiences because of your increased energy level. When this experience is absorbed at a soul level, you are adding another tool for growth to occur.

Healing requires feeling. The most intense feeling is experienced through grief and loss. The opportunities for healing from the crossing over of a loved one, or any loss that triggers grief, are immense. It is important to stress how vital it is to process the feelings that occur as a result of grief. This is the primary reason why I am focusing on this critical emotion once again.

When you initially lose a loved one or a vital aspect of yourself, your grief is all-consuming and extremely intense. You will miss this person your entire life, but the severe acute grief will gradually fade over time. For this to occur, it is beneficial to acknowledge, process and release all the emotions that emerge from grief and loss. These emotions may also be elicited from the loss of a relationship, loss of innocence, loss of health, or any loss you feel deeply in your being. If your emotions are denied and repressed, they may return in many unhealthy avenues. Choosing mind-altering substances like alcohol or drugs to lessen your grief will only delay the inevitable and add many more obstacles that interfere with your healing journey. To heal you must feel. There is no shortcut or any other avenue to work through grief. It is soul work at an incredibly intense level. It may take a significant amount of time to work through complicated emotions that arise from a loved one's crossing or from any critical loss in your life.

When we resist distressing emotions, we give them strength. When we suppress those emotions, they become entrenched into our being, and we can lose control over when they decide to emerge. These repressed emotions may then appear as depression, anxiety, mental or physical illnesses at any time they choose. Accepting and processing the pain and associated feelings of grief will help resolve the emotions that do not serve you in a healthy way. Even the redirection for your grief will initiate the healing process. You can elicit growth merely by focusing on the emotions that require healing to discover a concrete plan.

As you heal, it is important to be able to distinguish between grief and sadness. Complicated grief is based on fear and elicits feelings of blame, anger, guilt and many paralyzing emotions. Your spirit can become stuck in an incapacitating cycle of negativity. This is where grief may immobilize your ability to experience the life you were destined to live. Sadness is natural with any loss and is based on missing the physical and emotional aspects of your loved ones. We intensely miss their hugs, kisses and presence in our lives. Remember, we are forever intertwined with our loved ones' souls, and they continue to live through us. Our emotional and spiritual connection remains forever. When your heart is open, you create a direct spiritual link with your loved one. By releasing your extreme grief, you are allowing the soul of your loved one to freely do the work they choose to do in the Afterlife. You are not releasing the love or memories of your loved one; you are opening the door for greater love and joy to potentially enter into your life. This is one of the most important gifts you can receive and give. Complicated grief is not only paralyzing for us on Earth, but it also delays the souls who have crossed over from accomplishing their goals and plans in Heaven. Our loved ones in the Heavenly Realm are patient and hold no judgment around how we choose to grieve. They are aware of and support us on our healing journey at all times.

In many cases, the souls of our dear loved ones will wait to reincarnate until we have crossed over. We are honoring and respecting our loved ones by releasing our debilitating grief, so they are able to prepare our place beside them in Heaven. This enables us to reincarnate into our next life all together if we so choose. They will continue to grow and learn from us through our releasing of overburdening emotions attached to their crossing over. The best way to honor our loved ones in the Afterlife is to live a joyous and heartfelt life here on Earth. When we release the pain and anguish from their passing, we allow love back into our hearts. Love that is unconditionally given and received is eternal. Our bonds with our crossed-over loved ones continually strengthens. Upon entrance into the Afterlife, all unfavorable emotions are washed away. They hold no blame, guilt, pain or shame. They certainly do not want anyone left on Earth to carry any of those emotions that hold us back from living our most authentic lives. All is forgiven, and the only thing that remains is love.

By healing ourselves, we allow our soul vibration to elevate. This in turn increases the vibration of the Universe. By elevating our spiritual energy, we become more energetically connected to our loved ones in the Afterlife. Meditation, prayer and intentional dreams can further increase our spiritual energy. Our loved ones' souls embrace this and pull their energy down to meet ours. Intentional dreaming is when you ask crossed-over loved ones questions before falling asleep. Write down any answer you receive immediately upon waking. Keep a journal or your phone at your bedside to record any response you get. You will receive the answer you need, not necessarily the ones you think you want. It is important to note that your crossed-over loved ones will send messages that facilitate your spiritual journey. Asking for wealth, power or earthly rewards are ego-driven desires and not necessarily soul-driven priorities. You are still free to ask for anything your heart desires, and you do not have to censor your requests or communication. Spirit ensures you will receive what you require on your soul journey. The road that leads us to our life purpose may take many twists and turns. Remain open to the experience and all the lessons along the way. Trust that Spirit knows what is best for us even when we can't see it. We are always able to communicate with our beloved soul family, and now you may experience their presence. We will explore that concept in greater detail in later chapters. We can continue to strengthen our connection with our loved ones even after they have transitioned to the Higher Realms. Their great hope is that you live a life of joy, love, forgiveness and compassion.

For us to heal from a soul level, we must embrace the necessity for adverse life experiences. The ego is in contrast to love and alerts us to our healing journey. To live without fear, we must be willing to release the mental burdens of ego. With knowledge comes the power to change and accept that we chose this in our pre-life soul plan. When we recognize that every experience is for a higher purpose—our soul's growth—we begin to heal. We can now take control of a situation we have previously felt victimized by. If we acknowledge what requires our attention and commit to the healing process, the lessons will be embraced by our soul for all time. All the lessons learned are imprinted within our being and are archived for eternity. This permanent record on our soul is available for us to use as a tool for healing in this life and in all our lives.

It is important to stress once again that guilt is an emotion that may be devastating to our soul growth. When our energy center is consumed with guilt, it is very difficult to heal. When we sit in this paralyzing emotion, we deprive ourselves of discovering our pure essence and authentic purpose. For the great majority of us, guilt is an ego-driven emotion that serves little purpose in our evolution as a loving soul and is destructive in our healing process. Understand guilt as merely the catalyst to begin our mending journey. It is the trigger to alert us to what requires healing in our life. Release guilt with forgiveness and compassion, and allow love to fill that space for growth to occur.

Judgment is often another emotion that remains unhealed for many of us. It is easier to condemn and blame others instead of facing our own infallibility. Judgment of others comes from criticizing ourselves. We must acknowledge our low energy emotions before we can heal. When we project our thoughts onto others, they absorb the energy of that action. Becoming aware of this triggers our ability to send loving and forgiving messages into the Universe. When we collectively participate in this positive action, everyone benefits by embracing a higher and more loving energy.

The feelings we deny within ourselves will be projected onto others until we are able to heal ourselves. This is true for all our adverse emotions. Condemning others may originate from our personal feelings of low self-worth or possibly a variety of unresolved injurious feelings. If we find ourselves in situations where we are judging others or feel hostility towards others, realize resolving our underlying debilitating emotions is a critical aspect of our life plan.

Recently, I experienced a revealing situation that reinforced how judgment consumes and alters our life experiences. We were attending a dinner where many strong personalities created a chaotic and revealing pattern. One family member had a history of disapproval and distrust towards another person in attendance. I attempted to objectively view this situation and absorb the dynamics with compassion and understanding. I soon became aware of where the fear and anger my family member was projecting may be originating from. I sensed her loss of control of a situation she felt threatened by, which resulted in alerting unresolved emotions to emerge from within herself.

I was given insight into why this person kept returning to my loved one's space. The Universe continually brought this person back for my family member to confront her own pain and resolve what she had arranged to do in her pre-life plan with this soul. I believe when my loved one begins to heal her pain, this person will have honored her part of the bargain and will have no need to remain in my family member's life.

I am very hopeful that my family member will discover how to mend herself with forgiveness and love by becoming aware of her own emotional need for healing. She is a beautiful soul who requires some direction in resolving her personal internal distressing messages so she may create love and forgiveness for herself and others.

Another dynamic that I observed that day was the power of projecting low energy sentiments onto others. One person in the group was particularly abrasive and overbearing in her communication. There was much judgment towards this person during the day. The general atmosphere of negativity was palpable by all those present. By evening, she felt the energy of others towards her and became very sad and hurt. There was no direct verbal confrontation with her, but the adverse sentiment was internalized by this woman on a deep level. This is a profound example of how our energy projected into the Universe affects the vibration of the atmosphere and that of an individual.

If we collectively could have seen how this person was feeling insecure and sad, we all could have changed the dynamic of that entire day. If we had approached her with compassion and not judgment, it would have resulted in a more favorable experience for all. We were collectively responsible for creating a low vibrational milieu and detrimental environment. I realized how quickly a group mentality can influence every person's response in any given situation. When we are in the moment of an escalating distressing event, it is important to attempt to pull away from the influences of that unfavorable energy. Only then can we attempt to insert our positive intentions to help alleviate some of the adverse energy surrounding all of us.

By becoming aware of these types of situations, we are empowered to change the dynamic of any life event. It takes confidence and courage and will result in creating an optimistic flow of energy into our Universe. Imagine if we all did this, even on a small scale, how our world energy would elevate and improve our earthly experiences.

To resolve the painful emotions of self-judgment and judgment of others, you must bravely initiate your healing journey. Acknowledge, heal and release underlying painful emotions to allow a space for peace and forgiveness. Healing has occurred when you become aware that you feel an absence of condemnation or hostility towards your fellow human beings. Your heart is open to love and compassion, and you may feel compelled to be of service to others. This is forgiveness and healing at a soul level.

When we vibrate in love and gratitude, we are rewarded with genuine reciprocal energy. When we veer off our chosen path, the Universe sends us messages to return to our life's plan. There is no judgment on our souls if we choose not to listen. It is simply in our best interest to open ourselves to learning and understand how to mend our inner being. Since we are all energetically connected, when we heal ourselves, we begin to heal all.

Our intuition and deep inner place of all-knowing will guide us to our soul plan. Having the tools of awareness of how our soul operates is a great starting point. When you incorporate a plan of action into your process, you are on your way to achieving soul growth and fulfilling your life's objectives. With all the knowledge and tools presented to you, coupled with your courage and faith, you are equipped to realize your life's purpose. When you feel you are veering off your chosen path, return to your inner place of forgiveness, healing and love. Wrap yourself in a warm and loving emotional blanket. Go into nature or your safe place to ground yourself. With renewed strength, you are able to tackle life's challenges once again.

Healing may also come in very subtle manifestations. Sometimes the messages come in whispers, and other times the Universe sends such powerful communication it is difficult to deny. Train your intuition to accept and embrace these heartfelt messages. They are critical tools in discovering your life's purpose and keep you on a forward path when you are led astray. I will share with you significant life experiences that triggered my healing journey in profound ways. My hope is that you may recognize potential events in your life that create awareness of your personal healing journey.

About a year after my dad crossed over, we received a beautiful healing message from his soul. My brother and his family were experiencing a very difficult grieving journey. They were not fully able to express their grief or process their painful emotions. Then along came a sickly little piglet named Lentil. Despite my brother's physician skills and loads of love from the family, Lentil died a couple of weeks later. The intensity of their grief overwhelmed and perplexed them.

During the aftermath of this event, I experienced visits from the soul of Lentil. I had not previously been aware that the souls of all animals crossed over. I have since been shown that all souls go to Heaven, and animal souls have a special area that is designated specifically for them. The messages I received were initially quite subtle. When I informed my brother's family that I saw Lentil was at peace and with no more pain, they were relieved. Lentil kept appearing during my meditation, which for me meant there was another message I needed to pass on. I finally got the full impact of this message and was truly amazed. I discovered that our dad had sent Lentil to my brother's family as a healing gift. The imagery dad sent me was magical. In my vision, I saw the soul of Lentil morph into my father. Then my dad took on the image of an eagle and flew upwards into the Higher Realms. My father was giving us an avenue for our grief to be released. Dad saw the incredible pain his son and family were holding onto from his passing. He sent Lentil as a catalyst to allow my brother's family to fully express their grief. They had inadvertently buried the painful emotions attached to our father's crossing over. It felt safer to grieve Lentil, and in doing so, they were able to begin the healing journey over the loss of our dad.

When we suppress our emotions attached to numerous losses in our life, we are creating the potential for great pain and hardship in our being. Grief is accumulative if not processed and released. When we bury the emotions associated with any loss in our lives, we create the potential for any future loss to exponentially be experienced. By releasing the emotions attached to any critical incident in our lives, we are freeing our souls to learn our intended lessons. We also decrease the incidence of repeating experiences that emphasize these devastating emotions. The pain may be a result of multiple losses in this lifetime and may also include unresolved emotional trauma from many past lifetimes. By beginning your healing journey today, you are alerting the Universe to your intention to create enlightened change for your soul's growth.

Regardless of where we are in our spiritual journey, healing at a deep soul level is attainable. We are never alone on this seemingly daunting voyage. The souls of our crossed-over loved ones are always around us to envelop each individual in love and understanding. Even when our loved ones' soul journeys take them to the ascending Higher Realms, we retain that deep connection with them. In the Afterlife, our loved ones continue on their journey of learning and achievement. They advance to Higher Energy Realms once they reach their soul goals. Each advancement reflects an elevation in the level of their soul's progression. This is similar to receiving a promotion here on Earth or graduating from an educational program. When we stagnate in profound unresolved grief and debilitating emotions, we hinder the soul journeys of our loved ones in the Afterlife. Once we begin the process of working through releasing our grief, we are freeing our loved ones' souls to continue on their journey. It is challenging for our crossed-over loved ones to break through relentless grief. There is no blame or animosity felt by them, as they are patient and compassionate towards us at all times. By processing our grief, we are creating an opening for their souls to communicate with us and to freely continue on their journey. It is human to mourn our loved ones' passings, but remaining in paralyzing grief serves no higher purpose for anyone. Our loved ones will always be present for us, even from their advancing higher energy placement. In the Afterlife, our souls can freely move from one energy realm into another. They are able to return to our lower energy dimension so they can support and communicate with us on this earthly plane at will.

There will come a time when the happy memories with our loved ones outweigh the sadness we feel. This is a true measure that we are on a healing path. Through meditation, prayer or thought we can release the soul of our loved one from their earthly obligations. This in no way means we are releasing the connection and love we have with them. This merely enhances and strengthens our ongoing connection for love to flourish. We are releasing the residual low energy emotions that may have blocked our ability to experience their soul's spiritual essence. This is truly a gift for all to embrace on our spiritual voyage.

Every individual will discover their own unique path for their healing journey. There are numerous avenues available for mending our wounded hearts. Embrace and implement the method that seems most authentic for you. You must begin to heal yourself before you attempt to support others on their mending venture. Self-forgiveness at a soul level opens the door to forgiveness of others. Use all the tools presented that are appropriate for you on your healing journey. The first step may be to acknowledge that Divine Healing opens a space in your heart for recovery to occur. Professional therapists, group therapy, meditation, prayer, Eastern Medicine, reiki, Body Talk, hypnotherapy, past-life regression or any modality you feel comfortable with are all beneficial for healing.

If you wish to explore meditation, a basic understanding of chakras is helpful. An important aspect of meditation is to clear your brain from the chatter that may interfere with your ability to calm your mind. Visualize the frontal brain as the ego center. Shut off that area so you may access the stillness of self. When you have invasive interfering thoughts, allow them to enter, honor every thought and gently release them. Forgive yourself for any setback, as this is the most challenging aspect of meditation. With practice, the chatter in your mind will eventually decrease and become less of an issue. I still have to work on those thoughts that do not serve a higher purpose for me. I send them on their way to make room for healing messages to enter. It is important to note that meditation is not an absence of thought, but is a journey to explore a single avenue of thought.

Start by breathing intentionally and begin to visualize your chakras. Pull each chakra into your center of being to help maintain balance in your life. When you work on aligning your chakras, you will be empowered to elevate your spiritual awareness from a heart-centered energy. Imagine pulling a string from your feet, through the center of your body, and out the top of your head. I have discovered that when I visualize my chakras, I can feel when one is out of balance. I literally envision a specific chakra being to the left or right of my central core body. I can then focus on prioritizing that appropriate chakra to maintain a balance in my life. I have had to work primarily with my throat chakra, because I have been reluctant to speak my truth throughout my lifetime. I am alerted to heal that aspect of myself and actively work on guiding my throat chakra into the center of my being once again. This is a tool to utilize in conjunction with the intentional spiritual healing you are working on. As you become more comfortable with this practice, you will experience a palpable shift in your soul center. When we are able to meditate in nature, I strongly believe this is a great method to achieve grounding and return to our Higher Soul Self. Grounding simply means being present in the moment. Concentrate on your breathing to bring you back to that peaceful state of being. This is a practice that requires repetition, patience and commitment. Meditation is available for you to implement in a variety of formats. You can meditate during exercise, complete rest, or by repeating a phrase or single word. You can begin your meditation practice with a time commitment of only five minutes a day. The most crucial aspect of meditation is to remain consistent in your practice. You are the best authority to understand what works for your purpose. Research different methods and institute what resonates for you. There is no wrong way to meditate, just follow your intuitive inclinations.

    Begin by preparing your environment to be a place of calmness and tranquility. This can be accomplished by making space in a special room in your home or in nature. Start by breathing deeply and clearing your mind of any residual thought. Continue with opening and aligning your chakras from the base level and work up from there. I find it helpful to visualize the colors each chakra represents while embracing what each chakra embodies for me personally. When you reach the crown chakra (top of your head), pull energy from the upper realm to meet your energy. It may also be beneficial to generate energy from nature. Feel her strength starting from your feet flowing through to the top of your head. The following are a basic explanation for what each individual chakra represents for me:

ROOT: RED
    Also called the base chakra
    Area around the pelvic floor
- grounding: connects all energy to Earth
- stabilizing: financial and emotionally
- balanced=secure, peace, accomplished
- out of balance=digestive issues, lower back pain, hip pain, ovarian or prostate issues, anxiety, fear
- get in balance by finding a solid connection between your inner soul self and Earth

SACRAL: ORANGE
    Area around lower abdomen
- Pleasure: sex, food
- balanced=creative energy, enjoyment of life
- out of balance=obesity, addiction, restless, hormone disorder
- get in balance by expressing yourself through creative activities; such as writing, sport, dance, painting, or any art form you choose

SOLAR PLEXUS: YELLOW
    Area around stomach
- identity, personal power, self-confidence
- balanced=gut feeling, intuition, confidence, wisdom
- out of balance=controlling, micromanage, greed
- get in balance by exercise, yoga, positive affirmations, remain open to your inner voice messages

HEART: GREEN
Area around heart center
- love, compassion, kindness
- balanced=love of self is equal or greater than love for others
- out of balance=put needs of others first, increased heart rate, heartburn, relationship issues
- get in balance by loving yourself first

THROAT: BLUE
Area around neck
- gives voice to personal truth, clarity
- balanced=speak clearly with kindness, truth and love
- out of balance=throat pain, infections, cavities, mouth ulcers, digestive issues (swallow our truth)
- get in balance by authentically expressing ourselves verbally or through writing (speaking our truth)

THIRD EYE: INDIGO/ PURPLE/ PINK
Area in center of forehead, just above eye level
- opens mind beyond fifth sense and material world
- extrasensory perception (ESP), intuition and psychic energy come from third eye
- balanced=feel in tune with physical/spiritual realms
- out of balance=anxiety, depression, mental fog, headaches, insomnia, sinus issues
- get in balance by meditating, yoga, grounding, following your intuitive inner voice

CROWN: VIOLET
Area around top of head
- pure consciousness energy, connects us to the entire Universe
- balanced=will align all chakras, good health, wisdom, joy, connection with spiritual supports

- out of balance=feeling of apathy and disconnect which results in a lack of direction or purpose in life
- get in balance by expressing gratitude through meditation or sending beautiful intentions into the Universe

Approach every aspect of healing with a positive and enlightened attitude. This is a critical lesson for our lives on this Earth. It is imperative to mend so that we may embrace our life purpose and soul growth. Forgiveness and healing are essential aspects in realizing our soul journey. The tools presented enhance our ability to fulfill our pre-life birth plan and earthly purpose.

Knowledge of the Afterlife and recognition of our pre-life soul plan assist us on our healing journey. Discovering our life purpose through resolving past and present trauma will help us become aware of our intended path. Relinquish control of the external world and accept that the only thing we can control is ourselves. Do not set out to change others; we can only change ourselves. When we increase our vibration, others around us will be positively influenced to raise theirs. We will then attract similar situations and people who radiate a higher enlightened frequency. When we project forgiveness and love into the Universe, the world grows in love and compassion for all humanity.

Acceptance of a Higher Power that loves us unconditionally will strengthen our faith and purpose. Accept that we are all connected to every soul, and we are all an essential part of Source. Our relationship with our Creator is a symbiotic connection. We are all on this journey together. We are never separate from other souls or from Source. I will use the analogy of a large body of water representing Source to help us understand our spiritual unity. Every drop of water is an individual soul. We become one within that body of water yet always maintain our unique characteristics. No drop of water can exist without the other to create the whole. When we begin to heal ourselves, our vibrational energy will influence the collective towards healing the Universe.

COMMUNICATION WITH SOULS IN THE AFTERLIFE

Communication with spiritual beings is possible for everyone. Love is the language of the soul. When we embark on our journeys of soul healing, we open space in our hearts for connection with our crossed-over loved ones' spiritual essence. This can occur at any time in our spiritual journeys, and manifests uniquely to each individual. Finding our highest truth through healing our most painful emotions will open a greater path for communication to develop.

Realizing that we co-exist in a physical world of humanity and a spiritual world of divine knowing is an essential tool in this process. As humans, we experience life through our senses in a low-density state. As spiritual beings, we are vibrating at a higher intensity, which enables us to discover our deepest purpose and truth. Prayer, meditation, intentional thought and gratitude are all methods of accessing awareness of a Higher Power and spiritual communication. The veil between our two worlds is progressively becoming thinner. When we open our hearts to this realization, our communication with the Spiritual Realm becomes less complex and more transparent. Our crossed-over loved ones will relay messages in a variety of forms. While we meditate or dream, we may visualize pictures or images. We can relate to these images because they have specific meaning to us personally. Our loved ones will often send symbols that you individually can best understand. A yellow rose, for example, may signify their favorite flower. It could also represent a gesture of forgiveness. You are the most reliable source for decoding these messages.

Communication predominantly comes in the form of telepathic messages, but you may occasionally hear spoken words. Generally, this manifests as a single word and not complete phrases or sentences. Most communication comes from a place of inner knowing or a sensation of receiving a message unlike any other form of communication on Earth. Attempt to view this form of communication as heart centered and not brain dominant. Try to accept these messages with openness and gratitude, as it takes an enormous amount of energy from the spirit of our loved ones to convey this precious gift to us.

Spiritual beings use many forms of energy to create a conduit of spiritual communication. They may send meaningful songs when you are thinking of them or to get your attention. Embrace how you feel during these moments, as that is the intention of all spiritual communication. Do not allow your ego to cast doubt around these occurrences. You may also notice a number or sequence of numbers consistently in a variety of circumstances. Remember, there are no coincidences. This is all synchronicity playing out for your enlightenment. My dad alerts us to notice repeating numbers on a daily basis. His favorite is 11:11. Interestingly, November 11th is his birthday. In Canada, we celebrate this day as Remembrance Day. This number also has sentimental ties to my childhood that I hold dear to my heart. There is an emotional energy connected to all communications from spiritual beings. Pay special attention to those feelings, as this is the most important aspect of the message. Our crossed-over loved ones main intent is to infuse you with their unconditional love and protection. Love is the foundation that everything else is built upon. The underlying theme to all communication is to reassure us that they are joyous and content in their heavenly home. It takes faith, trust and acceptance to fully receive messages from our crossed-over loved ones. There is a unique quality to the message being sent that alerts us to "hear" this communication. Use your intuitive instincts to dominate your ego-based brain. Think less; feel more. This is heart-centered expression at the highest soul level.

I have been blessed with the ability to communicate with souls in the Afterlife. I strengthen my gift by putting into practice the tools and knowledge I am sharing with you. One form of communication is through automatic writing, where crossed-over souls can tap into my abilities to transmit their messages from the Heavenly Realm. I am the vessel they use to convey their messages to loved ones here on Earth. Spirit can be quite persistent in getting their intentions across to me. There are times I wake in the middle of the night to write down a message being sent to me. When I read the communiqué in the morning, I am often amazed at the information I have received. I am also blessed to be able to communicate directly with souls who have crossed over. They send messages through visions, spoken words, symbols, smells and through a "knowing" internal sensation that reverberates within my soul. I am especially sensitive to a soul's underlying individual characteristics and who they are at their core essence. The messages are of a healing nature and have a positive emotional underlying note.

Highly intuitive people may also have strong empathic abilities. I have always internalized the emotions of others around me and can become overwhelmed with the intensity of their feelings. If you have the trait of being an empath, ensure that you are grounding and protecting yourself from the acute and powerful emotions of others in the Earthly and Heavenly Realms. This can be accomplished by going into nature and absorbing her energy and healing power. Meditation, prayer, and purposeful thought are also grounding techniques. Orientate yourself to the here and now to achieve instantaneous grounding when you become overwhelmed with intense emotion. I will visualize wrapping myself in a protective fluffy white blanket of positive love energy to block out the messages I am not ready to receive at that time. You may also "zip up" a virtual sweater to block out energy that does not serve you.

Learn to distinguish your emotions from those around you. This can be challenging and requires active participation to be able to process your personal feelings from someone else's emotions. As an empath, we must understand that our intentions and motivations are powerful. It is not our job to take away any person's pain or interfere with their healing journey. We must allow others to embrace and resolve their personal challenges through the avenue that is most effective for them. When we internalize their suffering, we are creating a negative balance within ourselves and are selfishly denying our loved ones their learning and growing opportunities. As we know, life will soon create another circumstance for that person that may be even more challenging to resolve. This is one of the most important realizations an empath must consider while attempting to assist others on their healing journey. You can remain a support person as they navigate the hardships of life, but remain vigilant to not inserting your strong empathic influences into their process. Create balance, boundaries and awareness to effectively use empathy as a healing skill without giving your power away.

I am eternally grateful for my ability of being able to communicate with Spirit. I work diligently on strengthening my skills when I am called to do so. We all have the capability, on some level, to connect with our loved ones in the Heavenly Realm. As spiritual beings, we are all gifted with varying degrees of psychic skill. As individual as each person is, so are our abilities and potential. We become aware of our spiritual proficiency in a variety of formats. Highly evolved souls recognize their capabilities from a very early age. Many people have been alerted to their abilities through extreme life events. Near-Death Experiences, Out-of-Body Experiences, traumatic experiences in childhood, war and extreme violence are only a few of these circumstances. We may also become enlightened to our spiritual strengths through deep meditation, dreams, hypnosis, yoga or prayer that connect us to our Higher Soul Selves.

As spiritual beings, we all possess the potential to have psychic or intuitive knowing. Simply being aware of this knowledge allows us to access and develop these abilities. We are all capable of enhancing our innate psychic strengths through a variety of methods. Embrace the avenue you feel most comfortable with. Release the fear to come from a love-centered approach. When you receive positive affirmations, you may want to explore more advanced forms of spiritual communication in the future.

Mediums have psychic awareness and are also blessed with the ability to communicate with those who have crossed over into the Higher Realms. All mediums are psychic, but not all people with psychic abilities naturally have mediumship capability. Mediums are unique individuals with varying degrees of expertise and proficiency. All psychic mediums are not created equal. Some mediums choose to be in the spotlight, but many talented mediums will never publicly expose themselves. It is a brave soul who shares their gifts with the world. The more the exposure, the increased possibility of ridicule and cruelty exist. Historically, people with psychic mediumship abilities were marginalized to the fringes of society, tortured and even murdered.

There are so many misconceptions regarding what a medium is in our society today. This prevents many mediums from fully declaring our abiities or acknowledging ourselves as mediums. I know that I have had much reluctance in accepting myself as a medium and publicly exposing my strengths, even to those in my inner circle. Many people base their knowledge about mediumship from movies and media that present a warped view in contrast to what a medium truly is. There is also the historical representation of mediums being opportunistic frauds in undesirable roles in society. One of the most damaging perceptions of mediums originates from biblical misinterpretations. In actuality, mediums receive their abilities and communication through the Highest Power in the Universe. We have been blessed with the most precious God-given skills available to humankind. Authentic mediums receive their communications from a heart-centered love energy that is divinely inspired.

When I discussed mediumship with my cousin, he was unsure about the term medium. In spiritual mediumship, prophet may be a more accurate description for these divine abilities. From a theological perspective, prophets receive their direction through a Higher Power to help the collective navigate life challenges. Prophets are individuals who are in communication with a Divine Being and serve as an intermediary with humanity to deliver messages of a healing nature. There are people who gravitate to lower energy experiences, but these individuals are not considered mediums or prophets in the true sense of the word. It is perfectly acceptable to be skeptical regarding the authenticity of some people who claim to be mediums. Research and investigate any person that you are inquiring about for a professional reading. Some mediums have deep generational abilities that enhance their mediumship skill level. The majority of mediums have to work very hard at perfecting their craft. I like to use the analogy of how people learn to play an instrument. Some people are born with incredible natural capability, but the majority of us have to practice many hours before we are able to reasonably play that instrument. Mediumship is similar in many ways. Mediums must continually work on becoming more proficient in their stengths. With each reading with a fellow human being, we learn and grow. Even mediums who have an innate ability will continue to expand their knowledge and skills through growing and learning like everyone else on Earth. We are mothers, sons, friends, firefighters, social workers, nurses, and ordinary people you encounter in your daily life. Mediums are represented by normal human beings who are blessed with a beautiful skill from God. Society is only recently recognizing the great contribution people with these abilities can have in our daily existence.

One of the most challenging skills for a medium is to learn the language of Spirit. Spiritual communication often comes in the form of symbols. Every symbol has a specific meaning for each individual medium. It may take years to fully comprehend this spiritual foreign language. Every soul in the Afterlife has their unique way of communicating. Their communication strengths often reflect how they spoke in the Earthly Realm. Some souls are proficient in their communication competency, and others may struggle. As mediums, we must be sensitive to the underlying intent of the message without inserting our personal interpretations. This can be a very difficult aspect of the process to perfect. Our mission as mediums is to convey the message from a crossed-over soul with honesty and as directly as possible. It is a delicate process that will never be perfect. On this Earthly Realm, we misinterpret communication every day with people we are conversing with face to face. Imagine how difficult it is to communicate with spiritual beings who have to use alternate modes of relaying messages to us on Earth.

Each medium develops their unique personalized communication with souls in the Higher Realms. Many develop their intuitive expressions through a portal commonly referred to as a "Claire." The predominant Claires are: clairvoyance, which is a psychic site or seeing images; clairaudience is hearing voices; clairsentience is recognizing feelings and claircognizance is an internal knowing. Clairalience is psychic smelling and clairgustance is the ability to psychically taste. Mediums are able to access these avenues of communication with varying degrees of strength and competency. Most mediums have a few predominant Claires that they are proficient in and use for their communication. Spiritual beings choose which mode of expression they are strongest in and recognize what Claire the medium excels at. Every situation is unique, and both Spirit and mediums have to work very hard at receiving and relaying messages.

    I have been blessed to experience all these forms of Claires with crossed-over souls during my lifetime. Some I experience only on rare occasions and others are present during most communications with spiritual beings in the Afterlife. I work to strengthen all my abilities, but I ultimately have little control around how crossed-over souls convey messages. There are times when Spirit may call my name, send me a telepathic message, make me taste a certain food and create a sensation of how they crossed over, all within seconds of coming into my awareness. As mediums, we have to adapt to a variety of communications simultaneously and then be receptive to the message being conveyed. My father presenting himself physically after his passing was my most profound spiritual experience. I will share that amazing visit with my dad later in the chapter. I am grateful for every communication in any format that I receive from Spirit. I am often alerted to an incoming message initially by a smell or a knocking sound. Insistent spirits will occasionally call my name out loud. When a spiritual being is very close by, I experience a ringing in my ears and a distinct shivering sensation throughout my body. I have tasted blood or vomit if this was significant to that soul's crossing. I have also tasted wonderful food and beverages in celebratory settings. I often smell cigarette smoke prior to my mother-in-law's communications. My paternal grandmother precedes her arrival through the smell of insulin. It is interesting to note that many smells that other people tolerate overwhelm me and often make me nauseous. It is like the dial for my senses is frequently turned on ten. I am an introvert at heart, and it is often challenging to be in large groups. I love the smell of leather, wood, or smoke from wood fires and do not find many natural smells as offensive as some people do.

    My most predominant abilities are being able to feel a spiritual being's personality and emotions they wish to convey. I receive their communication through an internal knowing and even directly through words or phrases. I believe my calling as a medium is to channel messages from the Spiritual Realm and to mainly convey these revelations through my writing. My strengths are not in doing individual readings for people, although if a spiritual being is insistent, I am able to relay messages to a loved one. As mediums, we must all recognize where our capabilities are best utilized. There are so many talented and amazing mediums, but you must do your research to find one that suits your needs the most appropriately.

There are great responsibilities that are a critical aspect of having psychic mediumship abilities. We must always be considerate to balancing the messages received and when to relay the information to loved ones in this Earthly Realm. Those in deep grief may not be receptive or able to hear from their crossed-over loved ones immediately. It can be very challenging to know when the most appropriate time is to convey the messages to loved ones here on Earth. As mediums, we all must incorporate our abilities into our daily lives and learn to be comfortable with the role we embrace. It is difficult to imagine all the challenges that mediums face. Spirit can be very intrusive in our daily existence. Many mediums find it arduous to balance receiving spirit messages and maintaining a normal routine. The process of receiving, understanding and relaying spirit communication can be very exhausting. Many deny their gifts due to the prejudice and fear surrounding those that are perceived as unique in this world. Whatever our role in this realm is, some people can be judgmental and cruel towards anyone they do not understand or view as being different. We are all spiritual souls in human bodies trying to navigate our place in this extremely challenging existence.

As humans, we are all blessed with innate psychic knowing. Everyone has the potential to strengthen their skills to enhance their daily lives, regardless of their current psychic knowledge. All of us are capable, on some level, to be able to communicate with our crossed-over loved ones. By raising our vibration through forgiveness, gratitude and love, we are increasing the probability for communication with our spiritual loved ones to occur. The closer we get to our Higher Soul Self, the thinner the veil to the Afterlife becomes. We do not have to reach the highest state of Nirvana to accomplish this level of awareness. Simply alerting the Universe of our intent to begin our journey will activate a shift into a higher enlightened energy state. It is possible to increase our ability through repetition and perseverance to strengthen our psychic muscle.

Now that we have been given knowledge on how to develop our psychic awareness and how communication works with our loved ones in the Spiritual Realm, we can take steps to strengthen our bond with people in our lives today. This is an opportunity to restructure our relationship with family and friends here on Earth and begin to initiate our eternal connection with them. This dialogue can take place as soon as you feel comfortable. When we become aware of the inevitable crossing over of a loved one, we are given a great opportunity to open our communication with them now and into the Afterlife. It may initially be uncomfortable speaking to our loved ones who are nearing the end of their time on this Earthly Realm, but the rewards can be life-altering. Our society is so afraid of death, and many fear even speaking about a subject that has been taboo for many years. When we are able to discuss our fears and concerns about dying, we are able to alleviate some of the fear surrounding this very natural aspect of living. The discussions we have before our loved ones end their journey on Earth can greatly increase our ability to communicate with them in the Heavenly Realm.

Prior to my father crossing over, we discussed how he would let us know when he arrived in Heaven. We reviewed about five specific events that may occur after a soul reaches the Afterlife. My father's strict Catholic upbringing had not prepared him for this concept, so I had to encourage him to speak openly about this subject. I mentioned that spiritual beings may manipulate energy; place money in the path of family members (like quarters or dimes); find misplaced items; move objects; or direct feathers, birds or butterflies towards loved ones. Dale mentioned he would love to come back as an eagle, and my dad thought that was a great idea. This became a very beautiful memory for all of us present. It does not have to be a threatening situation and can be approached with a lighthearted attitude to alleviate the heaviness of speaking to loved ones about the demise of our earthly life.

Astoundingly, within weeks of my father crossing over, he fulfilled all five of the scenarios that we discussed. He still continues to send us many validating signs and symbols, even seven years after the anniversary of his transition to the Higher Realms. The first incident occurred the evening of his funeral. I had placed my dad's R.C.M.P. boots on a table as part of a display to honor him. When we returned home, I heard "check the boot." I immediately discovered $100 secured in a money clip in the toe of the boot. As a police officer, my father never hid money in their home, as he knew this was a dangerous practice. My mom has moved twice in the past six years, and she does not have access to cash due to her dementia. Despite that, we still find money in the most unusual locations in her small apartment.

The next validation was through a set of keys. My parents had misplaced their lock box keys for the safe at their bank. While dad was alive, we had searched for two months to find those keys. A few days after dad's passing, I was compelled to walk into his office. It was a cloudy day, but there was a stream of light focused on a container on a top shelf. I heard "look in the container." When I did, I found two sets of keys for their bank lock box. We had previously looked in that location multiple times.

The following incident occurred around electricity. The heater in my mom's bedroom started making loud banging noises around four o'clock a.m. for a few nights in a row. This was witnessed by my sister, who was visiting with my mom after dad's passing. Maintenance checked, and there were no issues with her heating system. I suggested to Mom to acknowledge Dad if this happened again. Interestingly, this was the same time my dad got off his shift when they were a young honeymoon couple. Mom and Dad always joked that this was the reason they had three children in under three years. The next night at the same time, the banging began again. Mom thanked Dad for coming to her but gently informed him that she needed her sleep. He did not choose this method of getting Mom's attention again but instead insinuated his presence in many other formats in the future.

One evening, we all went out for a family dinner. When we returned to Mom's apartment after supper, five pictures hanging on the wall were tilted sideways. They were all pictures of family. The scenery pictures were not altered, except for a picture of an eagle that I had never noticed before. My cousin, who knew nothing of my conversation with Dad, told me of an eagle sitting on her fence for over twenty-four hours shortly after my dad's crossing over.

My father sends white feathers to many members of our family. This began immediately after his passing and occurs regularly to this day. Many times, there are no pillows or any viable source that would contain feathers anywhere near the vicinity where they are found. My grandchildren call all white feathers "Papa feathers," because we find so many of them. My granddaughter's young friend handed me a large white feather while we were walking along the beach. She stopped and told me, "Your daddy wants you to have this feather." She had no knowledge of my father's crossing over, and we were not discussing my dad at the time. I still have that feather on my meditation table. When I spiritually questioned my father why he sent feathers, my dad manifested a vision from my early childhood. I saw my grandma and myself on a dirt floor basement. We were filling pillows with feathers taken from the chickens on their farm. This is one of my prominent memories with my grandma, and I still have that pillow today. This is the same grandmother who had diabetes and comes to me by first infusing the air with the smell of insulin. I can readily identify her through this scent and an emotional gentleness that is uniquely her.

My granddaughter began "playing games with" and talking to her papa within days of his passing. She would act out "Ring around the Rosie" and tickle games with papa in her crib. I have multiple documented events that are communications from my dad with our grandchildren and family. My father's soul is very strong, and he is a great communicator from the Afterlife. This has been confirmed through many incidents, my personal communications with my dad and through mediums we have had readings with. My dad's strong energy and dynamic personality have remained consistent on both sides of the veil. Our souls do not lose their core essence and always retain who we are at a deep heartfelt level.

The personal gift I cherish the most from my dad is the strengthening of my medium and psychic abilities. After Dad passed, he opened a portal to the Higher Energy Realms for me to access. He has sent me so many spiritual revelations and personal strengths. With my spirit team, my dad is instrumental in supporting me with writing this book. My dad knows me better than anyone from the other side of the veil. I believe he gently controls how much knowledge and information I am given. He understands that I would completely exhaust myself if I was given my abilities all at once. I am so blessed to have the support and love of my father from before and after his transition. I feel my relationship with my dad is stronger in spirit than it ever was here on Earth. It is possible for every person to have a connection with loved ones who have crossed over to the other side of the veil. Stay open and committed to the process, and you will achieve a bond that is unique to you.

Our spirit guides also attempt to communicate with us from the Heavenly Realm. You are encouraged to make requests and ask questions of your spirit guides. Do not block the answers out of fear. Ask for positive and loving messages. You will not receive messages that do not serve your higher purpose. You will receive what you need, not necessarily what you desire. The messages are gifts to help us realize our soul's life plan. By placing our ego to the side, we are more receptive to the healing messages. Approach this as an exercise for your soul. Build the muscle for spirituality by repetition and calling on your guides to assist you. This is similar to strengthening your physical body through repetitive exercises, except now you are building up your spiritual strength. Gain trust and confidence in what your spirit guides are telling you. You will recognize the positive sensation within your solar plexus (gut) when the message resonates with you. I will often get chills or a sensation along my spine and goose bumps or shivers throughout my body to validate the message I am receiving. You may visualize images or words through your "third eye," which is located between your eyes and slightly above the brow line. While meditating, center your energy here. If you experience an uncomfortable feeling, know that this is your ego interfering.

Everyone is capable of experiencing communication with our loved ones' souls and spirit guides. It requires faith, trust, hard work, repetition and an open heart and mind. Each occurrence will be as unique as you are. Be grateful for even the most subtle messages, as our loved ones have to work extremely hard to connect with us. Receive every communication with love, compassion and gratitude.

Our loved ones may use dreams to alert us of their existence. Dreams create the ideal environment for a visit or vision to occur. The characteristics of a visit or vision from spiritual beings are more organized, realistic and usually contain a theme that has an emotional component. Words may not be spoken, but there is always an underlying message through feeling or sensing an emotion of love and compassion. Dreams tend to be bizarre and disorganized and are generally forgotten upon awakening. You may witness a visit within a dream state, but you will remember the visit and its significance. Visits and visions are recalled in vivid detail for a lifetime, and the emotional impact is everlasting. Your crossed-over loved ones are communicating with you to help alleviate your fear about the death of the body. They reassure us that our soul continues on forever and we have nothing to be afraid of. They want us to know that all is forgiven, and they see the whole picture for the purpose of our lives from the other side. They understand their role in our life journeys and know the intention of our interactions is ultimately to discover our Higher Soul Selves and return to divine love that we all are at the core of our being.

Ask your loved ones to come through before you fall asleep or while meditating. Do not be discouraged if you do not get an immediate response. There are many factors in our lives that contribute to our ability to receive messages. Accepting the truth of eternal life, learning how to raise our vibration, connecting our energy level with our crossed-over loved ones and patience in the process are all components that contribute to communication. Even with my dedication and abilities, it may be months before a crossed over soul responds to my messages. I understand that I am not meant to receive a message at that time or my loved one is creating an alternative method of responding to my request. It is crucial to note that our crossed-over loved ones are acutely aware of what is required for our growth. They will not interfere if it does not serve a higher purpose for us or others close to us. If you are not meant to receive a direct message, your loved ones will find another method of communication that is less threatening to you. Avoid dismissing any information as insignificant or irrelevant. Our loved ones are aware of the method that is best suited to us. Many people would be overwhelmed to receive direct communication with a spiritual being, so a soul may choose a more subtle approach. There are very few people who are prepared and capable of receiving messages from the Heavenly Realm in a straightforward manner.

Remember, it takes an enormous amount of energy for our loved ones to slow their vibration to meet ours. It is important to directly request assisstance from our loved ones in the Heavenly Realm. They are with us when we require their presence in our lives, but will not interfere unless we are open to their guidance. This does not mean you need to censor your communication with your crossed-over loved ones. They love when we speak to and think of them or celebrate the life we shared with them. When you speak about your crossed-over loved ones, do so in the present tense. They appreciate being a part of celebrations and during important milestones in our lives.

Our vibrational energy increases during meditation, in a dream state or with intentional thought. Alcohol or drug usage decreases our ability to connect with crossed-over loved ones. I have noted that caffeine, in moderation, may increase our ability to raise our vibration. To synchronize our vibration with theirs takes work and patience on both sides of the veil. A very effective way of raising our vibration in our daily lives is through blessings and gratitude. When we send messages of gratitude into the Universe for our loved ones and for our life experiences, we increase our energy frequency. By sending blessings or positive intentions to those we feel have done us wrong, we exponentially increase our vibrational frequency. When we consistently activate these practices in our lives, with pure and loving intentions, our vibrational levels increase. The Universe responds by sending us positive people and experiences. We are also increasing the likelihood of communicating with our crossed-over loved ones and spirit guides.

Our ability to communicate with spiritual beings varies greatly with each individual. I strengthen my skill by consistently using all the tools I have shared with you. We all receive messages from our crossed-over loved ones. We can fine tune our potential to recognize and receive these communications by opening our hearts and minds. Look for synchronicity in your daily experiences. These are safe and acceptable methods for our loved ones to send us messages. Synchronicities may alert you to more intense communication from the souls of your crossed-over loved ones. Place ego and fear to the side and allow faith and love to take their place. Messages may come in direct ways but will likely take a unique path to get your attention. Attempt to remove any self-doubt around receiving messages from loved ones. Embrace the emotion experienced, as that is their primary motivation for all communication.

My most vivid and concrete communication came in the form of a visitation from my dad. My sister noticed an open house for the home we grew up in during our teenage years. My mom, brother, sister and I decided to go to our previous home together. The memories flooded back for all of us. My heart and soul were exceptionally open on this day. As we were preparing to leave, I felt a sharp increase in vibrational energy. Directly in front of me, shimmering particles of light began to take shape. I felt an electrical buzzing energy at a level I had never experienced before. This molecular formation took on a human form, and my handsome father was standing in front of me. He radiated an inner light that was difficult to look at directly. His brilliant blue eyes and beautiful smile were shining the brightest. He appeared around thirty-five years old and was wearing his Red Serge (the formal Royal Canadian Mounted Police uniform). I have never seen my father look more radiant and filled with such pure joy. At the exact moment I visualized Dad, my mom said, "Nick is here." Keep in mind, my mom's ability to express emotions was compromised due to her dementia. She felt my dad as clearly as I saw and experienced his presence. My siblings did not visualize him but also felt his energetic peacefulness and overwhelming love. This miraculous event will forever be engraved on my heart. I am eternally grateful to have been given this incredible gift of witnessing my father's earthly presence once more. He never spoke a word, but the love and peace he radiated will forever be imprinted on all our souls.

When I receive messages from spiritual beings, I will often ask for clarification. I request simple and meaningful validations when I am unsure of the message being given. Many times, the communication is so precise that clarification is not necessary. Every soul has their own unique way of transmitting information. Some are great communicators and others struggle. How effectively they spoke with people in the Earthly Realm is often indicative of how effective their spiritual language is from the Heavenly Realm. Also, the more advanced the soul is, the better their communication skills become. As previously stated, understanding spiritual language is similar to learning a foreign language on Earth. Spirit may send symbols or images, and it can be challenging to comprehend the underlying messages of those symbols. With perseverance and practice, it is possible to learn this unique language of spiritual communication. When you have a close relationship with a spiritual being, communication may flow smoother and with greater clarity once the intensity of grief lifts.

It is natural for communication with our intimate crossed-over loved ones to not be received while in the immediate depths of grief. Even the most gifted mediums may not be able to initially contact their closest loved ones. It is very difficult for spiritual beings to break through relentless grief. I am truly blessed to have been able to communicate with my father so soon after his crossing over. My initial communication occurred at four o'clock a.m. while writing his eulogy. He surrounded me in a fog or cloud-like embrace that felt like a warm and loving hug. I experienced a love energy from every single particle within that haze surrounding me.

Receiving messages through electricity, radio or phone waves is quite common. The vibration of the electrical energy is helpful for increasing spiritual energy. Spirit may cause clocks to stop or fast-forward at will. A significant song may play repeatedly on the radio, whether the radio is turned on or not. The song may have a personal meaning or contain a special message when most needed. Cell phones are also a popular tool for spirit communication. Spiritual beings are resourceful and will use whatever energy source is available to them at the time. Electrical surges or outages occur frequently around people with strong psychic and mediumship abilities. My Spiritual Self is grateful for any communication with spiritual beings, but my human self gets distracted when I am inconvenienced by electrical manipulations. These energy surges occur quite regularly in my daily life.

Messages will often be received more intensely when we are in a relaxed state. While I was getting a massage, the clock on the wall rapidly began progressing ahead in time. My therapist was quite shocked by this, especially when the clock returned to the appropriate time the moment my treatment was complete. I love to share my spiritual experiences with other people and help them accept what they are witnessing is a miraculous event.

The most incredible electrical experience occurred about eighteen months after my dad crossed over. My brother was still in deep grief and felt guilt surrounding our dad's passing. I asked Dad to send me a message reassuring my brother that he was at peace and was not holding any negative emotions around his crossing over. During meditation, my dad sent me an explosion of electrical fireworks in my mind. I told my brother to look for electrical signs confirming our dad had no ill will surrounding his passing. Within hours, my brother's medical clinic lost all electricity. It was restored in under thirty minutes, but losing electricity in the clinic had never previously occurred. Within twenty-four hours, my mom's apartment block lost all its power as well as the city block my son and his family lived on. The electricity also went out in my nephew's home thousands of kilometers away in Vancouver, Canada. The next morning the power went out in my gym. The bizarre part of that is it only occurred in the room where I was participating in a group class. When I stepped out of the gym that morning, there were hundreds of white feathers lining the curb in the parking lot. I still have a picture of that amazing site. The weather was beautiful with no storms in the forecast, and all our locations were miles apart. My dad has always had a larger-than-life personality and that continues into the Afterlife in many meaningful experiences. My brother received our father's messages with love, self-forgiveness and acceptance. This was a pivotal incident that helped our entire family continue on our healing journey. By becoming aware of everyday miracles, you can recognize and celebrate your connection to loved ones who have crossed over.

I was hesitant to include this next communication from Spirit, as this person is well known and beloved. I heard, "I want to be included." This spiritual being strongly encouraged me, on numerous occasions, that his soul message was important to convey to the world. I feel this Spirit trusted me with his message for a variety of reasons. I have had many synchronicities in my life with this soul being. I understand on a deep level why this spiritual being feels safe with me and trusts that his message will be heard in an intentional and loving way. He took me through his transition to the Afterlife in a clear and unemotional recounting of his last moments on Earth. He spoke of his loved ones with heartfelt emotion and tenderness. He informed me that his "life and death was pre-planned so many others would learn and live." To see a personality so seemingly invincible cross over influenced many to cease their destructive behaviors and choose to live a healthier lifestyle. He also informed me, "I have not reincarnated because I have much to recover from." He stressed that his soul is at peace and we should not mourn his passing. Since his crossing over, people have given testimonials about how this person's demise directly influenced their decision to radically change their lives in a healthy way.

When I asked this person why he chose me to relay his message, he informed me that my dad was instrumental in his choice to use me as a vessel. He said that my writing would bring an important message to the world, and he would like to be a part of that. He stated that he felt close to my dad in spirit. There are many parallels with this person and my father when they were in this Earthly Realm and in the Afterlife. He informed me that my dad "mirrored the life he could have led in a different time."

His most important message is one of awareness to humanity. He confirmed that "this time is a critical moment for us to awaken to our personal spiritual identity. If we do not confront what is painful and traumatic in our life today, we will miss a great opportunity to heal the Universe." He stressed that the thinning of the veil is a temporary occurrence and that we must take advantage of this great awakening now.

I am eternally grateful that this powerful soul shared so many inspirational messages with me. His communication was very clear and definitive, but I still requested validation because of the importance of his message. The next night, I had a confirming and meaningful vision that left a lasting impression on me. I rarely dream in full color, but on this night I visualized a gorgeous double rainbow with shades I had never witnessed here on Earth. Each spectrum of color had multitudes of other hues that do not exist on this Earthly Realm. This symbol of a rainbow has a few validating messages within the image for me personally. It is an emotional memory I share with my father from a family vacation in Hawaii. It is also a confirming personal validation from the sender of this message.

He then elaborated on the original message he sent me. He stressed once again that "these are crucial times. The veil is thinning and an opening is being created, like a portal, to the other side. This is the moment to confront the fear, the pain and the traumatic in your life." He confirmed that our Universe performs in cycles, and if we do not act at this time we will have missed a great opportunity to heal individually and collectively. I felt his passion and urgency in getting his message across to me.

This soul worked very persistently and uniquely in his communication with me. He was able to penetrate my self-doubt to have his message heard. His confidence in me keeps me strong and focused on my mission to spread soul knowledge and Divine Love into the Universe.

I am amazed and grateful for any positive interaction I have with each spiritual being from the Afterlife. Every experience is distinctive and leaves an imprint on my soul. Even when the loss of a loved one is extremely painful, the messages I receive fill me with a sense of joy and peace. Soon after a good friend of ours crossed over, I began to receive multiple messages from him. He actually took me through his passing, where two separate events led to the demise of his earthly body. I felt chest pain followed by overwhelming vertigo and weakness all over my body. He reassuringly conveyed to me that he was totally at peace and was truly happy. I told my husband immediately about our friend's visitation. Later that evening, Dale was notified about all the details of our friend's passing. My vision was accurate in great detail. It was important for our friend to let me know how he crossed, but he quickly made me feel that it was only an instant in time. His main focus was to instill an enormous sense of joy within me that he was experiencing in the Afterlife. His fun and flirtatious personality infiltrates all our communications. His teasing ways come through in unique avenues. While riding my bike along a path parallel to the Gulf of Mexico, he will send me to specific "In memory" benches which have elements of his name on them. I will then hear his wonderful laugh and feel his delight. He has also shown me that he connects with my dad in the Heavenly Realm. My father is as socially active in Heaven as he was on Earth. My dad throws great Afterlife parties, and our friend is always invited!

Throughout the years, my first boyfriend occasionally reached out to me from the Spiritual Realm. He had crossed over to the Heavenly Realm at a young age. Very recently, he sent me a message wanting to be included in the documenting of my spirit communications for my book. Many of the memories we experienced together came rushing back.

First love often leaves a lasting and impressionable impact, which was definitely true for me. I was young and fell in love quickly and intensely. Unexpectedly, he broke my heart when he decided to date my younger sister. I was devastated and quickly learned a lesson to protect my heart in future relationships.

Years later, we serendipitously met up and were able to honestly discuss our past history. We were able to overcome our past and had a wonderful evening of dancing and laughter with our friends. That was the last time I saw him on this Earthly Realm.

He has occasionally sent me lighthearted messages from the Spiritual Realm over the years. Recently, he sent me a very strong message of apology for hurting me so long ago. His visitation occurred within a dream state. My sister, myself and my old boyfriend were all sitting on a couch together, and I was joking about how he left me for her. He then looked up at me with tears in his eyes and sincerely asked for my forgiveness. I granted him that forgiveness without hesitation. We embraced, and I felt a powerful love infused into my being. This was not a romantic love but a much more meaningful soul love that I carry with me to this day.

I recognized that the hurt I experienced from this incident as a young woman influenced future relationships for me. I became more cautious and guarded my heart with vigilant awareness. This was not a negative lesson and felt like one that I required during this lifetime. I now understand that part of our soul contract was to alert me to what required healing within myself. Retrospectively, I realized that in relationships I would change critical aspects of myself to attempt to be the person I felt my partner wanted me to be. I also put up barriers to protect my heart and shield my truth. It took many years and a few crucial relationships for me to be confidently myself and to allow someone fully into my heart.

The only person to penetrate all those vulnerabilities is my husband, Dale. In the early years of our marriage, this came out in sometimes intense ways. It was a challenge for both of us to balance our strong personalities and insecurities. I am now able to accept love without giving up a core aspect of myself. I am once again reminded that every critical interaction in our lives is a pre-planned event to alert us to the lessons we need to learn in this lifetime. I am eternally grateful for all those experiences, even when they were extremely painful and challenging at the time.

There is another aspect to soul communication that I feel is important to convey. It reinforces how the power of prayer is not just a platitude but has the potential to create miraculous results. This became evident during the birth of our good friend's grandchild. Prior to his entrance into this world, I had received a spiritual message that there were going to be serious challenges surrounding his birth. Our friend's grandson became critically ill shortly after delivery. His grandma immediately started a prayer chain, which grew to include people from around the world.

I remained awake during most of the night to actively pray and worked tirelessly to surround the baby with love and strength. I became a vessel to help direct and channel all the prayer energy manifested into a direct path towards this innocent soul. Early the following morning, I witnessed an incredible vision. The baby's soul was surrounded by angels and close family members that had previously crossed over. I also observed the power of all the prayers being sent. It came across as not just a feeling but an actual tangible event that cocooned the baby in the most exquisite love energy. I viewed the baby's soul teetering on the edge of the veil to the Heavenly Realm. The soul appeared peaceful and comfortable with either decision. I truly felt the power of prayer gently guide the baby's soul back over to this side of the veil. His soul has shown us the miracle of prayer and faith, and I feel his journey here will have a beautiful impact on this Earthly Realm.

There are times when the message received from a crossed-over soul is so strong that it amazes me to the core of my being. Last summer, I was riding my bike behind my late mom-in-law's previous residence. I heard my mother-in-law and her mom giggling, and they were both super excited to tell me some great news. The message was very clear and direct. They informed me about my niece becoming pregnant that upcoming fall. They also confirmed that this baby would be a healthy little girl. I immediately pulled over and sent a text message to my sister-in-law about being a grandma to her first granddaughter. Also, it was her son's birthday that day, which I had not been previously aware of.

Around Christmas time, we found out that our niece was three months pregnant. Shortly after, it was confirmed they were having a baby girl. This message was incredibly powerful for me in many ways. I loved the joy surrounding this communication. I was truly amazed at how my crossed-over mother-in-law was aware of this soul entering into a future child. This confirmed my truth regarding soul knowledge, pre-life planning and soul family. It brings me overwhelming joy to know that my mom-in-law and her mom are aware of and already have a relationship with this soul who recently entered our lives. I once again send gratitude to my family in the Afterlife for entrusting me with this miraculous news and confirmation of the cycle of our soul journey.

This next interaction with a crossed-over soul occurred just as I was finishing my book. This soul sent a clear and firm message that he wanted to share his message with family and friends.

Our experience began while we were vacationing at our winter home. Dale received a phone call from his good friend and mentor from his law enforcement days. Dale's friend sadly informed us that he was very ill with terminal cancer and only had months to live. Dale immediately booked a flight home to spend some time with him.

Two mornings later, I awoke from hearing a loud rhythmic whistling in my ear. I then heard a tinging metal sound followed by 1980s music. I immediately sensed our friend's soul energy and I strongly suspected that he had crossed over to the Afterlife. Dale had not received any further news regarding his friend's health status, so he decided to fly back home as scheduled.

The next morning, I woke up to the same whistling and the "knowing" that it was our friend. Dale was back at home waiting to hear from his buddy. I knew in my heart that our friend had crossed over, and Dale validated the sad news later that day. The information of his passing was delayed due to the family being in such shock around the very rapid demise of their loved one.

About two weeks later, our friend came to me in another visitation. He confirmed that it was definitely he who woke me up those two mornings. Our friend verified that the reason he used whistling was because he knew it would get my attention quickly. Our friend must have been aware of my strong aversion to whistling. My sister and I would relentlessly tease my younger brother when we were kids. My brother would retaliate by whistling in a very irritating way. This would immediately silence my sister and me. To this day, I find whistling very annoying, and it definitely gets my attention.

When a soul dies suddenly, there is sometimes a period of adjustment to their new surroundings in the Heavenly Realm. They have to find an alternative way to communicate that is understandable to us on Earth. Initially, our friend sent me auditory messages that he knew I could identify with. He was now able to communicate clearly and in a direct soul language that came through loud and clear. He confirmed with me that the tinging was from the sound heard after shutting off a Harley Davidson motorcycle. This was a memory we shared, as well as The Blues Brothers' 1980s music. He also informed me that he would send Dale dragonflies, as these were not as "wussy" as butterflies or birds. Our friend jokingly reprimanded Dale for not initially trusting my message from him weeks before. His comical personality and use of "colorful" language comes through strongly in all our communications. It is interesting to note that we can still swear in the Afterlife, and it is totally acceptable.

The next day I asked our friend for validation of all his messages to me. As I was riding my bike, he sent me to a memory bench along my morning path. This bench was the only bench he sent me to and was much further along the route than I normally would ride. Not only did this bench have his first name on it but also every letter of his last name contained within the name on the bench. I immediately took a picture of this and was overwhelmed with emotion from this concrete form of validation. There is obviously an attachment I have with souls and these special benches.

A few days later, I was on my daily bike ride when I witnessed a large dragonfly carrying a huge bug. I heard our friend clearly say, "That is nothing, wait 'till you see what I will show Dale today." My husband was with a friend golfing on a new course. A couple of hours later, Dale texted me and was shocked by the enormous number of dragonflies on the fairway. Neither of us have witnessed dragonflies in these numbers since coming to this area over twenty years ago. I had not even had time to inform Dale about my most recent message from our friend. These are all beautiful gifts from our crossed-over loved ones that we may celebrate as everyday miracles.

One of the most memorable aspects of our friend's message to me was "shutting off the Harley." He informed me that this was symbolic of his earthly life. He told me he "shut down" his physical life here on Earth but that he would be riding his Harley during many exciting adventures in the Afterlife. This is the same symbolism my father used when he sent me the image of an eagle soaring into the Higher Realms. I could feel the strong love our friend has for his family remaining here, and he wants them to know he will always be with them as their support and protector from the Heavenly Realm. Once again, our friend was persistent and determined to send his loving message across to me.

Our crossed-over loved ones souls can also be very helpful in everyday life occurrences. I will get messages that have a practical application, with instructions given in a direct manner. When items go missing, I will ask for soul support to help me find them. Because of my mom's dementia, she occasionally misplaces personal items. At one point she had lost her wedding rings for several days. I asked Dad for help in locating them and he replied, "under the bed." I knew my mom was not physically capable of placing her rings there, so I began by looking in her bathroom. I heard my dad chuckle and repeat that they were under the bed. I looked there and saw nothing, but I trusted my father, so I crawled under the bed. Embedded in the rug, in the center under her bed, were not only her wedding rings but also my father's. I will never know how they got there or why they were there. My mom was so thankful that her husband was still caring for her from Heaven. I believe that was the intended loving message from my dad to my mom.

Another form of communication is presentation of meditative visions manifesting into actual life events. My daughter's very good friend passed away as a young mother. She had been in our life for many years, and her passing was devastating. She came to me soon after her crossing over and was insistent on getting her message across. She brought me through a series of stunning visions. She took the form of a beautiful dove, soaring in peace and love. The day after I received that strong vision, my husband and I went out for dinner. I was sitting outdoors facing a large mirrored window. In the reflection, I saw a beautiful white bird soaring towards me from behind. It was so majestic and magical; I initially thought it was an illusion. I then noticed my husband's face and realized that he saw it too. This beautiful creature landed on a glass partition directly behind me and above my head. I could see this incredible image in the reflection but was unable to look directly at it. The energy and light that this being radiated was overwhelming for me. She stayed for a moment and then soared away. I knew in every fiber of my being that she was sent by my daughter's friend. My previously skeptical husband also felt that a powerful event had occurred.

The next day, I was telling my mom what had taken place the evening before. As we walked to my car, we were surrounded by fluffy white feathers. I had never seen feathers like this before. I accepted this as being a beautiful validation for the events experienced the night before. Later that day, my granddaughter told my daughter, "Mommy your friend went home, home to Heaven. She is happy there." When my daughter went to sleep that night, she was awakened with a song that was meaningful to her and her friend who had crossed over. The amazing aspect of this communication was that my daughter's phone was completely shut down and powered off.

My daughter and her best friend here on Earth often visit the graveside of their special friend. The three were inseparable in their high school years. Without fail, they are accompanied by three deer who present themselves during each visit to the gravesite. The deer represent the close friendship and bond these three young women will forever share. Her soul is exceptionally strong and remains a beautiful presence in all our lives. These are all messages and validations from the souls of our crossed-over loved ones. I am filled with love and gratitude for all my experiences and especially those of my family and friends.

Soul communication often manifests in subtle ways that may initially be challenging to recognize. Animals are a link to our spiritual connection through many avenues. They are sent to trigger awareness and faith in the Heavenly Realm. Animals may be used as a conduit to accept indirect messages that may not be received in other formats. Children who have experienced NDEs will often return and speak of animal spirits greeting them during their journey into the Spiritual Realm. My granddaughter recently told me that we meld our souls to spirit animals before we ascend to the Higher Realms. Her exact words were, "Grammy, after we die we meet up with our animals in Heaven. We mix together and then fly up into the sky."

We all have spirit animals that are powerful connections between Earth and the Heavenly Realm. Discovering our spirit animal is similar to becoming aware of our spirit guide. Use your tools of meditation, intentional thought, prayers and dreams to discover your spirit animal. Recall animal dreams, animals you are drawn to and those who are drawn to you and past connections to specific animals. In Indigenous culture, our spirit animal is our guardian spirit. When you discover your spirit animal or animals, seek what characteristics are significant to you and your life. Spirit animals may reflect traits and characteristics that alert us to aspects of ourselves that need to be acknowledged and healed. As we learn and grow in this lifetime, our primary spirit animal may change to help us recognize deeper issues that require addressing. Discovering our spirit animal is another tool in realizing our life purpose and triggers us to understand what requires healing within ourselves. My animal spirit guide is a deer. They are sensitive and highly intuitive. Deer represent a balance between confidence and success and gentleness and grace. I embrace these characteristics with love and recognize that confidence is an area that I must focus on. By becoming aware of all these spiritual supports through many unique avenues, we are empowering ourselves with the realization of our life purpose and who we truly are on a soul level.

Messages will also come through our pets and children. Our pets will often look into an empty space and start barking. They may also be reluctant to enter an area they have been in many times before. This is a sign to realize spirit energy may be present at that moment. Take time to attempt to raise your vibration to receive any messages being sent. It may be as simple and beautiful as experiencing a sensation of love and peace wash over you. Animals and children have a deeper sense for those who are in the Heavenly Realm. Children have a remarkable ability to hear and see our loved ones who have crossed over. Embrace and encourage their experiences without putting pressure on them to perform. Do not allow fear to interfere with the precious gift of receiving messages through our children and pets.

Our eldest granddaughter is exceptionally gifted in being able to communicate with crossed-over souls. I believe she chose me, in our pre-life plan, as her grandmother to help guide her in her spiritual journey. Our eldest grandson has wonderful adventures that are very detailed and accurate beyond his age and knowledge ability. I also sense each of my grandchildren have their own unique spiritual gifts that will develop as they get older. I feel blessed in the role of their mentor and guide but most importantly their Grammy.

Soon after my father passed, we noticed an elevation in spiritual occurrences involving our eldest granddaughter. She was around sixteen months old and still in her crib. We would occasionally observe her on the baby monitor after she would wake up from a nap. At one point she began to kiss the air and giggle. We would watch her turn around in circles with her arms up in the air, seemingly holding hands with someone. She would say "Papa," "love" and "tickle" and laugh out loud. When her vocabulary improved, she would often speak of souls from the Afterlife. Early on in my visits with my granddaughter, I would find I quickly became mentally and physically exhausted. Her spiritual abilities seemed to strengthen whenever I was around her. I eventually realized that she was unknowingly draining my energy to enhance her own. I now know how to ground myself so that I can stay strong to guide her without depleting my energy levels.

When my granddaughter was around two, my daughter and I witnessed how strong her connection to crossed-over loved ones was. My granddaughter was just beginning to learn her colors and knew purple and pink, but the other colors were unfamiliar to her. My daughter and I prayed to my dad to communicate the color brown. We then asked my granddaughter what color Papa was wearing in Heaven. She immediately responded: "Papa says brown." This was very emotional and validating for us. Around the same time, I was showing my granddaughter a photo album she had never seen before. She went directly to a picture of my maternal grandmother and said, "She is my angel." We had not discussed angels or crossed-over souls in any capacity with her at this stage in her life.

When my granddaughter was about four years old, we went to my father's gravesite. She ran directly to it and had only seen it once before. What truly amazed us is when I asked her to find my maternal grandparents' graveside, she ran to it without any hesitation. I didn't even remember exactly where it was at that time. We had never shown it to her previously, and there were over a hundred graves in the area. When I asked her how she found their graves, she shrugged her shoulders and replied, "They told me." My granddaughter has experienced many other wonderful events with crossed-over loved ones souls.

My eldest grandson also shares a gift with spiritual beings and has had many validating experiences. His spirit guide is very present in his life. My grandson has often spoken of "John" since he began to verbalize at a very young age. I love to hear about the exciting adventures John and my grandson embark on. He has traveled to the Wild West, Africa and into space with John on numerous occasions. When my grandson tells me about these journeys, the details are astounding, and his knowledge far exceeds the normal comprehension for his age. There is a distinct quality to these memories that is unique and flows in a rhythm that is consistent with this type of communication. When relaying these recollections, children speak with confidence and consistency that is not normally present in their daily language. It is fascinating to witness this aspect of their personalities develop.

Messages from crossed-over souls come in many varied manifestations. Embrace and express gratitude for every positive experience you have with them. They are truly gifts from Heaven. If you ever encounter a spirit that makes you feel uncomfortable, surround yourself and them in God's white light and send them on their way towards the light. Some souls are so enthusiastic to make contact, their energy may feel overwhelming and even frightening. You are always the one in control and have the power to orchestrate how this experience will play out. It is very rare for a soul to have negative intent or malicious motivation. Do not hesitate to send any soul on their way if you are unsure of their motive or uncomfortable with their presence. Your loved one's spirit will find another way to contact you that is less threatening to you. These visits are meant to enhance your life, not bring fear into a situation that is meant to be joyful.

My most recent and incredibly rewarding gift I have been blessed with occurred quite unexpectedly. I had no previous experience with this type of spiritual visit and was unaware that this form of communication even existed. Needless to say, I was initially overwhelmed and cautious when my first interaction occurred. I woke up around three o'clock a.m. to a heavy energy accompanied by a grey cloud-like image along my bedroom wall. Initially, I felt confusion and anger surrounding this soul. I quickly realized that this was a soul who had recently passed and was reluctant about leaving his earthly existence and fully crossing over. I heard him say "too soon," and deeply felt his emotions of frustration, angst and a resistance to move on. After my confusion lifted, I realized he was someone familiar to me personally. I then gently bathed his soul in white light and soothingly reassured him that this was his soul's journey. I assured him that he would soon be reunited with all his loved ones, both those who were awaiting him in Heaven and those who would join him later. I could sense his spirit calming and begin to accept his earthly demise. I guided him into the light and felt a radiant love and tranquility with this phase of his transition. I then recognized this soul as someone I knew many years ago. The next morning, I became aware, through social media, that my friend had passed away during the night. I felt honored and blessed for the opportunity to help his soul cross over. After my initial confusion, I soon understood what I was being called to do. I intuitively realized that this experience was preparing me for a much more complicated transition in the future.

I usually discourage souls from waking me up during the night, but sometimes they are very insistent and assertive. Crossed-over souls love to present themselves to me between three and four o'clock a.m. There are many reasons for this particular time period, but for me it is when I am most open to absorb spirit messages. It seems souls are at their strongest frequency and I am best able to raise mine. This particular soul attempted to wake me on a few occasions. A couple of times they even knocked on my headboard to get my attention. I obviously did not respond quickly enough, and finally this soul demanded my attention in a unique way. I woke up at three o'clock a.m., hearing what sounded like my husband's voice calling my name. Dale had fallen asleep on the couch downstairs, so was nowhere near me. I then asked this soul what they needed from me because now they had my full attention. I instantly smelled vomit and was infused with a feeling of anguish, deep sadness and fear. I knew this spirit was male and had taken his own life. His fear of transitioning was palpable and terrifying. I bathed him in white light and calmly reassured him that he would only find forgiveness and unconditional love on the other side of the veil. I could feel his trust in me strengthening and his fear slowly subsiding. I encouraged him to enter into the light, which he cautiously did. I heard him say "I see her," and felt overwhelming love and gratitude exude from his being. He looked back at me with a gentle smile as he entered the light. The next day, my husband informed me about his friend who had passed away a few weeks prior. He was from another country, and there was a delay in our receiving notification of his passing. My husband did not know how his friend had crossed over at this time. I realized that this was the person I had encountered during the night. I informed my husband that his friend had died by suicide and told him about what I had experienced the previous night. Later that evening, my husband confirmed his friend's crossing over through notification he received from another friend. The details I had received were astoundingly accurate. We were also aware that this friend's wife had crossed over a year prior. That evening Dale was acutely mourning his friend's passing. I heard his friend's soul being, in a very enthusiastic and positive communication with me, express his joy about being reunited with his wife. He thanked me profusely for helping him cross over. He confirmed that he had been accepted with forgiveness and unconditional love in the Afterlife. He wanted to reassure Dale that he was joyous and content in the Heavenly Realm. About a week after this incident, my husband's friend came through once again. He gifted me with a beautiful vision of his wife reaching for him hand in hand. They joined in a spiritual and loving embrace. He again conveyed his gratitude for my help and asked that my husband not grieve his passing. He informed me that he is blissfully happy and at peace. He still occasionally communicates with me to reassure us how joyful he is. I feel deep in my being that assisting souls in their transition into the Afterlife is a crucial aspect of my life purpose. I am grateful to those souls who trust me to aid in their transition into the Heavenly Realm.

    Initially, I was not going to write about my personal interactions with crossed-over souls or divulge any of my life experiences. Fear has traditionally held me back from fully sharing my abilities, but now I feel empowered to do so. My guides spoke clearly to me during my writing and meditation. They told me to "draw on your own experiences," and said, "your life matters." They also reassured me that "you have the power to help change the world." I have faith and trust in my guides and in my loved ones on the other side of the veil. I am also aware that not all people will accept my messages without skepticism and questioning on this Earthly Realm. I only ask for respect for all and to approach this information with an open heart and mind. I hope to open the dialogue on spirituality so we may all come together with a common goal of spreading the message of forgiveness and love into the Universe.

I have discovered other members of my family also have spiritual abilities. My maternal great-grandmother had "the gift." My mom said that when my great-grandma looked at her, "She was able to see into my soul." People came from neighboring communities to receive spiritual guidance from my great-grandmother. This is the same great-grandmother who came to me with my great-grandfather when I was around three years old. She was gently pushing me on a swing, and I later described her to my mom. My mom verified that I described her grandparents and that they were both deceased before I was even born. We never discussed this again as I strongly felt my mom's confusion and fear. My mother had an experience shortly after her mom crossed over that terrified her. My mom was driving home late one evening and saw my deceased grandmother in the back seat. My grandmother said, "Do not be afraid; I am fine." My mom screamed and asked her mom to never do that again. She never came to my mom again in that format. My grandmother comes to me in very subtle communications and has confirmed that she is my granddaughter's guardian angel.

I also have cousins and close family members who are gifted but are reluctant to fully embrace their abilities. My very closest cousin is able to see auras around people. He will use this gift as a tool to trust a person in personal or business matters. There is often a practical purpose for our spiritual skills that we may use to enhance our daily lives. My family members fear negative reprisal from family and society in revealing their abilities. My daughter as well as my eldest and youngest sons have abilities to connect with crossed-over souls. As a very young child, my eldest son spoke of his experience in the womb. His account was very accurate regarding an incident I had while experiencing premature labor with him. When my daughter was about five years old, she saw her deceased aunt and described her perfectly. At that time, we had not been notified about her passing, and my daughter had only met her once. My youngest son has a connection with animal spirits and receives communication within dream states. My husband has a strong ability to communicate with crossed-over loved ones through visions within dreams. When my family members are ready, I hope they are able to share their gifts to help heal the collective. The greater number of people who come out to share this awakening of spiritual enlightenment, the more empowered our society will become to create positive change for all.

    Communication with souls comes in many varied and unique formats. We are all blessed with the ability to connect with our loved ones on the other side of the veil. Simply understanding that our loved ones hear us and feel our love within the Heavenly Realm is an inspirational message. When we are alerted to our Higher Soul Self and the unconditional love of Source, we are empowered to strengthen our ability for spiritual communication to occur. Our initial step is to remove the blockages of fear and ego. Still your mind and open your heart to experience the love sent from the Heavenly Realm. There is no wrong way to proceed in the process of connecting with your loved ones' soul energy. Enter with a pure beautiful intention of love, and you will achieve your heart's desire.

    We are now aware it takes an enormous amount of energy for our loved ones to send us messages. It also requires patience, awareness and effort for us to receive and accept this miraculous form of communication. Every individual soul in the Afterlife has their own unique way of communicating. Their personalities will shine through, and you will be able to recognize their distinctive characteristics as your abilities strengthen. An open heart, acceptance and perseverance are all critical elements in achieving spiritual communication. Speak with your crossed-over loved ones as you did on this Earthly Realm. They are still the same people, except now they are gentler and kinder. Do not allow fear to prevent you from attempting to continue the relationship you have with your loved one.

Wherever you are at on your spiritual journey, understand that you are always heard by Source and your crossed-over loved ones. Communication is sent and received telepathically, through prayer, meditation, dreams or the spoken word. Embrace even the most subtle forms of communication, and trust that it is the love energy internalized by your soul being that is the true message. It may help to understand that we are never alone on our journey. We are always surrounded and embraced with the unconditional love of Source and our crossed-over loved ones' spiritual energy.

PAST-LIFE EXPERIENCES AND REINCARNATION

For some, the idea of past lives is a difficult concept to grasp. I believe that to fully embrace the meaning of life, spirituality, our purpose in this Universe, faith and deep soul love, we must be open to acknowledging the significance of past lives. We are all given glimpses into our past lives in a variety of avenues. Déjà vu and dreams may provide flashes into lives we have previously led. Déjà vu literally means already seen. I believe that there are no coincidences in life and that major life events were pre-planned by us in an intentional way. A vital contributing motivation for our life purpose is to resolve key issues from our past lives, which materialize as specific characteristics requiring healing in this lifetime. Attempt to change your perspective on the negative perception society has placed on past lives. Remove the fear and false assumptions that are attached to this belief. Approach reincarnation as a critical aspect of our soul's journey. View your past-life experiences as a glimpse into the window of your soul so that you may be alerted to what requires healing in this lifetime.

Our soul families are active participants and a strong influence during the pre-planning of our next lives to reincarnate into. We will often choose generations of the same family to rejoin a soul that is still on Earth. Therefore, a soul who once resided in a great-grandfather may return as the grandson years later. When this occurs, we will often see traits of previous ancestors in our loved ones today. DNA and environment influence our earthly bodies, but a primary factor in realizing recurring traits is due to a soul retaining its past memories. I believe the reason why the nature vs. nurture debate has never achieved a resolution is due to an important factor that has been overlooked. That consideration is the element of reincarnation and soul memory having a dominant influence in our core personality. It is interesting to note that our souls carry talents, personality traits, unresolved emotional trauma and passions into every life. If we are alert to recognize these signs, we are given another tool to understand the evolution of our souls. It is not a coincidence that our son has a passion for the military, just as his grandfather and great-grandfather did before him. This also helps to explain how young children are able to play a musical instrument flawlessly or sing like they have had years of training. We can understand this because their soul has experienced potentially many lifetimes immersed in their passion or life purpose.

Children are revealing past-life memories with more frequency and clarity. They detail accurate events and emotions that far exceed their preschool abilities and experiences. My eldest grandson speaks of his previous life in Africa with details I was able to verify regarding specific animals and customs to the region he lived in. My eldest granddaughter has revealed multiple past lives, some in detail and others with fragments of recollection. My confirmation for past life experiences for myself and others encapsulates the emotion these memories contain. There are many verifiable physical details which are fascinating, but it is the emotional attachment that accompanies these past-life memories that convince me they are genuine. When we can open our mind to the inevitability of reincarnation, we become aware of a cycle of eternal life that is difficult to dispute.

When we are able to release some of the restrictions and rules imposed by society and organized religion, we open ourselves to a world of less fear and more joy. Society wants us to conform to the idea that we only have one life to fulfill all our goals. We are placed in a controlled and limited box to perform these duties. We are groomed to achieve wealth and power under extreme stress and unrealistic expectations. This detracts from realizing our true purpose on Earth. We are here to rediscover our Spiritual Soul Self and become aware of our purpose in this lifetime. When we embrace the truth that our soul continues on forever, we are given the freedom to think and live outside of this conforming structure. This is the secret that society and many organized religions have tried to conceal. As the veil thins and we all become aware that our lives continue on, we are blessed with the realization of eternal soul energy. I only ask that you open your heart to this reality. Release the cloak of fear to reveal a life of endless possibilities. This creates less anxiety around the death of this body and a hopeful newfound purpose for the life we are living now. When we are able to remove the apprehension surrounding reincarnation, we open ourselves up to living an enlightened and more joy-filled existence.

There is anecdotal evidence and verifiable factual documentation that past lives exist. Children's past-life memories have been studied for many decades. These children are from all over the world and come from various faiths, nationalities and diverse family dynamics. Researchers have been able to validate specific aspects of these children's memories. There is often trauma associated with a past-life memory. Once the experiences of the past lives are acknowledged or verified, the person is released from the debilitating residual energy of that past lifetime. One aspect I find fascinating is that there is often a correlating birthmark, unexplained skin condition or other physical characteristics that are relevant to how the soul crossed over in a previous life. These memories are the most vivid between the ages of two to six years of age, because young children are not tainted by societal prejudice and are closer in time to their pre-birth memories. When we can open our hearts and minds to the possibility of past lives, we can make sense of many of the mysteries that plague us today.

How else can we explain small children possessing incredible talents and skills far surpassing their age or capabilities? We all have interests and sometimes obsessions surrounding specific periods in history or places and people from the past. Where do our innate passions originate from? Where do our "irrational" fears come from? Why do specific situations bring terror into our being without having an experience with that event in this lifetime? Why do we have seemingly illogical fears of spiders, snakes, mice, drowning, heights, confined spaces or the dark? Have you ever been to a city or region and felt immediately at home or instinctively knew your way around? Have you envisioned or dreamt of frequently being present in specific periods of history? These are all potential glimpses into our past lives. The concept of past lives answers these questions and many more. It also flows beautifully when we consider the entire cycle of eternal life and provides answers to our most perplexing questions about our existence.

My daughter and I experienced a simultaneous past-life memory many years ago. At the time, neither of us were aware of the significance or underlying meaning of this event or even had awareness of the concept of past lives. I had started using a new natural product for cleaning that had scents derived from ancient essential oils. My daughter had such a severe emotional and physical reaction to these scents that I was unable to use them again. Both of us independently and spontaneously had a vision of her being violated by someone who strongly had this scent attached to them. When I later researched the origin of the product, I discovered an interesting historical link to these essential oils. During the Black Plague, there was a group of people who stole from the dying and dead victims. These thieves would saturate themselves in the same oils that this cleaning product contained. The oils naturally have antiviral and antimicrobial properties contained within them. This was how the thieves were able to steal from deceased victims without contracting the deadly plague. They may also have built up immunity against this disease. Both my daughter and I instinctively felt that she had been victimized by these thieves during a previous life. At the time, we did not have the information or knowledge that we presently have. It is interesting to note that even without the tools and insight I have now, we both came to the same conclusion regarding a life and time we had no previous awareness of. This event occurred over fifteen years ago, yet still has profound significance in my life today.

Recently I was in a Body Talk counselling session, and what was revealed was life-altering. I have a great relentless fear of losing members of my family to an uncontrollable tragedy. Whenever there is a normal threat to my family, especially my children or grandchildren's health, I internally react with a panic that is disproportionate to the reality of their illness. I have not revealed the intensity of the emotions I experience to anyone, as I have felt it is an irrational fear I had to deal with. During my counselling session, my therapist mentioned a possible past-life connection to the Black Plague. The memory of that past life came back in an instant of vivid detail. I recalled losing my entire family to this horrific disease in history. The emotions rushed back and felt momentarily overwhelming. The realization that this had occurred in a previous life allowed me an outlet where I could now process my emotions around this critical incident in my past. I am hopeful that, with time, the disproportionate emotions I experience around my family's well-being will eventually subside to a more appropriate level. This past-life memory also gave me insight into why I experienced such an intense reaction to being "locked up" during Covid. I now have clarity regarding the impending doom feeling I had during the isolation period of Covid. I recently researched and discovered that during the Black Plague, families were literally locked in their homes from the outside. The sick and healthy members of the family could only come out once all the members were either dead or had miraculously survived this intolerable situation. My once "irrational" fears now seem like a tangible distant memory I can now process and move on from.

There are many prompts that may alert us to a past life. Scent, visions, current experiences, meeting a stranger who we know at a deeper level but have never met in this lifetime are all triggers that may instantly connect us to a past-life memory. Do not dismiss these occurrences, as they may be sending you a message that opens a path to healing or discovering an important aspect towards your life purpose.

We are blessed to live in a time where we can access our past lives with relative ease. Hypnosis, with the intention of discovering past lives, is potentially the most direct means. Meditation, with practice, is another method of discovering potential past lives. When you research hypnotherapists, confirm they have specific training in past-life regression. This is a valuable tool for potentially resolving trauma or phobias. There are many documented cases where a person's deep relentless fears were alleviated after experiencing a previous life through hypnosis. The past life contained specific events which held traumatic memories. These unresolved emotions were carried on the soul into their current lifetime and surfaced as "irrational" fears. When we release these past-life memories through hypnosis or regression, it often results in our fears being resolved in this lifetime. The lives that emerge through past-life regression often have a direct link to help us discover our life purpose by resolving past and present trauma. When you are open to discover your past-life memories, attempt to determine their significance in your current life. The past-life memories that enter our consciousness have a direct link to resolving current life emotions that may have plagued us for our entire existence and potentially many lifetimes.

Hypnosis is relaxing and invigorating all at once. It is not forceful or manipulative. You are always in control of your experience. You are aware of your connection to the present but are still able to encounter the past. The positive impact may be instantaneous or just require self-reflection for healing to occur. It is important to follow up with counselling and seek support when repressed memories emerge that have a strong emotional impact. Once again, the reason for these memories is to alert you to the emotions that require releasing and healing in this lifetime.

Children are receptive to remembering their past lives with clarity and without provocation for a variety of reasons. Their openness and innocence allow their authentic memories to come forward without the restrictions of societal prejudices. Their past-life memories are also still fresh in their consciousness. Recently, my eldest granddaughter said to me, "We live many lives, and you and me know this Grammy." On another occasion, I saw her switching the bodies of her dolls onto the same head. When I asked her why she did this, she answered, "We always have the same head but many different bodies." She delivers this information in a straightforward and emotionless way. We do not prompt her or ask for clarification. From the age of two, she has conveyed glimpses of several past lives. She does this spontaneously, and we do not ask any leading questions. My granddaughter appears to go into a light meditative state when she discusses past-life experiences. She communicates with the maturity of a person well beyond her years during these specific conversations. She is always in a safe and quiet space when she speaks of these memories. Driving in the car with her family or snuggling under a blanket seem to be her favorite comfort zones.

At around two years old, my granddaughter started talking about her other mother and father and older sister. At that time, my granddaughter was an only child. About every six months, new details emerged from that previous-life memory. I have consistently documented and journaled all my personal experiences and those of family and friends that are spiritual in nature. Her recollection never wavered in the details. When she turned four and a half, we received her full memory of that past-life experience. I will relay her account from her perspective as accurately as I recorded and recall it. She told us, "My mother and father were downstairs with my little brother. My older sister hid me behind a wall in our upstairs bedroom. I heard the bad men come into our house. I heard their loud boots walking downstairs. My mother, father and brother went to Heaven. My sister came to get me from behind the wall after the bad men left. My sister took care of me." Months later, my granddaughter said to her mom, "My older sister said it was okay to steal." My granddaughter had no concept of death or stealing at that time in her life. Later, my granddaughter told me that I was her mother in that life and her mom now was her older sister in the same previous life. She has never referred to her parents in this life as mother and father. She only calls them mommy and daddy. Since she told us the entire memory of her past-life recollection, she has never spoken of this again in any capacity. There appears to be no residual trauma or even recall of that lifetime in her memory now.

My immediate instinct was that her previous life occurred during the Holocaust. I have not directly experienced a past-life regression or memory during the Holocaust, but I am fascinated with that time period. I am always drawn to the Jewish section of every historical city we have travelled to. We have recently been to Auschwitz in Poland and previously toured the Holocaust museum in Berlin. I have always had great respect and compassion for the Jewish culture and people.

Around five years old, my granddaughter had another clear memory of a past life. She and I were playing in the backyard when she began digging in the grass. I asked her what she was doing, and she replied, "I am a pauper, digging for coins." I asked what that meant to her. She said, "We were so poor, we had to steal to eat and live." She talked about stealing money from people's pockets and that they were not liked by these people. She said they lived in an alley with dirt floors. When I later asked her parents if they knew what a pauper was, they both were unaware of that term. My granddaughter had never heard or spoken the word pauper before and hasn't since. Her memory and recollection of being a pauper is astoundingly accurate. The terminology she used was a popular term around the 19th century in England. These destitute people had to rely on charity or stealing to survive. She relayed this story with little emotional relevance and quickly went on to playing and having fun with Grammy.

Another revelation came when my granddaughter was around three years of age. She informed my daughter that she chose her to be her mommy from Heaven before she was even born. Recently, my granddaughter told her mom (my daughter), "Of all the moms and dads I have ever had, you and Daddy are my favorite. I will always remember you best when I think of my mommies and daddies." When my daughter asked her how many mommies and daddies she has had, she replied, "Oh Mommy, I have had so many." My granddaughter is seven years old now and rarely speaks of past-life experiences and spiritual encounters. This is common at this age, and hopefully she will be open to her strengths when she is older. We do not place any expectations on her or pressure her in any way. This is her journey, and we are here to support her whenever she needs us. Interestingly, her abilities still shine through when her guard is down. My granddaughter recently got upset with her mom and shouted at my daughter, "I will never pick you as my mommy ever again!"

I have been told by independent mediums over the years that I have had many lives with my daughter and eldest granddaughter. I have predominantly been in a teacher or mentorship role with my granddaughter. I have strong memories of experiencing past lives with many of my loved ones from this life. My understanding of my past lives enhances the faith and love I experience today. The lessons I am learning from recalling past lives help to validate my experiences and visions I have had in this lifetime. I feel I have been brought full circle in my spiritual journey through my recollection of past lives. As I am writing this, I am getting clarification regarding my life purpose today. The information I am receiving is that my current life is an accumulation of many significant previous lives. The reason I have such a large unique family is because many members of my soul family wanted to be included in this current life. We all wanted to be present because of the significance of this critical time in history. I also believe that I am coming nearer to my last reincarnations on this Earth. I have been blessed with the information I am sharing with you, so I am able to inform the collective about the truth around our eternal life. I will further explore these insights during meditation, as they are coming very strongly as a message I need to pursue in more depth.

During deep reflection, I have had glimpses into a multitude of previous lives. I have predominantly been female in these lives. I appear to have been a healer in many, both as female and male. A majority of my healing lives involve being a midwife. My entire career in this current life was as a high-risk obstetrical and gynecologic oncology and palliative care nurse. This was a passion I felt called to from a very early age. In grade two, I wrote a story about becoming a nurse or a nun. Interestingly, the hospital I worked at for over twenty-five years was established and run by the Catholic Grey Nuns. I still have that story I wrote. I have recalled several lives as an Indigenous person in North America on the midwestern plains and on the west coast of Florida, an African woman in several lives, a peasant in biblical times in astounding detail, a male blacksmith in the 1700s with my brother from this lifetime, a midwife with my niece in a remote forested area, a nurse on an aviation base in the First World War with Dale and my best friend from this lifetime and many other ordinary lives. I have never seen myself as famous or in a notable life in history. I recall being a storyteller, either verbally or through writing, as a common theme in many of my lives. Some of these lives were extremely challenging, but I always felt an underlying emotion of positive hopefulness within my soul.

I strongly believe that we are primarily shown past lives that relate to challenges in our current lives. They are gifts to help us resolve issues we are experiencing today or to guide us to our life purpose. This became evident during my experience with a past-life regression therapy session. I went with no expectations or preconceived ideas or thoughts about what this experience would entail. I recalled three distinct previous life events that were all significant to my life today. I have discussed aspects of these lives previously but will now focus on how they gave me insight and healing into my current life.

The first regression was as a caregiver to my mom. It began in France and concluded on the desolate prairies in central northern Canada. After my father crossed over in that life, I was put in charge of caring solely for my mother. I lived a lonely life of resentment and died an angry and frustrated old woman. When I became aware of that past life, I was alerted to the emotions that required healing in this lifetime. I was able to successfully resolve old karma and come to a place of peace in my caretaking role as a caregiver to my mom once again. I was very fortunate to resolve many of the residual issues from that lifetime that had carried over into my current life. I believe that this past-life memory was the catalyst that motivated me to recognize my healing journey in this life. This did not happen immediately and took much communication with my family members and personal self-reflection to alert me to my role in this recurring theme in my existence.

My next recollection of a previous life was that of a wealthy and carefree young female in the early 1900s. I have vivid memories of being present in downtown Toronto, Canada during a catastrophic fire. I recall the remainder of this life being very positive and joyous. I believe I chose this life to recover from the bitterness of my previous life. This life reflected the period of my current life where I was most carefree. In this past life, I recall driving an open model T-Ford car with the wind blowing in my hair. In my current lifetime, I used to own and ride a Harley Davidson. I recognized many of my friends from that lifetime who are currently friends from this life. I believe that past-life memory was there to remind me to have fun and enjoy all aspects of my existence on this Earth.

The third life I recalled occurred in the Scottish Highlands in the 1700s. This was the most detailed regression. I remembered many facts from that time period, in details I recorded and later verified. This past-life recollection confirmed that my husband today is my soulmate. His scent and characteristics triggered other lives that we have lived together, including this present one. Many of my children from that life are in my life today. I vividly recall assisting my daughter in her delivery of my granddaughter through a very difficult birth in that past life. In this life, I experienced a strong urgency to be present during all my grandbabies' births. This was most intensely felt with my first granddaughter. In that life, I was a midwife and healer and collected herbs for my craft. I recalled many details of that past life like it occurred yesterday. I crossed over from that life with a peaceful transition, surrounded by my family, into the Afterlife. I knew that my soul would live on and conveyed that to my family before I crossed over. This entire experience brought me full circle to my life today.

The last past-life regression was the most profound. Recalling that past lifetime with my husband has strengthened our relationship today and given me a new understanding regarding our challenges. My connection with my children and grandchildren has been enhanced and deepened. After I crossed over in that last past-life regression, I felt my soul ascend towards a beautiful light-filled love. I wanted to explore my soul's journey at that moment, but the therapist quickly brought me back to the present. This requires a very intense hypnotic state to be able to explore our exploits in the Afterlife. I have been blessed with experiencing glimpses of the Heavenly Realm through Out-of-Body journeys and deep meditation with my spirit team. We are given insight into the Afterlife to enhance the critical lessons we need to learn in this lifetime. I will definitely be pursuing my soul's journey into a life between past lives in a future session. It promises to be a fascinating adventure.

During this experience, I was also shown an important aspect of our soul families. Our children in any lifetime do not have to be biological to be part of our soul family. My children today are a mix of biological, stepchildren and foster children. Every significant individual in our lives today is connected to us by our original soul family or close soul group. Biological connection is an earthly phenomenon, not a spiritual concept. Spouses, children, siblings, and best friends are often part of our soul family. I have learned that the eldest child appears to have a pivotal role in orchestrating the primary family members. There are no concrete rules, and every lifetime is evaluated for the unique experience it is meant to become. Our roles continually change to best accommodate the lessons we require to learn and grow in each lifetime. It is interesting to note that as our soul progresses to the Higher Realms, we decrease the critical intense relationship we have with our soul family. We are forever connected to our soul family through a divine energy, but we become increasingly focused on pursuing our individual soul professions. Our role then encompasses being a leader and mentor to younger souls as we are elevated to a position within Source's inner circle. We are less inclined to reincarnate on Earth and have graduated from student to master status in the Heavenly Realm. This is the goal for all the soul work we experience on Earth and within the Universe.

It is a fascinating exercise to place people in your current life into separate soul group categories. Use your instinct and intuition. We have approximately five to twenty people in our core soul family. There are also close peripheral groups and a specific study group. Each of these adjacent groups consist of five to fifteen souls. While doing this exercise, the results may be very revealing and enlighten you on your close personal relationships. This may also trigger memories of being with these people in different roles in a variety of lifetimes.

Recently, my father confirmed my feelings about the soul connection I previously experienced with my great-grandfather Michael. Dad came to me in a very clear vision with his and Michael's souls blended together. I now have confirmation that my great-grandfather and father are the same soul. Michael also crossed over from stomach cancer, or "stomak" cancer as it was originally recorded. I have also become aware of Michael being the father I lost in my first life regression. This is the life I recalled being a caregiver to my mom during my initial experience. My dad then sent me a validating message to confirm all these visions. He took me back to an incident in this lifetime before he crossed over. He made me aware that on a soul level, he remembered the connection he had with his grandfather's (his) life. I distinctly recall a look in my dad's eyes that confirmed his unwavering conviction that he had experienced a similar life journey before. He instilled a validating message and accompanying emotions of peace and tranquility that I still carry within me today.

Another phenomenon to support the continuation of our soul's journey through a myriad of lifetimes is the concept of Near-Death Experiences. Millions of people all over the world have had similar experiences after their heart and brain ceased to show any signs of life. A great deal of those people have had glimpses into past lives during their NDEs. There is much documentation of verifiable anecdotes that occurred during a multitude of fascinating NDEs. The accounts are enlightening and affect each person profoundly. Many people uncover spiritual gifts of psychic and mediumship abilities after their NDEs. Others have discovered great artistic or musical talents that were not previously present in this lifetime. There are countless books and stories available for everyone to access and learn more about NDEs.

Another validating occurrence for many people is through an Out-of-Body Experience (OBE). NDEs and OBEs create the ideal circumstances for a past-life memory or vision to occur. It is reported that over ten percent of the world's population experience

OBEs. People experience these episodes during a dream state or while in deep meditation, immediately following extreme exercise, in conjunction with NDEs, under anesthesia, during childbirth, hypnosis, accidents or situations creating severe stress. There have also been reported incidents of people experiencing OBEs during a mental or physical health crisis. People have also experienced Out-of-Body adventures while under the influence of hallucinogenic drugs. Pilots and astronauts may have seemingly unexplained occurrences through sensory deprivation or overload and strong g-forces. I have been shown that the incidence of NDEs, OBEs, astral projection, shared death experiences, and simultaneous or individual past-life memories is significantly higher than what is recorded. Our human selves have a difficult time recognizing these incidents or fully appreciating the transcendent nature of an OBE or NDE. By keeping an open mind and heart, we can embrace the awareness for our soul's journey through many wondrous avenues.

I have been blessed with having a few OBEs in my lifetime. The most profound one occurred during a deep meditative session. I suddenly felt myself being transported through a series of doors, similar to a progression of falling dominoes. I traveled through dozens of these doorways and was surrounded in darkness, not light. The darkness was comforting and not at all threatening. I was accompanied by my advanced spirit guide named Scalion during this transformative personal experience. When the final door fell, I saw light-centered souls floating in peace and harmony. They were all connected by a luminescent gossamer web. The souls were linked freely within this web, and all were intertwined with an ascending shimmering ray of light and connected to the most exquisite Source of unconditional love and compassion. A pulsing energy radiated from within this Highest Power and enveloped every soul with great love and light. The souls were energized by Source, and Source was invigorated by the souls. This Highest Power once again presented as an energy and not an entity unto itself. It was a glorious symbiotic relationship to witness. Emanating within this great energy was a darker-skinned, light-eyed ethereal figure with shoulder-length wavy hair. No words were spoken, yet I knew this to be Jesus. He slowly turned his head and gave me an imperceptible nod. The pure divine love I experienced was indescribable. I understood his message without question. He wanted me to continue on my journey to spread love and awareness into the Universe. I am eternally grateful for this miraculous experience. He infused me with confidence and strength that I required at that moment in my life. He removed doubt and has given me courage to continue on my mission of assisting others on their spiritual journey.

When we open ourselves to spiritual awakening, we are presented with many opportunities for growth and understanding. Embrace the beautiful gift of knowledge and faith that you have been blessed with. Every aspect of spirituality contains an enlightened message of love and self. When we embody these lessons, the clarity for our soul journeys and life purposes emerges. The greater our faith, the higher probability for spiritual connection and enlightenment. Do not allow your ego to bring fear into this process. We are in control of every aspect of our personal journeys. Empower yourselves with the knowledge and tools available. We are never alone in our mission. When we access the connection to the Higher Realm, we will remember the love of Source and return to our Spiritual Soul Self. When we absorb that love, we will radiate love and compassion from our inner core. The Universe will embrace that love and begin to heal, one soul at a time.

OUR LIFE PURPOSE REVEALED

We are in a critical time for universal consciousness to be recognized. The veil is thinning, and a portal to our spiritual awareness is being created. We are the chosen souls who have been gifted this monumental opportunity for learning, awareness and growth. We have been blessed with the key of knowledge to unlock our souls' life purposes. Our most crucial goal is to confront the traumatic and painful emotions that paralyze us on our life journeys. If we choose to not process these emotions now, we will have missed a vital opportunity to awaken ourselves and the universal collective. If we miss this opening for extreme growth and learning, we will have to wait for a whole new cycle to occur in the Universe.

A powerful initial step in this journey is to alert the Universe of our intent to heal. This will trigger our spirit to recognize the memory of our pre-life soul plan. Empower yourselves with all the knowledge available to you. The Universe will present learning opportunities that best suit your personal journey. Attempt to remain open to this process and do not allow ego and fear to interrupt you on your healing path. Send forgiveness into the world's energy by releasing your pain and despair. Fill that space in your hearts with love and compassion. Remain open to all the tools presented and the knowledge you have been blessed with to assist you in discovering your life purpose. Embrace the truth that you pre-planned every challenge and experience to alert you to what requires healing for your soul's learning and growth in this lifetime. Immerse your Higher Soul Self in forgiveness and love. Be patient and kind during this lifelong process. For your journey to be successful, it is not imperative to experience every opportunity presented. We are all unique souls, and the Universe will provide us with what we require to learn the lessons we set out to embrace. We are empowered through knowledge and our willingness to remain open throughout this process. Accept that you will be challenged and will falter. Understand that there are no coincidences or failures. Focus on how you respond to every experience and what you learn through every stage of development. You always have been and will forever be the master of your destiny.

Embrace the knowledge that every person and experience that elicits a strong emotional response was pre-planned by your Higher Soul Self. This was done out of love for the purpose of soul learning and growth and for karmic release to occur. With faith and spiritual awareness, discovering your life purpose is accessible to every single person. When we embrace how this process works, we can all begin our journey of enlightenment. We attract people and experiences that reflect the qualities that are most in need of healing within ourselves. When we practice Divine Healing, we are releasing our victim mentality and embracing the true intention of healing, learning and growth. When we choose to ignore our emotions elicited from these experiences, we are only inviting the inevitable re-occurrence of these challenges in our lives. It is imperative that we eliminate blame for our life's detrimental interactions. No higher purpose is served when we blame God, society, other individuals or ourselves for life's adverse experiences.

To grow, we must accept responsibility and control over all our earthly opportunities. Even when we achieve a goal that we immediately perceive as trivial, the eventual outcome may produce a monumental influence on the Universe. When our intentions are pure and divinely inspired, we may be creating an opportunity for tremendous genuine change without being fully aware of the end result. It is never too late to adjust the trajectory of your life. By altering our perception on any life event, we are taking a critical step towards healing. When we put in the work with an open heart, we will sense a shift in energy and spiritual awareness. When we lean into love and service towards others, we are fulfilling not only a great part of our life's purpose but also the collective universal purpose.

We have all chosen to be on this Earth at this exact moment in time. We have left the bliss of our Eternal Home to participate in a potential monumental shift in our world's consciousness. This epic mission was not only agreed upon by individual soul groups but was also embraced by the entire spiritual community in the Heavenly Realm. There are very few times in our world's history where this has occurred. We are the chosen ones. We are the strongest and bravest of souls. This is one of the most challenging times in the history of our Universe. Earth is the most formidable and demanding learning center in all the galaxy. The opportunity for immense growth and knowledge is within our power. Individually and collectively, emotions that have been repressed and buried for generations are now surfacing. It is our responsibility to acknowledge, process and release the emotions that do not serve a higher purpose so that we may heal ourselves as well as the collective community.

Despite the hate and anger in the world, we are capable of love and understanding in far greater capacities. Release the desire to attempt to control others or your environment. We are only in control of how we respond to any life event or individual. We are accountable, during our life review in the Heavenly Realm, for every single interaction we participate in on Earth. We will deeply feel every emotion experienced by others during that interaction. We will not be judged in the Afterlife, except by ourselves. This form of judgment is on a very different level in the Heavenly Realm than what we understand on Earth. Our lives will be recorded and evaluated for our soul's placement, advancement, learning and growth.

Living in this imperfect world is required for us to work towards enlightenment. We are always striving for balance. There is no growth in neutrality. Change is the catalyst for achieving our soul goals. Human ego sends us messages of fear, greed and selfishness. Ego is necessary as a contrast to love and helps us recognize the need for healing. Fear is necessary in the biological sense to alert us to danger on a physical level. Releasing fear and ego in the spiritual sense is essential for soul growth to occur and for spirituality to soar.

It is acceptable and fair to feel skeptical regarding some aspects of spirituality presented here. Allow yourself the time to absorb the concepts that may be new to you. Embrace the tools and truths that you choose to support yourself with on your healing journey. The groundwork is there for you to choose which fork in the road you wish to explore. All spiritual roads lead back to love, even when we encounter detours and bumps along the way. There is no real downside to embracing this alternative perspective on how to discover your life's purpose.

As you navigate your journey through spiritual awakening, celebrate every milestone with gratitude. The concepts presented may be new territory for many people and will require time and acceptance of a new perspective. Be confident that you will gain what you desire to enhance your soul's journey. We are not expected to act on every trigger or to apply all the tools presented to become aware of our life purpose. We are given many options to use for enhancement of our personal journey. Our spiritual supports are acutely aware of what serves our individual needs and creates openings for us to embrace those opportunities. If we are bombarded with these tools all at once, we may be too overwhelmed to process them and have them be valuable to our journey.

As you adopt one truth, you will discover it is easier to accept concepts that may initially have felt foreign to you. As you experience the expansion of your soul, other doors will open to alert you to recognize and embrace your life purpose. The clarity to discover who you truly are will emerge as you continue on your life journey. Every spiritual experience builds on the next experience to return you to self. When you rediscover your Highest Soul Self, you are alerted to your purpose in this lifetime. It may be beneficial to return to the beginning of the book for you to process every step in a new light. You will find that as your spiritual growth expands, you will become more aware of your purpose and how to use the tools presented in an enlightened way. Embrace every revelation and supportive concept that you feel comfortable with, and relinquish your need for control to our Higher Power.

We are now empowered with the knowledge and tools to achieve our soul's mission and life purpose. The intention of the veil of amnesia is that we may rediscover ourselves as the powerful spiritual beings we are. The purpose of our existence is to return to our Highest Soul Self through the awareness of love. The emotional love we encounter on Earth is a trigger for us to be alerted to the elevated state of Source's love that encapsulates our entire soul essence. It transcends even the greatest love we experience here on Earth. As we elevate the frequency of our soul's energy with learning, love, forgiveness and gratitude, we get closer to knowing our truth. Our soul vibration, at its core, is unique to every individual and will continue on for all of eternity.

One of our primary goals on Earth is to embrace and grow towards Divine Love. This is the energy of supreme love that encapsulates all creation. It is the pinnacle of spirituality. This is our Nirvana, the highest state of enlightenment. The Divine Love of Source is a state of consciousness or a state of being that resonates within each individual and throughout the Universe. For this awareness to occur, we must first create an opening for healing and forgiveness to enter our soul center. The foundation of Divine

Healing embraces the truth that all souls are created equally from the energy of Source's unconditional love. The core purpose of Divine Healing is to release the restrictive emotions that have previously paralyzed our journey towards spiritual awareness. Through this process, we are also given the opportunity to clear past karmic debt. When we are releasing the unpleasant emotions of anger, sadness, guilt, shame, unworthiness, hopelessness and pain, we are freeing our souls to learn the lessons we came here to embrace. Everything meaningful in life first presents itself as a challenge. There are no mistakes, only opportunities for learning and growth. Each lesson is imprinted on our soul for eternity. This is the foundation for the core strength we draw from when life gets challenging.

During pre-birth planning, our soul places triggers and soul memories to alert us to our life purpose. Our soul planned many experiences that mirror aspects of ourselves that require healing. Through repetitive experiences that evoke recurring emotions, we become aware of what requires our attention. Only we have the power to release our soul from the cycle of perpetual adverse experiences. This is a pattern that will not change until we create the change required to resolve this paradigm. If we truly embrace the knowledge that we choose our path and our life lessons, it allows us to accept and grow from every experience. Remember, we pre-planned experiences that trigger our soul to opportunities to work through and release emotions that hold us captive from our truth.

We have many opportunities to perfect our lessons on Earth. The choice of how we accomplish that is in our control. When we accept ourselves as loving and beautiful souls, we are empowered to deliver that message to all humanity. We are never alone on our journey. When we heal and love ourselves first, we then have the ability to help heal and send love into the Universe. This raises our soul vibration and inevitably raises the vibration of humankind. By maintaining a high vibration, genuine high vibrational experiences and people will be attracted back to us.

We have now successfully broken out of the negative cycle of ego, pain, victimization, judgment and hate. We have entered a renewed state of forgiveness, love, gratitude and service. It is important to accept ourselves as lovingly connected to all that is (Source) and that everything we do on Earth matters in a profound way. We are in control of how we live out this life. It requires an open heart and mind, the dedication to work on ourselves and the faith that our survival as a human race is dependent on our ability to heal ourselves and humanity. It is powerful to recognize our life path and initiate the steps to fulfilling our prearranged destiny. Purpose is restored in our life, and we are empowered to follow our soul's pre-planned voyage. Now that we know better, we must be better.

My sincere prayer is that you have been enlightened on many aspects of your soul's journey. I have attempted to clarify our adventures into the Afterlife in a clear and concise manner. I strived to convey an open and loving relationship with Source that is accessible to each and every person. My great desire was to offer you a completely new and alternative perspective on dealing with the critical challenges in your life. The knowledge and tools we embrace along this path are present to strengthen our commitment to rediscover our Higher Soul Self. When we return to our Higher Soul Self, we become aware of our existence and purpose in this lifetime. The simplicity of this realization is so beautiful and meaningful in the flow of our spiritual journey. When we embrace this truth, we are empowered to fulfill our soul plan and life purpose.

With every life challenge we achieve on Earth, we elevate our station in the Afterlife. The ultimate goal of all soul work is to ascend towards our position at the side of Source's pure light and love. Our greatest triumph will be to sit within our Creator's inner circle as an Ascended Master or one of Source's enlightened spiritual beings.

    We are now granted the knowledge and tools to fulfill our ultimate destiny. Simply by initiating the process, we are activating a shift in our consciousness and alerting the Universe towards our intention of soul growth and learning. Through Divine Healing, we are opening a space for self-love and forgiveness on a level never previously imagined. We are increasing our vibrational energy, which escalates enlightened authentic experiences in our life and contributes to elevating universal positive energy. As we work through the process, we discover our life purpose. We are solidly on the path to achieving our soul's mission to unearth who we truly are on a deep spiritual level. As we heal one soul at a time, we are empowered to share that love with every soul through all our Beautiful Intentions.

THIS IS THE BEGINNING, NOT THE END...

CITATIONS

Serendipity: "Moments where we discover something meaningful while seeking something else." Horace Walpole (1717-1797)

Karma: "Intent and actions of an individual (cause) influence the future of that person (effect)." en.m.wikipedia.org

"We are all spiritual beings having a human experience": Pierre Teilhard de Chardin (May 1881-April 1955) en.m.wikipedia.org

"Looking for love in all the wrong places" song by Johnny Lee, 1980. Songwriters, Wanda Mallette, Bob Morrison, and Patti Ryan. Label: Full Moon 47004. en.m.wikipedia.org

"Daniel" song by Elton John and Bernie Taupin (1973). Album "Don't shoot me I'm only the piano player; MCA (US)

Blue's Brothers: Dan Aykroyd and John Belushi (1978)

Jackson Kiddard (- 1901): Philosopher who wrote "Anything that annoys you is teaching you patience..."

Elizabeth Kubler-Ross (1926-2004): "On Death and Dying" (1969)

"Prophet" definition: en.m.wikipedia.org

"Deer Spirit" definition: www.mindbodygreen.com

"OBE" definition: en.m.wikipedia.org

ACKNOWLEDGEMENTS

I would love to thank all my family and friends who were invaluable support in writing my truth. To my husband, Dale, who never gave up on me; even when I wanted to give up on myself. To my beautiful children who were always there for moral and technical support whenever I called them in a panic. Justin and Josh, you saved me on so many occasions. Thank you to all my loved ones who continually encouraged me and trusted me with their personal stories. I am indebted to all of you.

I would also like to thank my incredible team at Tellwell Publishing. You have been supportive with every hurdle I faced, and I have faced many.

When I began my spiritual journey, I was inspired by three authors who were aligned to my personal enlightenment. Those authors are: Michael Newton, PhD; Robert Schwartz; Colin C. Tipping.

Milton Keynes UK
Ingram Content Group UK Ltd.
UKHW012008170124
436226UK00003B/37